J.M. Dent

The high history of the Holy Graal

J.M. Dent

The high history of the Holy Graal

ISBN/EAN: 9783744776783

Printed in Europe, USA, Canada, Australia, Japan

Cover: Foto ©ninafisch / pixelio.de

More available books at **www.hansebooks.com**

THE TEMPLE CLASSICS

Edited by
ISRAEL
GOLLANCZ
M.A.

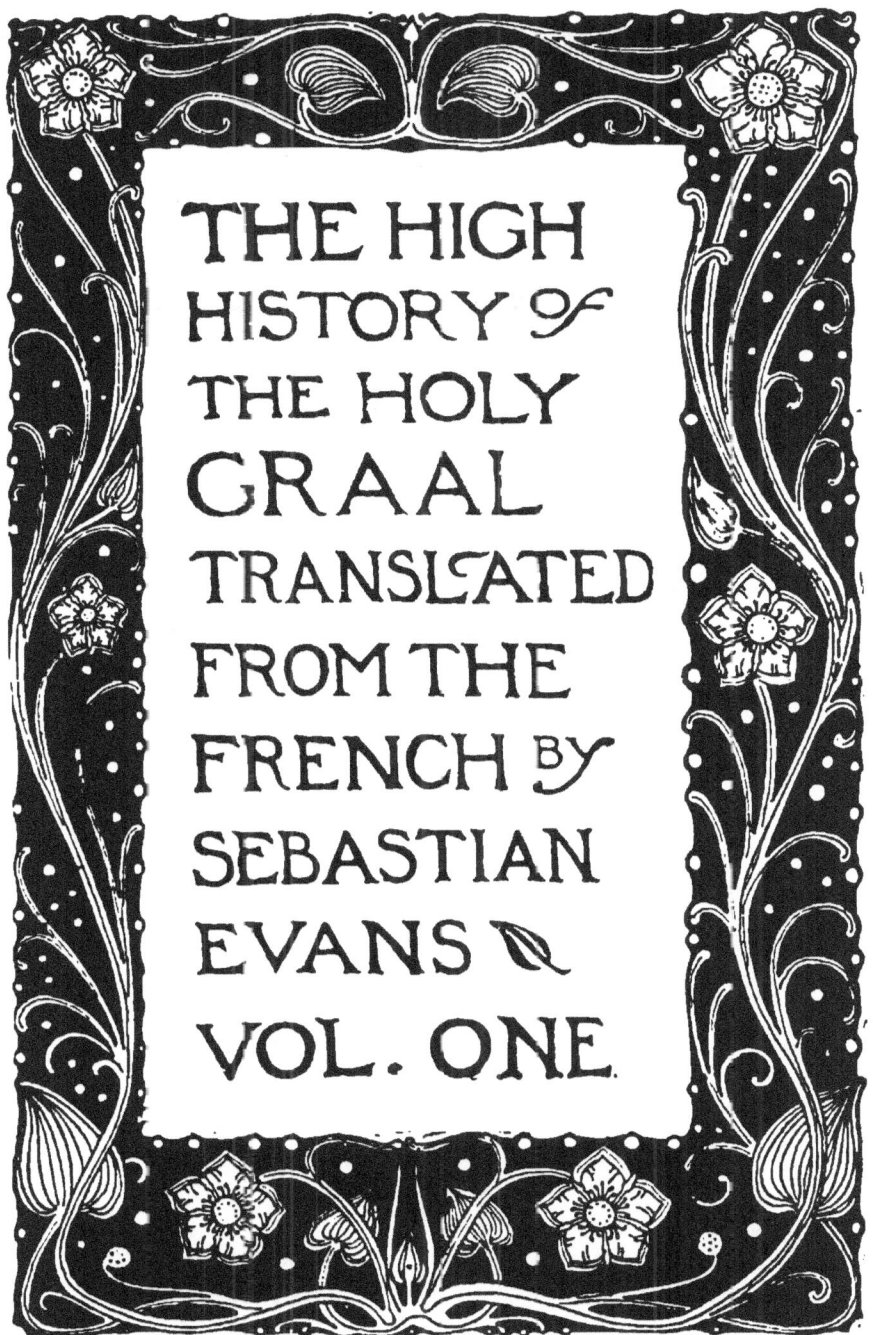

MDCCCXCVIII PUBLISHED BY J·M·DENT
AND·CO: ALDINE·HOUSE·LONDON·E·C

THE HIGH HISTORY OF THE HOLY GRAAL

BRANCH I

INCIPIT

HEAR ye the history of the most holy vessel that is called Graal, wherein the precious blood of the Saviour was received on the day that He was put on rood and crucified in order that He might redeem His people from the pains of hell. Josephus set it in remembrance by annunciation of the voice of an angel, for that the truth might be known by his writing of good knights and good worshipful men how they were willing to suffer pain and to travail for the setting forward of the Law of Jesus Christ, that He willed to make new by His death and by His crucifixion.

The Book of the Graal

TITLE I

The High Book of the Graal beginneth in the name of the Father and of the Son and of the Holy Ghost. These three Persons are one substance, which is God, and of God moveth the High Story of the Graal. And all they that hear it ought to understand it, and to forget all the wickednesses that they have in their hearts. For right profitable shall it be to all them that shall hear it of the heart. For the sake of the worshipful men and good knights of whose deeds shall remembrance be made, doth Josephus recount this holy history, for the sake of the lineage of the Good Knight that was after the crucifixion of Our Lord. Good Knight was he without fail, for he was chaste and virgin of his body and hardy of heart and puissant, and so were his conditions without wickedness. Not boastful was he of speech, and it seemed not by his cheer that he had so great courage; Natheless, of one little word that he delayed to speak came to pass so sore mischances in Greater Britain, that all the islands and all the lands fell thereby into much sorrow, albeit thereafter he put them back into gladness by the authority of his good knighthood. Good knight was he of right, for he was of the lineage of Joseph of Abarimacie. And this Joseph was his mother's uncle, that had been a soldier of Pilate's seven years, nor asked he of him none other guerdon of his service but only to take down the body of Our Saviour from hanging on the cross. The boon him seemed full great when it was granted him, and full little to Pilate seemed the guerdon; for right well had Joseph served him, and had he asked to have gold or land thereof, willingly would he have given it to him. And for this did Pilate make him a gift of the Saviour's body, for he supposed that Joseph should have dragged the same shamefully through the city

[margin: Sir Perceval's good conditions]

of Jerusalem when it had been taken down from the cross, and should have left it without the city in some mean place. But the Good Soldier had no mind thereto, but rather honoured the body the most he might, rather laid it along in the Holy Sepulchre and kept safe the lance whereof He was smitten in the side and the most Holy Vessel wherein they that believed on Him received with awe the blood that ran down from His wounds when He was set upon the rood. Of this lineage was the Good Knight for whose sake is this High History treated. Yglais was his mother's name: King Fisherman was his uncle, and the King of the Lower Folk that was named Pelles, and the King that was named of the Castle Mortal, in whom was there as much bad as there was good in the other twain, and much good was there in them; and these three were his uncles on the side of his mother Yglais, that was a right good Lady and a loyal; and the Good Knight had one sister, that hight Dindrane. He that was head of the lineage on his father's side was named Nichodemus. Gais li Gros of the Hermit's Cross was father of Alain li Gros. This Alain had eleven brethren, right good knights, like as he was himself. And none of them all lived in his knighthood but twelve years, and they all died in arms, for their great hardiment in setting forward of the Law that was made new. There were twelve brethren. Alain li Gros was the eldest; Gorgalians was next; Bruns Brandalis was the third; Bertholez li Chauz the fourth;

Sir Perceval's kindred

8   THE HIGH HISTORY OF

King Brandalus of Wales was the fifth; Elinant of
Arthur's Escavalon was the sixth; Calobrutus was the
court seventh; Meralis of the Palace Meadow was
the eighth; Fortunes of the Red Launde was
ninth; Melaarmaus of Abanie was the tenth;
Galians of the White Tower the eleventh;
Alibans of the Waste City was the twelfth.
All these died in arms in the service of the
Holy Prophet that had renewed the Law by
His death, and smote His enemies to the utter-
most of their power. Of these two manner of
folk, whose names and records you have heard,
Josephus the good clerk telleth us was come
the Good Knight of whom you shall well hear
the name and the manner presently.

II

The authority of the scripture telleth us that
after the crucifixion of Our Lord, no earthly
King set forward the Law of Jesus Christ so
much as did King Arthur of Britain, both by
himself and by the good knights that made
repair to his court. Good King Arthur after
the crucifixion of Our Lord, was such as I tell
you, and was a puissant King, and one that well
believed in God, and many were the good
adventures that befel at his court. And he had
in his court the Table Round that was garnished
of the best knights in the world. King Arthur
after the death of his father led the highest life
and most gracious that ever king led, in such
sort that all the princes and all the barons took
example of him in well-doing. For ten years
was King Arthur in such estate as I have told

you, nor never was earthly king so praised as he, until that a slothful will came upon him and he began to lose the pleasure in doing largess that he wont to have, nor was he minded to hold court neither at Christmas-tide nor at Easter nor at Pentecost. The knights of the Table Round when they saw his well-doing wax slack departed thence and began to hold aloof from his court, insomuch as that of three hundred and three-score and six knights that he wont to have of his household, there were now not more than a five-and-twenty at most, nor did no adventure befal any more at his court. All the other princes had slackened of their well-doing for that they saw King Arthur maintain so feebly. Queen Guenievre was so sorrowful thereof that she knew not what counsel to take with herself, nor how she might so deal as to amend matters so God amended them not. From this time beginneth the history.   *The King waxeth slothful*

III

It was one Ascension Day that the King was at Cardoil. He was risen from meat and went through the hall from one end to the other, and looked and saw the Queen that was seated at a window. The King went to sit beside her, and looked at her in the face and saw that the tears were falling from her eyes. 'Lady,' saith the King, 'What aileth you, and wherefore do you weep?' 'Sir,' saith she, 'And I weep, good right have I; and you yourself have little right to make joy.' 'Certes, Lady, I do not.' 'Sir,' saith she, 'You are right. I have seen on this

The Queen giveth counsel high day, or on other days that were not less high than this, when you have had such throng of knights at your court that right uneath might any number them. Now every day are so few therein that much shame have I thereof, nor no more do no adventures befal therein. Wherefore great fear have I lest God hath put you into forgetfulness.' 'Certes, Lady,' saith the King, ' No will have I to do largesse nor aught that turneth to honour. Rather is my desire changed into feebleness of heart. And by this know I well that I lose my knights and the love of my friends.' ' Sir,' saith the Queen, 'And were you to go to the chapel of S. Augustine that is in the White Forest, that may not be found save by adventure only, methinketh that on your back-repair you would again have your desire of well-doing, for never yet did none discounselled ask counsel of God but He would give it for love of him so he asked it of a good heart.' 'Lady,' saith the King, 'And willingly will I go, forasmuch as that you say have I heard well witnessed in many places where I have been.' ' Sir,' saith she, ' The place is right perilous and the chapel right adventurous. But the most worshipful hermit that is in the Kingdom of Wales hath his dwelling beside the chapel, nor liveth he now any longer for nought save only the glory of God.' 'Lady,' saith the King, 'It will behove me go thither all armed and without knights.' ' Sir,' saith she, ' You may well take with you one knight and a squire.' 'Lady,' saith the King, 'That durst not I, for the place is perilous, and the more folk one should take **Of Chaus** thither, the fewer adventures there should he **the squire** find.' 'Sir,' saith she, 'One squire shall you take by my approval, nor shall nought betide you thereof save good only, please God!' 'Lady,' saith the King, 'At your pleasure be it, but much dread I that nought shall come of it save evil only.' Thereupon the King riseth up from beside the Queen, and looketh before him and seeth a youth tall and strong and comely and young, that was hight Chaus, and he was the son of Ywain li Aoutres. 'Lady,' saith he to the Queen, 'This one will I take with me and you approve.' 'Sir,' saith she, 'It pleaseth me well, for I have heard much witness to his valour.' The King calleth the squire, and he cometh and kneeleth down before him. The King maketh him rise and saith to him, 'Chaus,' saith he, 'You shall lie within to-night, in this hall, and take heed that my horse be saddled at break of day and my arms ready. For I would be moving at the time I tell you, and yourself with me without more company.' 'Sir,' saith the squire, 'At your pleasure.' And the evening drew on, and the King and Queen go to bed. When they had eaten in hall, the knights went to their hostels. The squire remained in the hall, but he would not do off his clothes nor his shoon, for the night seemed him to be too short, and for that he would fain be ready in the morning at the King's commandment. The squire was lying down in such sort as I have told you, and in the first sleep that he slept, seemed him the King had gone without him.

The squire was sore scared thereat, and came to his hackney and set the saddle and bridle upon him, and did on his spurs and girt on his sword, as it seemed him in his sleep, and issued forth of the castle a great pace after the King. And when he had ridden a long space he entered into a great forest and looked in the way before him and saw the slot of the King's horse and followed the track a long space, until that he came to a launde of the forest whereat he thought that the King had alighted. The squire thought that the hoof-marks on the way had come to an end, and so thought that the King had alighted there or hard by there. He looketh to the right hand and seeth a chapel in the midst of the launde, and he seeth about it a great graveyard wherein were many coffins, as it seemed him. He thought in his heart that he would go toward the chapel, for he supposed that the King would have entered to pray there. He went thitherward and alighted. When the squire was alighted, he tied up his hackney and entered into the chapel. None did he see there in one part nor another, save a knight that lay dead in the midst of the chapel upon a bier, and he was covered of a rich cloth of silk, and had around him waxen tapers burning that were fixed in four candlesticks of gold. This squire marvelled much how this body was left there so lonely, insomuch that none were about him save only the images, and yet more marvelled he of the King that he found him not, for he knew not in what part to seek him. He taketh out one of the tall tapers, and layeth

The squire his dream

hand on the golden candlestick, and setteth it betwixt his hose and his thigh and issueth forth of the chapel, and remounteth on his hackney and goeth his way back and passeth beyond the grave-yard and issueth forth of the launde and entereth into the forest and thinketh that he will not cease until he hath found the King. *The stolen candlestick*

IV

So, as he entereth into a grassy lane in the wood, he seeth come before him a man black and foul-favoured, and he was somewhat taller afoot than was himself a-horseback. And he held a great sharp knife in his hand with two edges as it seemed him. The squire cometh over against him a great pace and saith to him, 'You, that come there, have you met King Arthur in this forest?' 'In no wise,' saith the messenger, 'But you have I met, whereof am I right glad at heart, for you have departed from the chapel as a thief and a traitor. For you are carrying off thence the candlestick of gold that was in honour of the knight that lieth in the chapel dead. Wherefore I will that you yield it up to me and so will I carry it back, otherwise, and you do not this, you do I defy!' 'By my faith,' saith the squire, 'Never will I yield it you! rather will I carry it off and make a present thereof to King Arthur.' 'By my faith,' saith the other, 'Right dearly shall you pay for it, and you yield it not up forthwith.' Howbeit, the squire smiteth with his spurs and thinketh to pass him by, but the other hasteth him, and smiteth the squire in the

The dream cometh true left side with the knife and thrusteth it into his body up to the haft. The squire, that lay in the hall at Cardoil, and had dreamed this, awoke and cried in a loud voice: 'Holy Mary! The priest! Help! Help, for I am a dead man!' The King and the Queen heard the cry, and the chamberlain leapt up and said to the King: 'Sir, you may well be moving, for it is day!' The King made him be clad and shod. And the squire crieth with such strength as he hath: 'Fetch me the priest, for I die!' The King goeth thither as fast as he may, and the Queen and the chamberlain carry great torches and candles. The King asketh him what aileth him, and he telleth him all in such wise as he had dreamed it. 'Ha,' saith the King, 'Is it then a dream?' 'Yea, sir,' saith he, 'But a right foul dream it is for me, for right foully hath it come true!' He lifted his left arm. 'Sir,' saith he, 'Look you there! Lo, here is the knife that was run into my side up to the haft!' After that, he setteth his hand to his hose where the candlestick was. He draweth it forth and showeth it to the King. 'Sir,' saith he, 'For this candlestick that I present to you, am I wounded to the death!' The King taketh the candlestick and looketh thereat in wonderment for none so rich had he never seen tofore. The King showeth it to the Queen. 'Sir,' saith the squire, 'Draw not forth the knife of my body until that I be shriven.' The King sent for one of his own chaplains that made the squire confess and do his houselling right well. The King himself draweth forth the knife of the body, and the soul departed *King* forthwith. The King made do his service *Arthur* right richly and his shrouding and burial. *goeth* Ywain li Aoutres that was father to the squire *forth* was right sorrowful of the death of his son. King Arthur, with the approval of Ywain his father, gave the candlestick to S. Paul in London, for the church was newly founded, and the King wished that this marvellous adventure should everywhere be known, and that prayer should be made in the church for the soul of the squire that was slain on account of the candlestick.

V

King Arthur armed himself in the morning, as I told you and began to tell, to go to the chapel of S. Augustine. Said the Queen to him: 'Whom will you take with you?' 'Lady,' saith he, 'No company will I have thither, save God only, for well may you understand by this adventure that hath befallen, that God will not allow I should have none with me.' 'Sir,' saith she, 'God be guard of your body, and grant you return safely so as that you may have the will to do well, whereby shall your praise be lifted up that is now sore cast down.' 'Lady,' saith he, 'May God remember it.' His destrier was brought to the mounting-stage, and the King mounted thereon all armed. Messire Ywain li Aoutres lent him his shield and spear. When the King had hung the shield at his neck and held the spear in his hand, sword-girt, on the tall destrier

King Arthur at the chapel armed, well seemed he in the make of his body and in his bearing to be a knight of great pith and hardiment. He planteth himself so stiffly in the stirrups that he maketh the saddlebows creak again and the destrier stagger under him that was right stout and swift, and he smiteth him of his spurs, and the horse maketh answer with a great leap. The Queen was at the windows of the hall, and as many as five-and-twenty knights were all come to the mounting-stage. When the King departed, 'Lords,' saith the Queen, 'How seemeth you of the King? Seemeth he not a goodly man?' 'Yea, certes, Lady, and sore loss is it to the world that he followeth not out his good beginning, for no king nor prince is known better learned of all courtesy nor of all largesse than he, so he would do like as he was wont.' With that the knights hold their peace, and King Arthur goeth away a great pace. And he entereth into a great forest adventurous, and rideth the day long until he cometh about evensong into the thick of the forest. And he espied a little house beside a little chapel, and it well seemed him to be a hermitage. King Arthur rode thitherward and alighteth before this little house, and entereth thereinto and draweth his horse after him, that had much pains to enter in at the door, and laid his spear down on the ground and leant his shield against the wall, and hath ungirded his sword and unlaced his ventail. He looked before him and saw barley and provender, and so led his horse thither and took off his bridle, and afterwards hath shut the door of the little house and locked it. And it seemed him that there was a strife in the chapel. The ones were weeping so tenderly and sweetly as it were angels, and the other spake so harshly as it were fiends. The King heard such voices in the chapel and marvelled much what it might be. He findeth a door in the little house that openeth on a little cloister whereby one goeth to the chapel. The King is gone thither and entereth into the little minster, and looketh everywhere but seeth nought there, save the images and the crucifixes. And he supposeth not that the strife of these voices cometh of them. The voices ceased as soon as he was within. He marvelleth how it came that this house and hermitage were solitary, and what had become of the hermit that dwelt therein. He drew nigh the altar of the chapel and beheld in front thereof a coffin all discovered, and he saw the hermit lying therein all clad in his vestments, and seeth the long beard down to his girdle, and his hands crossed upon his breast. There was a cross above him, whereof the image came as far as his mouth, and he had life in him yet, but he was nigh his end, being at the point of death. The King was before the coffin a long space, and looked right fainly on the hermit, for well it seemed him that he had been of a good life. The night was fully come, but within was a brightness of light as if a score of candles were lighted. He had a mind to abide there until that the good man should have passed away. He would fain have sate him down before the coffin, when a voice

A strife in the chapel

Our Lady giveth judgment warned him right horribly to begone thence, for that it was desired to make a judgment within there, that might not be made so long as he were there. The King departed, that would willingly have remained there, and so returned back into the little house, and sate him down on a seat whereon the hermit wont to sit. And he heareth the strife and the noise begin again within the chapel, and the ones he heareth speaking high and the others low, and he knoweth well by the voices, that the ones are angels and the others devils. And he heareth that the devils are distraining on the hermit's soul, and that judgment will presently be given in their favour, whereof make they great joy. King Arthur is grieved in his heart when he heareth that the angels' voices are stilled. The King is so heavy, that no desire hath he neither to eat nor to drink. And while he sitteth thus, stooping his head toward the ground, full of vexation and discontent, he heareth in the chapel the voice of a Lady that spake so sweet and clear, that no man in this earthly world, were his grief and heaviness never so sore, but and he had heard the sweet voice of her pleading would again have been in joy. She saith to the devils: 'Begone from hence, for no right have ye over the soul of this good man, whatsoever he may have done aforetime, for in my Son's service and mine own is he taken, and his penance hath he done in this hermitage of the sins that he hath done.' 'True, Lady,' say the devils, 'But longer had he served us than he hath served you and your Son. For forty years or more hath he been a murderer and robber in this forest, whereas in this hermitage but five years hath he been. And now you wish to thieve him from us.' 'I do not. No wish have I to take him from you by theft, for had he been taken in your service in suchwise as he hath been taken in mine, yours would he have been, all quit.' The devils go their way all discomfit and aggrieved; and the sweet Mother of our Lord God taketh the soul of the hermit, that was departed of his body, and so commendeth it to the angels and archangels that they make present thereof to Her dear Son in Paradise. And the angels take it and begin to sing for joy *Te Deum laudamus*. And the Holy Lady leadeth them and goeth her way along with them. Josephus maketh remembrance of this history and telleth us that this worthy man was named Calixtus.

The hermit Calixtus

VI

King Arthur was in the little house beside the chapel, and had heard the voice of the sweet Mother of God and the angels. Great joy had he, and was right glad of the good man's soul that was borne thence into Paradise. The King had slept right little the night and was all armed. He saw the day break clear and fair, and goeth his way toward the chapel to cry God mercy, thinking to find the coffin discovered there where the hermit lay; but so did he not! Rather, was it covered of the richest tomb-stone that any might ever see, and had on the top a red cross, and seemed it that the chapel was all incensed. When the King had made his orison therein, he cometh back again and setteth on his bridle and saddle and mounteth, and taketh his shield and spear and departeth from the little house and entereth into the forest and rideth a great pace, until he cometh at right hour of tierce to one of the fairest laundes that ever a man might see. And he seeth at the entrance a paled bar, and looketh to the right or ever he should enter therein, and seeth a damsel sitting under a great leafy tree, and she held the reins of her mule in her hand. The damsel was of great beauty and full seemly clad. The King turneth thitherward and so saluteth her and saith: 'Damsel,' saith he, 'God give you joy and good adventure.' 'Sir,' saith she, 'So may He do to you!' 'Damsel,' saith the King, 'Is there no hold in this launde?' 'Sir,' saith the damsel, 'No hold is there save a most holy chapel and a hermit that is beside S. Augustine's chapel.' 'Is this then S. Augustine's chapel?' saith the King. 'Yea, Sir, I tell it you for true, but the launde and the forest about is so perilous that no knight returneth thence but he be dead or wounded; but the place of the chapel is of so great worthiness that none goeth thither, be he never so discounselled, but he cometh back counselled, so he may thence return on live. And Lord God be guard of your body, for never yet saw I none aforetime that seemed more like to be good knight, and sore pity would it be and you were not, and never more shall I depart me hence and I shall have seen your end.'

The King meeteth a damsel

'Damsel,' saith the King, 'Please God, you shall see me repair back thence.' 'Certes,' saith the damsel, 'Thereof should I be right glad, for then should I ask you tidings at leisure of him that I am seeking.' The King goeth to the bar whereby one entereth into the the launde, and looketh to the right into a combe of the forest and seeth the chapel of S. Augustine and the right fair hermitage. Thitherward goeth he and alighteth, and it seemeth him that the hermit is apparelled to sing the mass. He reineth up his horse to the bough of a tree by the side of the chapel and thinketh to enter thereinto, but, had it been to conquer all the kingdoms of the world, thereinto might he not enter, albeit there was none made him denial thereof, for the door was open and none saw he that might forbid him. Sore ashamed is the King thereof. Howbeit, he beholdeth an image of Our Lord that was there within and crieth Him of mercy right sweetly, and looketh toward the altar. And he looketh at the holy hermit that was robed to sing mass and said his *Confiteor*, and seeth at his right hand the fairest Child that ever he had seen, and He was clad in an alb and had a golden crown on his head loaded with precious stones that gave out a full great brightness of light. On the left hand side, was a Lady so fair that all the beauties of the world might not compare them with her beauty. When the holy hermit had said his *Confiteor* and went to the altar, the Lady also took her Son and went to sit on the right hand side towards the altar upon a right

[marginal note: S. Austin's chapel]

The King seeth a vision. rich chair and set her Son upon her knees and began to kiss Him full sweetly and saith: 'Sir,' saith she, 'You are my Father and my Son and my Lord, and guardian of me and of all the world.' King Arthur heareth the words and seeth the beauty of the Lady and of the Child, and marvelleth much of this that She should call Him her Father and her Son. He looketh at a window behind the altar and seeth a flame come through at the very instant that mass was begun, clearer than any ray of sun nor moon nor star, and evermore it threw forth a brightness of light such that and all the lights in the world had been together it would not have been the like. And it is come down upon the altar. King Arthur seeth it who marvelleth him much thereof. But sore it irketh him of this that he may not enter there-within, and he heareth, there where the holy hermit was singing the mass, right fair responses, and they seem him to be the responses of angels. And when the Holy Gospel was read, King Arthur looked toward the altar and saw that the Lady took her Child and offered Him into the hands of the holy hermit, but of this King Arthur made much marvel, that the holy hermit washed not his hands when he had received the offering. Right sore did King Arthur marvel him thereof, but little right would he have had to marvel had he known the reason. And when the Child was offered him, he set Him upon the altar and thereafter began his sacrament. And King Arthur set him on his knees before the chapel and began to pray to God and to beat his breast. And he looked toward the altar after the preface, and it seemed him that the holy hermit held between his hands a man bleeding from His side and in His palms and in His feet, and crowned with thorns, and he seeth Him in His own figure. And when he had looked on Him so long and knoweth not what is become of Him, the King hath pity of Him in his heart of this that he had seen, and the tears of his heart come into his eyes. And he looketh toward the altar and thinketh to see the figure of the man, and seeth that it is changed into the shape of the Child that he had seen tofore.

The hermit speaketh with him

VII

When the mass was sung, the voice of a holy angel said *Ite, missa est.* The Son took the Mother by the hand, and they evanished forth of the chapel with the greatest company and the fairest that might ever be seen. The flame that was come down through the window went away with this company. When the hermit had done his service and was divested of the arms of God, he went to King Arthur that was still without the chapel. 'Sir,' saith he to the King, 'Now may you well enter herein and well might you have been joyous in your heart had you deserved so much as that you might have come in at the beginning of the mass.' King Arthur entered into the chapel without any hindrance. 'Sir,' saith the hermit to the King, 'I know you well, as did I also King

Uther Pendragon your father. On account of
your sins and your deserts might you not enter
here while mass was being sung. Nor will you
to-morrow save you shall first have made amends
of that you have misdone towards God and towards the saint that is worshipped herewithin.
For you are the richest King of the world and
the most adventurous, wherefore ought all the
world to take ensample of you in well-doing
and in largesse and in honour; whereas you
are now an ensample of evil-doing to all rich
worshipful men that be now in the world.
Wherefore shall right sore mishap betide you
and you set not back your doing to the point
whereat you began. For your court was the
sovran of all courts and the most adventurous,
whereas now is it least of worth. Well may
he be sorry that goeth from honour to shame,
but never may he have reproach that shall do
him ill, that cometh from shame to honour, for
the honour wherein he is found rescueth him to
God, but blame may never rescue the man that
hath renounced honour for shame, for the shame
and wickedness wherein he is found declare him
guilty.'

The King willeth to amend

VIII

'Sir,' saith King Arthur, 'To amend me
have I come hither, and to be better counselled
than I have been. Well do I see that the
place is most holy, and I beseech you that you
pray God that He counsel me and I will do
my endeavour herein to amend me.' 'God
grant you may amend your life,' saith the holy

hermit, 'In such sort that you may help to do **The** away the evil Law and to exalt the Law that **Black** is made new by the crucifixion of the Holy **Knight** Prophet. But a great sorrow is befallen in the land of late through a young knight that was harboured in the hostel of the rich King Fisherman, for that the most Holy Graal appeared to him and the Lance whereof the point runneth of blood, yet never asked he to whom was served thereof nor whence it came, and for that he asked it not are all the lands commoved to war, nor no knight meeteth other in the forest but he runneth upon him and slayeth him and he may, and you yourself shall well perceive thereof or ever you shall depart of this launde.' 'Sir,' saith King Arthur, 'God defend me from the anguish of an evil death and from wickedness, for hither have I come for none other thing but to amend my life, and this will I do, so God bring me back in safety.' 'Truly,' saith the hermit, 'He that hath been bad for three years out of forty, he hath not been wholly good.' 'Sir,' saith the King, 'You speak truth.' The hermit departeth and so commendeth him to God. The King cometh to his horse and mounteth the speediest that ever he may, and setteth his shield on his neck, and taketh his spear in his hand and turneth him back a great pace. Howbeit, he had not gone a bowshot's length when he saw a knight coming disorderly against him, and he sate upon a great black horse and he had a shield of the same and a spear. And the spear was somewhat thick near the point and burned with a great flame, foul and hideous, and the flame came down as far as over the knight's fist. He setteth his spear in rest and thinketh to smite the King, but the King swerveth aside and the other passeth beyond. 'Sir knight, wherefor hate you me?' 'Of right ought I not to love you,' saith the knight. 'Wherefore?' saith the King. 'For this, that you have had my brother's candlestick that was foully stolen from him!' 'Know you then who I am?' saith the King. 'Yea,' saith the knight; 'You are the King Arthur that aforetime were good and now are evil. Wherefore I defy you as my mortal enemy.' He draweth him back so that his onset may be the weightier. The King seeth that he may not depart without a stour. He setteth his spear in rest when he seeth the other come towards him with his own spear all burning. The King smiteth his horse with his spurs as hard as he may, and meeteth the knight with his spear and the knight him. And they melled together so stoutly that the spears bent without breaking, and both twain are shifted in their saddles and lose their stirrups. They hurtle so strongly either against other of their bodies and their horses that their eyes sparkle as of stars in their heads and the blood rayeth out of King Arthur by mouth and nose. Either draweth away from other and they take their breath. The King looketh at the Black Knight's spear that burneth, and marvelleth him right sore that it is not snapped in flinders of the great buffet he had received thereof, and him thinketh rather that it is a devil and a fiend. The Black

Knight is not minded to let King Arthur go so **and** soon, but rather cometh toward him a great **slayeth** career. The King seeth him come toward him **him** and so covereth him of his shield for fear of the flame. The King receiveth him on the point of his spear and smiteth him with so sore a shock that he maketh him bend backward over his horse croup. The other, that was of great might, leapeth back into the saddle-bows and smiteth the King upon the boss of his shield so that the burning point pierceth the shield and the sleeve of his habergeon and runneth the sharp iron into his arm. The King feeleth the wound and the heat, whereof is he filled with great wrath, and the knight draweth back his spear to him, and hath great joy at heart when he feeleth the King wounded. The King was rejoiced not a whit, and looked at the spear that was quenched thereof and burned no longer. 'Sir,' saith the knight, 'I cry you mercy. Never would my spear have been quenched of its burning, save it were bathed in your blood.' 'Now may never God help me,' saith King Arthur, 'Whenever I shall have mercy on you, and I may achieve!' He pricketh towards him a great run, and smiteth him in the broad of the breast and thrusteth his spear half an ell into his body, and beareth him to the ground, both him and his horse all in a heap, and draweth his spear back to him and looketh at the knight that lay as dead and leaveth him in the launde, and draweth him towards the issue incontinent. And so as the King went, he heard a great clashing of knights coming right amidst the

The forest, so as it seemed there were a good score
or more of them, and he seeth them enter the
launde from the forest, armed and well horsed.
And they come with great ado toward the
knight that lay dead in the midst of the launde.
King Arthur was about to issue forth, when the
damsel that he had left under the tree cometh
forward to meet him. 'Sir,' saith she, 'For
God's sake, return back and fetch me the head
of the knight that lieth there dead.' The King
looketh back, and seeth the great peril and the
multitude of knights that are there all armed.
'Ha, damsel,' saith he, 'You are minded to slay
me.' 'Certes, Sir, that I am not, but sore need
will there be that I should have it, nor never
did knight refuse to do the thing I asked nor
deny me any boon I demanded of him. Now
God grant you be not the most churlish.' 'Ha,
damsel, I am right sore wounded in the arm
whereon I hold my shield.' 'Sir,' saith she,
'I know it well, nor never may you be heal
thereof save you bring me the head of the
knight.' 'Damsel,' saith he, 'I will essay it
whatsoever may befal me thereof.'

The damsel craveth a boon

IX

King Arthur looketh amidst the launde and
seeth that they that have come thither have cut
the knight to pieces limb by limb, and that each
is carrying off a foot or a thigh or an arm or a
hand and are dispersing them through the forest.
And he seeth that the last knight beareth on the
point of his spear the head. The King goeth

after him a great gallop and crieth out to him: 'Ha, Sir knight, abide and speak to me!' 'What is your pleasure?' saith the knight. 'Fair Sir,' saith the King, 'I beseech you of all loves that you deign to give me the head of this knight that you are carrying on the point of your lance.' 'I will give it you,' saith the knight, 'on condition.' 'What condition?' saith the King. 'That you tell me who slew the knight whose head I carry that you ask of me.' 'May I not otherwise have it?' saith the King. 'In no wise,' saith he. 'Then will I tell you,' saith the King. 'Know of a very truth that King Arthur slew him.' 'And where is he?' saith the knight. 'Seek him until you shall have found him,' saith King Arthur, 'For I have told you the truth thereof. Give me the head.' 'Willingly,' saith the knight. He lowereth his spear and the King taketh the head. The knight had a horn at his neck. He setteth it to his mouth and soundeth a blast right loud. The knights that were set within the forest hear the horn and return back a great gallop, and King Arthur goeth his way toward the oak-tree at the issue of the launde where the damsel is awaiting him. And the knights come presently to him that had given the head to the King and ask him wherefore he hath sounded the horn. 'For this,' saith he, 'That this knight that is going away yonder hath told me that King Arthur slew the Black Knight, and I was minded you should know it that we may follow him.' 'We will not follow him,' say the knights, 'For it is King Arthur himself

The King winneth the knight's head

The damsel telleth of Perceval that is carrying off the head, and no power have we to do evil to him nor other sith that he hath passed the bar. But you shall aby it that let him go when he was so nigh you!' They rush in upon him and slay him and cut him up, and each one carrieth off his piece the same as they had done with the other. King Arthur is issued forth of the bar, and cometh to the maiden that is waiting for him and presenteth her the head. 'Sir,' saith the damsel, 'Gramercy.' 'Damsel,' saith he, 'With a good will!' 'Sir,' saith the damsel, 'You may well alight, for nought have you to fear on this side the bar.' With that, the King alighteth. 'Sir,' saith she, 'Do off your habergeon heedfully and I will bind up the wound in your arm, for of none may you be made whole save of me only.' The King doeth off his habergeon, and the damsel taketh of the blood of the knight's head that still ran all warm, and therewith washeth King Arthur his wound, and thereafter maketh him do on his habergeon again. 'Sir,' saith she, 'Never would you have been whole save by the blood of this Black Knight. And for this carried they off the body piecemeal and the head, for that they well knew you were wounded; and of the head shall I have right sore need, for thereby shall a castle be yielded up to me that was reft from me by treason, so I may find the knight that I go seek, through whom it ought to be yielded up to me.' 'Damsel,' saith the King, 'And who is the knight?' 'Sir,' saith she, 'He was the son of Alain li Gros of the Valleys of Camelot, and is named Perlesvax.'

'Wherefore Perlesvax?' saith the King. 'Sir,' saith she, 'When he was born, his father was asked how he should be named in right baptism, and he said that he would he should have the name Perlesvax, for the Lord of the Moors had reft him of the greater part of the Valleys of Camelot, and therefore he would that his son should by this name be reminded thereof, and God should so multiply him as that he should be knight. The lad was right comely and right gentle and began to go by the forests and launch his javelins, Welsh-fashion, at hart and hind. His father and his mother loved him much, and one day they were come forth of their hold, whereunto the forest was close anigh, to enjoy them. Now, there was between the hold and the forest, an exceeding small chapel that stood upon four columns of marble; and it was roofed of timber and had a little altar within, and before the altar a right fair coffin, and thereupon was the figure of a man graven. Sir,' saith the damsel to the King, 'The lad asked his father and mother what man lay within the coffin. The father answered: "Fair son," saith he, "Certes, I know not to tell you, for the tomb hath been here or ever that my father's father was born, and never have I heard tell of none that might know who it is therein, save only that the letters that are on the coffin say that when the Best Knight in the world shall come hither the coffin will open and the joinings all fall asunder, and then will it be seen who it is that lieth therein."'

Sir Perceval's childhood

X

How be knights made?

'Damsel,' saith the King, 'Have many knights passed thereby sithence that the coffin was set there?' 'Yea, sir, so many that neither I nor none other may tell the number. Yet natheless hath not the coffin removed itself for none. When the lad heareth his father and mother talking thus, he asketh what a knight may be? "Fair son," saith his mother, "Of right ought you well to know by your lineage." She telleth the lad that he had eleven uncles on his father's side that had all been slain in arms, and not one of them lived knight but twelve years. Sir,' saith she to the King, 'The lad made answer that this was not that he had asked, but how knights were made? And the father answered that they were such as had more valour than any other in the world. After that he said, "Fair son, they are clad in habergeons of iron to protect their bodies, and helms laced upon their heads, and shields and spears and swords girded wherewithal to defend their bodies."'

XI

'Sir,' saith the damsel to the King, 'When that the father had thus spoken to the lad, they returned together to the castle. When the morrow morning came, the lad arose and heard the birds sing and bethought him that he would go for disport into the forest for the day sith that it was fair. So he mounted on one of his father's horses of the chase and carried his javelins Welshman-fashion and went into the forest and found a stag and followed him a good four leagues Welsh, until that he came into a launde and found two knights all armed that were there doing battle, and the one had a red shield and the other a white. He gave up tracking the stag to look on at the melly and saw that the Red Knight was conquering the White. He launched one of his javelins at the Red Knight so hard that he pierced his habergeon and made it pass through the heart. The knight fell dead. Sir,' saith the damsel, 'The knight of the white shield made great joy thereof, and the lad asked him "were knights so easy to slay? Methought," saith the lad, "that none might never pierce nor damage a knight's armour, otherwise would I not have run him through with my javelin," saith the lad. Sir, the lad brought the destrier home to his father and mother, and right grieved were they when they heard the tidings of the knight he had slain. And right were they, for thereof did sore trouble come to them thereafter. Sir, the squire departed from the house of his father and mother and came to the court of King Arthur. Right gladly did the King make him knight when he knew his will, and afterward he departed from the land and went to seek adventure in every kingdom. Now is he the Best Knight that is in the world. So go I to seek him, and full great joy shall I have at heart and I may find him. Sir, and you should meet him by any adventure in any of these forests, he beareth a red shield with a white hart. And

Perceval slayeth the Red Knight

so tell him that his father is dead, and that his mother will lose all her land so he come not to succour her; and that the brother of the knight of the Red shield that he slew in the forest with his javelin warreth upon her with the Lord of the Moors.' 'Damsel,' saith the King, 'And God grant me to meet him, right glad shall I be thereof, and right well will I set forth your message.' 'Sir,' saith she, 'Now that I have told you him that I seek, it is your turn to tell me your name.' 'Damsel,' saith the King, 'Willingly. They that know me call me Arthur.' 'Arthur? Have you indeed such name?' 'Yea, damsel,' saith he. 'So help me God,' saith she, 'Now am I sorrier for you than tofore, for you have the name of the worst King in the world, and I would that he were here in such sort as you are now. But never again will he move from Cardoil, do what he may, such dread hath the Queen lest any should take him from her, according as I have heard witness, for never saw I neither the one nor the other. I was moved to go to his court, but I have met full a score knights one after other, of whom I asked concerning him, and one told me the same tale as another, for each told me that the court of King Arthur is the vilest in the world, and that all the knights of the Table Round have renounced it for the badness thereof.' 'Damsel,' saith the King, 'Hereof may he well be sorry, but at the beginning I have heard say he did right well.' 'And who careth,' saith the damsel, 'for his good beginning when the end is bad? And

much it misliketh me that so seemly knight Arthur
and so worshipful man as are you should have heareth
the name of so evil a king.' 'Damsel,' saith a Voice
the King, 'A man is not good by his name,
but by his heart.' 'You say true,' saith the
damsel, ' But for the King's name have I despite
of yours. And whitherward are you going?'
'I shall go to Cardoil, where I shall find King
Arthur when I shall come thither.' 'Go to,
then, and bestir!' saith she. 'One bad man
with another! No better hope have I of you,
sith that you go thither!' 'Damsel, you may
say your pleasure, for thither I go! God be
with you!' 'And may never God guide you,'
saith she, 'and you go to the court of King
Arthur!'

XII

With that the King mounted again and
departed, and left the damsel under the tree
and entered into the deep forest and rode with
much ado as fast as he might to come to
Cardoil. And he had ridden a good ten
leagues Welsh when he heard a Voice in the
thick of the forest that began to cry aloud:
'King Arthur of Great Britain, right glad at
heart mayst thou be of this that God hath sent
me hither to thee. And so He biddeth thee
that thou hold court at the earliest thou mayst,
for the world, that is now made worse of thee
and of thy slackness in well-doing, shall thereof
be greatly amended!' With that the Voice is
silent, and the King was right joyous in his
heart of that he had heard. The story speak-

Arthur cometh back to Cardoil

eth no more here of other adventure that befel King Arthur in his returning nor on his arrival. Anyway, he hath ridden so long that he is come back to Cardoil. The Queen and the knights made great feast of him and great joy. The King was alighted on the mounting-stage and went up into the hall and made him be disarmed. And he showed the Queen the wound that he had on his arm, that had been right great and painful, but it was healing full fairly. The King goeth into the chamber and the Queen with him, and doeth the King be apparelled in a robe of cloth of silk all furred of ermine, with coat, surcoat and mantle. 'Sir,' saith the Queen, 'Sore pain and travail have you had.' 'Lady, in such wise behoveth worshipful man to suffer in order that he may have honour, for hardly shall none without travail come to honour.' He recounteth to the Queen all the adventures that have befallen him sithence that he was departed, and in what manner he was wounded in the arm, and of the damsel that had so blamed him of his name. 'Sir,' saith the queen, 'Now may you well know how meet it is that a man high and rich and puissant should have great shame of himself when he becometh evil.' 'Lady,' saith the King, 'So much did the damsel do me well to wot, but greatly did a Voice recomfort me that I heard in the forest, for it told me that God bade me hold court presently, and that I shall see there the fairest adventure befal that ever I may see.' 'Sir,' saith she, 'Right joyous ought you to be that your Saviour hath had you in remembrance. Now, therefore, fulfil His commandment.' 'Certes, Lady, so will I do. For never had none better desire of well-doing than have I as at this time, nor of honour nor of largesse.' 'Sir,' saith she, 'God be praised thereof.'

The Queen rejoiceth

BRANCH II

INCIPIT

Arthur holdeth court NOW beginneth here the second branch of the Holy Graal in the name of the Father, and of the Son, and of the Holy Ghost.

TITLE I

King Arthur was at Cardoil with the Queen and right few knights. By God's pleasure, the wish and the will had come back to him to win honour and to do largesse as most he might. He made seal his letters and sent them throughout all his lands and all the islands, and gave notice to the barons and knights that he would hold court at Pannenoisance, that is situate on the sea of Wales, at the feast of S. John after Whitsuntide. And he was minded to put it off until that day, for that Whitsuntide was already too nigh, and they that should be present thereat might not all come by the earlier day. The tidings went through all lands, so that knights come in great plenty thereunto, for well-doing had so waxed feeble in all the kingdoms, that every one had avoided King Arthur as one that should do nought more for ever. Wherefore all began now to marvel whence his new desire had come. The knights of the Table Round that were scattered through the lands and the forests, by God's will learnt the tidings and right great joy had they thereof, and came back to the court with great ado. But neither Messire Gawain nor Lancelot came thither on that day. But all the other came that were then on live. S. John's day came, and the knights were come from all parts, marvelling much that the King had not held the court at Whitsuntide, but they knew not the occasion thereof. The day was fair and clear and the air fresh, and the hall was wide and high and garnished of good knights in great plenty. The cloths were spread on the tables whereof were great plenty in the hall. The King and the Queen had washen and went to sit at the head of one table and the other knights sate them down, whereof were full five score and five as the story telleth. Kay the Seneschal and Messire Ywain the son of King Urien served that day at the tables at meat, and five-and-twenty knights beside. And Lucan the Butler served the golden cup before the King. The sun shone through the windows everywhere amidst the hall that was strown of flowers and rushes and sweet herbs and gave out a smell like as had it been sprinkled of balm. And straightway after the first meat had been served, and while they were yet awaiting the second, behold you three damsels where they enter into the hall! She that came first sate upon a mule white as driven snow and had a golden bridle and a saddle with a bow of ivory banded with precious stones and a saddle-cloth of a red samite dropped of gold. The damsel that was seated on the mule was right

The Damsels of the Car

seemly of body but scarce so fair of face, and she was robed in a rich cloth of silk and gold and had a right rich hat that covered all her head. And it was all loaded of costly stones that flamed like fire. And great need had she that her head were covered, for she was all bald without hair, and carried on her neck her right arm slung in a stole of cloth of gold. And her arm lay on a pillow, the richest that ever might be seen, and it was all charged of little golden bells, and in this hand held she the head of a King sealed in silver and crowned with gold. The other damsel that came behind rode after the fashion of a squire, and carried a pack trussed behind her with a brachet thereupon, and at her neck she bore a shield banded argent and azure with a red cross, and the boss was of gold all set with precious stones. The third damsel came afoot with her kirtle tucked up like a running footman; and she had in her hand a whip wherewith she drove the two steeds. Each of these twain was fairer than the first, but the one afoot surpassed both the others in beauty. The first cometh before the King, there where he sitteth at meat with the Queen. 'Sir,' saith she, 'The Saviour of the world grant you honour and joy and good adventure and my Lady the Queen and all them of this hall for love of you! Hold it not churlishness and I alight not, for there where knights be may I not alight, nor ought I until such time as the Graal be achieved.' 'Damsel,' saith the King, 'Gladly would I have it so.' 'Sir,' saith she, 'That know I well, and may it not mislike you

The damsel greeteth Arthur

to hear the errand whereon I am come.' 'It
shall not mislike me,' saith the King, 'Say your
pleasure!' 'Sir,' saith she, 'The shield that
this damsel beareth belonged to Joseph, the
good soldier knight that took down Our Lord
of hanging on the rood. I make you a present
thereof in such wise as I shall tell you, to wit,
that you keep the shield for a knight that shall
come hither for the same, and you shall make
hang it on this column in the midst of your
hall, and guard it in such wise as that none
may take it and hang at his neck save he only.
And of this shield shall he achieve the Graal,
and another shield shall he leave here in the
hall, red, with a white hart; and the brachet
that the damsel carrieth shall here remain, and
little joy will the brachet make until the knight
shall come.' 'Damsel,' saith the King, 'The
shield and the brachet will we keep full safely,
and right heartily we thank you that you have
deigned to bring them hither.' 'Sir,' saith the
damsel, 'I have not yet told you all that I have
in charge to deliver. The best King that
liveth on earth and the most loyal and the most
righteous, sendeth you greeting; of whom is
sore sorrow for that he hath fallen into a grievous languishment.' 'Damsel,' saith the King,
'Sore pity is it and it be so as you say; and I
pray you tell me who is the King?' 'Sir,'
saith she, 'It is rich King Fisherman, of whom
is great grief.' 'Damsel,' saith the King, 'You
say true; and God grant him his heart's desire!'
'Sir,' saith she, 'Know you wherefore he hath
fallen into languishment?' 'Nay, I know not

Of King Fisherman

The damsel is bald at all, but gladly would I learn.' 'And I will tell you,' saith she. 'This languishment is come upon him through one that harboured in his hostel, to whom the most Holy Graal appeared. And, for that he would not ask unto whom one served thereof, were all the lands commoved to war thereby, nor never thereafter might knight meet other but he should fight with him in arms without none other occasion. You yourself may well perceive the same, for your well-doing hath greatly slackened, whereof have you had much blame, and all the other barons that by you have taken ensample, for you are the mirror of the world alike in well-doing and in evil-doing. Sir, I myself have good right to plain me of the knight, and I will show you wherefore.' She lifteth the rich hat from her head and showeth the King and Queen and the knights in the hall her head all bald without hair. 'Sir,' saith she, 'My head was right seemly garnished of hair plaited in rich tresses of gold at such time as the knight came to the hostel of the rich King Fisherman, but I became bald for that he made not the demand, nor never again shall I have my hair until such time as a knight shall go thither that shall ask the question better than did he, or the knight that shall achieve the Graal. Sir, even yet have you not seen the sore mischief that hath befallen thereof. There is without this hall a car that three white harts have drawn hither, and lightly may you send to see how rich it is. I tell you that the traces are of silk and the axletrees of gold, and the timber of the car is ebony. The car is covered above with a black samite, and below is a cross of gold the whole length, and under the coverlid of the car are the heads of an hundred and fifty knights whereof some be sealed in gold, other some in silver and the third in lead. King Fisherman sendeth you word that this loss hath befallen of him that demanded not unto whom one serveth of the Graal. Sir, the damsel that beareth the shield holdeth in her hand the head of a Queen that is sealed in lead and crowned with copper, and I tell you that by the Queen whose head you here behold was the King betrayed whose head I bear, and the three manner of knights whose heads are within the car. Sir, send without to see the costliness and fashion of the car.' The King sent Kay the Seneschal to see. He looked straitly thereat within and without and thereafter returned to the King. 'Sir,' saith he, 'Never beheld I car so rich, and there be three harts withal that draw the car, the tallest and fattest one might ever see. But and you will be guided by me, you will take the foremost, for he is scarce so fat, and so might you bid make right good collops thereof.' 'Avoid there, Kay!' saith the King. 'Foul churlishness have you spoken! I would not such a deed were done for another such kingdom as is this of Logres!' 'Sir,' saith the damsel, 'He that hath been wont to do churlishness doth right grudgingly withdraw himself therefrom. Messire Kay may say whatsoever him pleaseth, but well know I that you will pay no heed to his talk. Sir,' saith the damsel,

Arthur rebuketh Sir Kay

The damsels depart 'Command that the shield be hung on this column and that the brachet be put in the Queen's chamber with the maidens. We will go on our way, for here have we been long enough.' Messire Ywain laid hold on the shield and took it off the damsel's neck by leave of the King, and hung it on the column in the midst of the hall, and one of the Queen's maidens taketh the brachet and carrieth him to the Queen's chamber. And the damsel taketh her leave and turneth again, and the King commendeth her to God. When the King had eaten in hall, the Queen with the King and the knights go to lean at the windows to look at the three damsels and the three white harts that draw the car, and the more part said that the damsel afoot that went after the two that were mounted should have the most misease. The bald damsel went before, and set not her hat on her head until such time as behoved her enter into the forest; and the knights that were at the windows might see them no longer. Then set she her hat again upon her head. The King, the Queen, and the knights when they might see them no more, came down from the windows, and certain of them said that never until this time had they seen bald-headed damsel save this one only.

II

Hereupon the story is silent of King Arthur, and turneth again to speak of the three damsels and the car that was drawn by the three white harts. They are entered into the forest and ride on right busily. When they had left the castle some seven leagues Welsh behind them, they saw a knight coming toward them on the way they had to go. The knight sat on a tall horse, lean and bony. His habergeon was all rusty and his shield pierced in more than a dozen places, and the colour thereon was so fretted away that none might make out the cognizance thereof. And a right thick spear bore he in his hand. When he came anigh the damsel, he saluted her right nobly. 'Fair welcome, damsel, to you and your company.' 'Sir,' saith she, 'God grant you joy and good adventure!' 'Damsel,' saith the knight, 'Whence come you?' 'Sir, from a court high-plenary that King Arthur holdeth at Pannenoisance. Go you thither, sir knight,' saith the damsel, 'to see the King and the Queen and the knights that are there?' 'Nay, not so!' saith he. 'Many a time have I seen them, but right glad am I of King Arthur that he hath again taken up his well-doing, for many a time hath he been accustomed thereof.' 'Whitherward have you now emprised your way?' saith the damsel. 'To the land of King Fisherman, and God allow me.' 'Sir,' saith she, 'Tell me your name and bide awhile beside me.' The knight draweth bridle and the damsels and the car come to a stay. 'Damsel,' saith he, 'Well behoveth me tell you my name. Messire Gawain am I called, King Arthur's nephew.' 'What? are you Messire Gawain? My heart well told me as much.' 'Yea, damsel,' saith he, 'Gawain am I.' 'God

They meet Sir Gawain

Gawain joineth the damsels

be praised thereof, for so good knight as are you may well go see the rich King Fisherman. Now am I fain to pray you of the valour that is in you and the courtesy, that you return with me and convoy me beyond a certain castle that is in this forest whereof is some small peril.' 'Damsel,' saith Messire Gawain, 'Willingly, at your pleasure.' He returneth with the damsel through the midst of the forest that was tall and leafy and little haunted of folk. The damsel relateth to him the adventure of the heads that she carried and that were in the car, like as she did at the court of King Arthur, and of the shield and the brachet she had left there, but much it misliked Messire Gawain of the damsel that was afoot behind them. 'Damsel,' saith Messire Gawain, 'Wherefore doth not this damsel that goeth afoot mount upon the car?' 'Sir,' saith she, 'This shall she not, for behoveth her go not otherwise than afoot. But and you be so good knight as men say, betimes will she have done her penance.' 'How so?' saith Gawain. 'I will tell you,' saith she. 'And it shall so be that God bring you to the hostel of rich King Fisherman, and the most Holy Graal appear before you and you demand unto whom is served thereof, then will she have done her penance, and I, that am bald, shall receive again my hair. And so you also make not demand thereof, then will it behove us suffer sore annoy until such time as the Good Knight shall come and shall have achieved the Graal. For on account of him that first was there and made not the demand, are all the lands in sorrow and warfare, and the good King Fisherman is yet in languishment.' 'Damsel,' saith Messire Gawain, 'God grant me courage and will herein that I may come to do this thing according to your wish, whereof may I win worship both of God and of the world.'

<small>The Black Castle</small>

III

Messire Gawain and the damsels go on their way a great pace through the high forest, green and leafy, where the birds are singing, and enter into the most hideous forest and most horrible that any might ever see, and seemed it that no greenery never there had been, so bare and dry were all the branches and all the trees black and burnt as it had been by fire, and the ground all parched and black atop with no green, and full of great cracks. 'Damsel,' saith Messire Gawain, 'Right loathly is this forest and right hideous. Goeth it on far like this?' 'Sir,' saith she, 'For nine leagues Welsh goeth it on the same, but we shall pass not through the whole thereof.' Messire Gawain looketh from time to time on the damsel that cometh afoot, and sore it irketh him that he may not amend her estate. They ride on until that they come to a great valley and Messire Gawain looketh along the bottom and seeth appear a black castle that was enclosed within a girdle of wall, foul and evil-seeming. The nigher he draweth to the castle the more hideous it seemeth him, and he seeth great halls appear that were right foully mis-shapen, and the forest

<small>The Black Hermit's knights</small> about it he seeth to be like as he had found it behind. He seeth a water come down from the head of a mountain, foul and horrible and black, that went amidst the castle roaring so loud that it seemed to be thunder. Messire Gawain seeth the entrance of the gateway foul and horrible like as it had been hell, and within the castle heard he great outcries and lamentations, and the most part heard he saying: 'Ha, God! What hath become of the Good Knight, and when will he come?' 'Damsel,' saith Messire Gawain, 'What is this castle here that is so foul and hideous, wherein is such dolour suffered and such weary longing for the coming of the Good Knight?' 'Sir, this is the castle of the Black Hermit. Wherefore am I fain to pray you that you meddle not herein for nought that they within may do to me, for otherwise it may well be that your death is at hand, for against them will you have no might nor power.' They come anigh the castle as it were a couple of bow-shots, and behold, through the gateway come knights armed on black horses and their arms all black and their shields and spears, and there were a hundred and fifty and two, right parlous to behold. And they come a great gallop toward the damsel, and toward the car, and take the hundred and fifty-two heads, each one his own, and set them upon their spears and so enter into the castle again with great joy. Messire Gawain seeth the insolence that the knights have wrought, and right great shame hath he of himself that he hath not moved withal. 'Messire Gawain,' saith the

damsel, 'Now may you know how little would your force have availed you herein.' 'Damsel, an evil castle is this where folk are robbed on such wise.' 'Sir, never may this mischief be amended, nor this outrage be done away, nor the evil-doer therein be stricken down, nor they that cry and lament within the prison there be set free until such time as the Good Knight shall come for whom are they yearning as you have heard but now.' 'Damsel, right glad may the knight be that by his valour and his hardiment shall destroy so many evil folk!' 'Sir, therefore is he the Best Knight in the world, and he is yet young enough of age, but right sorrowful am I at heart that I know not true tidings of him; for better will have I to see him than any man on live.' 'Damsel, so also have I,' saith Messire Gawain, 'For then by your leave would I turn me again.' 'Not so, sir, but and you shall come beyond the castle, then will I teach you the way whereby you ought to go.'

Gawaine is challenged

IV

With that they go toward the castle all together. Just as they were about to pass beyond the castle wall, behold you where a knight cometh forth of a privy postern of the castle, and he was sitting upon a tall horse, his spear in his fist, and at his neck had he a red shield whereon was figured a golden eagle. 'Sir knight,' saith he to Messire Gawain, 'I pray you bide.' 'What is your pleasure?' 'You must needs joust with me,' saith he, 'and

Judas Machabee his shield conquer this shield, or otherwise I shall conquer you. And full precious is the shield, insomuch as that great pains ought you to take to have it and conquer it, for it belonged to the best knight of his faith that was ever, and the most puissant and the wisest.' 'Who, then, was he?' saith Messire Gawain. 'Judas Machabee was he, and he it was that first wrought how by one bird to take another.' 'You say true,' saith Messire Gawain; 'A good knight was he.' 'Therefore right joyful may you be,' saith he, 'and you may conquer the same, for your own is the poorest and most battered that ever saw I borne by knight. For hardly may a man know the colour thereof.' 'Thereby may you well see,' saith the damsel to the knight, 'that his own shield hath not been idle, nor hath the horse whereon he sitteth been stabled so well as yours.' 'Damsel,' saith the knight, 'No need is here of long pleading. Needs must he joust with me, for him do I defy.' Saith Messire Gawain, 'I hear well that you say.' He draweth him back and taketh his career and the knight likewise, and they come together as fast as their horses may carry them, spear in rest. The knight smiteth Messire Gawain on the shield whereof he had no great defence, and passeth beyond, and in the by-pass the knight to-brake his spear; and Messire Gawain smiteth him with his spear in the midst of his breast and beareth him to the ground over the croup of his horse, all pinned upon his spear, whereof he had a good full hand's breadth in his breast. He draweth his spear back to him, and when the knight felt himself unpinned, he leaped to his feet and came straight to his horse and would fain set his foot in the stirrup when the damsel of the car crieth out: 'Messire Gawain, hinder the knight! for and he were mounted again, too sore travail would it be to conquer him!' When the knight heard name Messire Gawain, he draweth him back: 'How?' saith he; 'Is this then the good Gawain, King Arthur's nephew?' 'Yea,' saith the damsel, 'He it is without fail!' 'Sir,' saith the knight to Messire Gawain, 'Are you he?' 'Yea,' saith he, 'Gawain I am!' 'Sir, so please you,' saith he, 'I hold me conquered, and right sorry am I that I knew you not or ever I had ado with you.' He taketh the shield from his neck and holdeth it to him. 'Sir,' saith he, 'Take the shield that belonged to the best knight that was in his time of his faith, for none know I of whom it shall be better employed than of you. And of this shield were vanquished all they that be in prison in this castle.' Messire Gawain taketh the shield that was right fair and rich. 'Sir,' saith the knight, 'Now give me yours, for you will not bear two shields.' 'You say true,' saith Messire Gawain. He taketh the guige from his neck and would have given him the shield, when the damsel afoot: 'Hold, sir knight, you that are named Messire Gawain! What would you do? And he bear your shield into the castle there, they of the castle will hold you recreant and conquered, and will come forth thence and carry you into the castle by force,

The knight's treachery

The knight yieldeth him and there will you be cast into his grievous prison; for no shield is borne thereinto save of a vanquished knight only.' 'Sir knight,' saith Messire Gawain, 'No good you wish me, according to that this damsel saith.' 'Sir,' saith the knight, 'I cry you mercy, and a second time I hold me conquered, and right glad should I have been might I have borne your shield within yonder, and right great worship should I have had thereof, for never yet hath entered there the shield of knight so good. And now ought I to be right well pleased of your coming, sith that you have set me free of the sorest trouble that ever knight had.' 'What is the trouble?' saith Messire Gawain. 'Sir,' saith he, 'I will tell you. Heretofore many a time hath there been a passing by of knights both of hardy and of coward, and it was my business to contend and joust with them and do battle, and I made them present of the shield as did I you. The more part found I hardy and well able to defend themselves, that wounded me in many places, but never was knight so felled me to the ground nor dealt me so sore a buffet as have you. And sith that you are carrying away the shield and I am conquered, never hereafter shall knight that passeth before this castle have no dread of me nor of no knight that is herein.' 'By my head,' saith Messire Gawain, 'Now am I gladder of my conquest than I was before.' 'Sir,' saith the knight, 'By your leave will I go my way, for, and I may hide not my shame in the castle, needs must I show it openly abroad.' 'God grant you do well!' saith Messire Gawain. 'Messire Gawain,' saith the Damsel of the Car, 'give me your shield that the knight would fain have carried off.' 'Willingly, damsel,' saith he. The damsel that went afoot taketh the shield and setteth it in the car. Howbeit, the knight that was conquered mounted again upon his horse, and entered again into the castle, and when he was come thereinto, arose a noise and great outcry so loud that all the forest and all the valley began to resound thereof. 'Messire Gawain,' saith the Damsel of the Car, 'the knight is shamed and there cast in prison another time. Now haste, Messire Gawain! for now may you go!' With that they all set forward again upon their way together, and leave the castle an English league behind. 'Damsel,' saith Messire Gawain, 'When it shall please you, I shall have your leave to go.' 'Sir,' saith she, 'God be guard of your body, and right great thanks of your convoy.' 'Lady,' saith he, 'My service is always ready at your command.' 'Sir,' saith the damsel, 'Gramercy, and your own way see you there by yonder great cross at the entrance of yonder forest. And beyond that, will you find the fairest forest and most delightsome when you shall have passed through this that sore is wearisome.' Messire Gawain turneth him to go, and the damsel afoot crieth out to him: 'Sir, not so heedful are you as I supposed.' Messire Gawain turneth his horse's head as he that was startled: 'Wherefore say you so, damsel?' saith he. 'For this,' saith

Gawain is heedless

Gawain departeth she, 'That you have never asked of my Damsel wherefore she carrieth her arm slung at her neck in this golden stole, nor what may be the rich pillow whereon the arm lieth. And no greater heed will you take at the court of the rich King Fisherman.' 'Sweet, my friend,' saith the Damsel of the Car, 'blame not Messire Gawain only, but King Arthur before him and all the knights that were in the court. For not one of them all that were there was so heedful as to ask me. Go your ways, Messire Gawain, for in vain would you now demand it, for I will tell you not, nor shall you never know it save only by the most coward knight in the world, that is mine own knight and goeth to seek me and knoweth not where to find me.' 'Damsel,' saith Messire Gawain, 'I durst not press you further.' With that the Damsel departeth, and Messire Gawain setteth him forward again on the way that she had taught him.

BRANCH III

INCIPIT

HERE beginneth another branch of the Graal in the name of the Father, and in the name of the Son, and in the name of the Holy Ghost.

Gawain findeth a damsel

TITLE I

Here is the story silent of the three damsels and the car and saith that Messire Gawain hath passed throughout the evil forest and is entered into the forest passing fair, the broad, the high, the plenteous of venison. And he rideth a great pace, but sore abashed is he of that the damsel had said to him, and misdoubteth him but he shall have blame thereof in many places. He rode hard the day long till that it was evensong and the sun was about to set. And he looketh before him and seeth the house of a hermit and the chapel in the thick of the forest; and a spring flowed forth in front of the chapel right clear and fresh, and above it was a tree full broad and tall that threw a shadow over the spring. A damsel sate under the tree and held a mule by the reins and at the saddle-bow had she the head of a knight hanging. And Messire Gawain cometh thitherward and alighteth. 'Damsel,' saith he, 'God give you good adventure!' 'Sir,' saith she, 'And

A hermit knight you always.' When she was risen up over against him, 'Damsel,' saith he, 'For whom are you a-waiting here?' 'Sir,' saith she, 'I am waiting for the hermit of this holy chapel, that is gone into the forest, and I would fain ask him tidings of a knight.' 'Think you he will tell you them and he knoweth any?' 'Yea, sir, I think so, according to that I have been told.' Therewithal behold you the hermit that was coming, and saluteth the damsel and Messire Gawain and openeth the door of the house and setteth the two steeds within and striketh off the bridles and giveth them green-meat first and barley after, and fain would he have taken off the saddles when Messire Gawain leapeth before: 'Sir,' saith he, 'Do not so! This business is not for you!' 'Hermit though I be,' saith he, 'yet well know I how to deal withal, for at the court of King Uther Pendragon have I been squire and knight two-score years, and a score or more have I been in this hermitage.' And Messire Gawain looketh at him in wonderment. 'Sir,' saith he, 'Meseemeth you are not of more than forty years.' 'That know I well of a truth,' saith the hermit, and Messire Gawain taketh off the saddles and bethinketh him more of the damsel's mule than of his own horse. And the hermit taketh Messire Gawain by the hand and the damsel and leadeth them into the chapel. And the place was right fair. 'Sir,' saith the hermit to Messire Gawain, 'You will disarm you not,' saith he, 'for this forest is passing adventurous, and no worshipful man behoveth be disgarnished.' He goeth for his spear and for his shield and setteth them within the chapel. He setteth before them such meat as he hath, and when they have eaten giveth them to drink of the spring. 'Sir,' saith the damsel, 'Of a knight that I go seek am I come to ask you tidings.' 'Who is the knight?' saith the hermit. 'Sir, he is the Chaste Knight of most holy lineage. He hath a head of gold, the lock of a lion, the navel of a virgin maid, a heart of steel, the body of an elephant, and without wickedness are all his conditions.' 'Damsel,' saith the hermit, 'Nought will I tell you concerning him, for I know not of a certainty where he is, save this, that he hath lain in this chapel twice, not once only, within this twelvemonth.' 'Sir,' saith she, 'Will you tell me no more of him, nor none other witting?' 'In no wise,' saith the hermit. 'And you, Messire Gawain?' saith she. 'Damsel,' saith he, 'As fainly would I see him as you, but none find I that may tell me tidings of him.' 'And the Damsel of the Car, Sir, have you seen her?' 'Yea, lady,' saith he, 'It is but just now sithence that I left her.' 'Carried she still her arm slung at her neck?' 'Yea,' saith Messire Gawain, 'in such wise she carried it.' 'Of a long while,' saith the damsel, 'hath she borne it thus.' 'Sir,' saith the hermit, 'how are you named?' 'Sir,' saith he, 'Gawain am I called, King Arthur's nephew.' 'Thereof I love you the better,' saith the hermit. 'Sir,' saith the damsel, 'You are of kindred to the worst King that is.' 'Of what

Perceval the Chaste Knight

<small>Arthur's name misliked</small> King speak you?' saith Messire Gawain. 'I speak,' saith she, 'of King Arthur, through whom is all the world made worser, for he began doing well and now hath become evil. For hatred of him hate I a knight that found me nigh St. Augustine's Chapel, and yet was he the comeliest knight that saw I ever. He slew a knight within the bar right hardily. I asked him for the head of the knight and he went back for the same and set himself in sore peril. He brought it me, and I made him great joy, but when he told me his name was Arthur I had no fainness of the bounty he had done me, for that he had the name of that evil King.'

II

'Damsel,' saith Messire Gawain, 'You may say your pleasure. I tell you that King Arthur hath held the richest court that he hath held ever, and these evil conditions whereof you blame him is he minded to put away for evermore, and more will he do of good and more of largesse than was ever known aforetime, so long as he shall live; nor know I none other knight that beareth his name.' 'You are right,' saith the damsel, 'to come to his rescue, for that he is your uncle, but your rescue will scarce avail him and he deliver not himself.' 'Sir,' saith the hermit to Messire Gawain, 'The damsel will say her pleasure. May God defend King Arthur, for his father made me knight. Now am I priest, and in this hermitage ever sithence that I came hither have I served King

Fisherman by the will of Our Lord and His commandment, and all they that serve him do well partake of his reward, for the place of his most holy service is a refuge so sweet that unto him that hath been there a year, it seemeth to have been but a month for the holiness of the place and of himself, and for the sweetness of his castle wherein have I oftentimes done service in the chapel where the Holy Graal appeareth. Therefore is it that I and all that serve him are so youthful of seeming.' 'Sir,' saith Messire Gawain, 'By what way may a man go to his castle?' 'Sir,' saith the hermit, 'None may teach you the way, save the will of God lead you therein. And would you fain go thither?' 'Sir,' saith Messire Gawain, 'It is the most wish that I have.' 'Sir,' saith the hermit, 'Now God give you grace and courage to ask the question that the others to whom the Graal hath appeared would ask not, whereof have many mischances sithence befallen much people.'

The chapel of the Graal

III

With that, they left of talking, and the hermit led Messire Gawain into his house to rest, and the damsel abode still in the chapel. On the morrow when dawn appeared, Messire Gawain that had lain all armed, arose and found his saddle ready and the damsel, and the bridles set on, and cometh to the chapel and findeth the hermit that was apparelled to sing mass, and seeth the damsel kneeling before an image of Our Lady, and she prayed God and the sweet Lady that they would counsel her of

Gawain goeth his way that whereof she had need, and wept right tenderly so that the tears ran down her face. And when she had prayed of a long space she ariseth, and Messire Gawain biddeth her God give her good day, and she returneth his salute. 'Damsel,' saith he, 'Meseemeth you are not over joyous.' 'Sir,' saith she, 'I have right, for now am I nigh unto my desolation, sith that I may not find the Good Knight. Now must I needs go to the castle of the Black Hermit, and bear thither the head that hangeth at my saddle-bow, for otherwise shall I not be able to pass through the forest but my body should there be cast in prison or shamed, and this shall be the quittance for my passing. Then will I seek the Damsel of the Car and so shall I go in safety through the forest.' With that the hermit had begun the mass and Messire Gawain and the damsel heard it. When mass was sung, Messire Gawain took leave of the hermit and the damsel also. And Messire Gawain goeth one way and the damsel the other, and either biddeth other to God.

IV

Hereupon the story is now silent of the damsel, and saith that Messire Gawain goeth through the high forest and rideth a great pace, and prayeth God right sweetly that He will set him in such way as that thereby he may go to the land of the rich King Fisherman. And he rideth until the hour of noon, and cometh into the fulness of the forest and seeth under a tree a squire alighted of a horse of the chase. Messire Gawain saluteth him, and the squire saith: 'Sir, right welcome may you be!' 'Fair sweet friend,' saith Messire Gawain, 'Whither go you?' 'Sir, I go to seek the lord of this forest.' 'Whose is the forest?' saith Messire Gawain. 'Sir, it belongeth to the Best Knight in the world.' 'Can you tell me tidings of him?' 'He ought to bear a shield banded azure and argent with a red cross thereon and a boss of gold. I say that he is good knight, but little call have I to praise him, for he slew my father in this forest with a javelin. The Good Knight was squire what time he slew him, and fain would I avenge my father upon him and I may find him, for he reft me of the best knight that was in the realm of Logres when he slew my father. Well did he bereave me of him what time he slew him with his javelin without defiance, nor shall I never be at ease nor at rest until I shall have avenged him.' 'Fair sweet friend,' saith Messire Gawain, 'Sith that he is knight so good, take heed you increase not your wrong of your own act, and I would fain that you had found him, so as that no evil had befallen him thereof.'

The Red Knight's son

V

'So would not I!' saith the squire, 'for never shall I see him in this place but I shall run upon him as my mortal enemy!' 'Fair sweet friend,' saith Messire Gawain, 'you may say your pleasure, but tell me, is there no hold in this forest wherein I may harbour me the night?' 'Sir,' saith the squire, 'No hold know I within

<small>The Widow Lady's castle</small> twenty league of your way in any quarter. Wherefore no leisure have you to tarry, for it is high noon already.' So Messire Gawain saluteth the squire and goeth a great pace as he that knoweth neither highway nor byway save only as adventure may lead him. And the forest pleaseth him well for that it is so fair and that he seeth the deer pass by before him in great herds. He rode on until it drew toward evensong at a corner of the forest. The evening was fair and calm and the sun was about to set. And a score league Welsh had he ridden sithence that he parted from the squire, and sore he misdoubted him that he should find no hold. He found the fairest meadow-land in the world, and looked before him when he had ridden a couple of bow-shot lengths and saw a castle appear nigh the forest on a mountain. And it was enclosed of high walls with battlements, and within were fair halls whereof the windows showed in the outer walls, and in the midst was an ancient tower that was compassed round of great waters and broad meadow-lands. Thitherward Messire Gawain draweth him and looketh toward the gateway of the castle and seeth a squire issue forth a great pace upon a hackney, and he came the way that Messire Gawain was coming. And when the squire seeth him and hath drawn somewhat anigh, he saluteth him right nobly.

VI

'Sir, right welcome may you be!' 'Good adventure may you have!' saith Messire

Gawain. 'Fair sweet friend, what is this Camelot castle here, sir?' 'Sir, it is the castle of the Widow Lady.' 'What is the name thereof?' 'Camelot; and it belonged to Alain li Gros, that was a right loyal knight and worshipful man. He is dead this long time, and my Lady hath remained without succour and without counsel. Wherefore is the castle warred upon of them that would fain reave her thereof by force. The Lord of the Moors and another knight are they that war upon her and would fain reave her of this castle as they have reft her of seven other already. Greatly desireth she the return of her son, for no counsel hath she save only of her one daughter and of five old knights that help her to guard the castle. Sir,' saith he, 'The door is made fast and the bridge drawn up, for they guard the castle closely, but, so please you, you will tell me your name and I will go before and make the bridge be lowered and the gate unfastened, and will say that you will lodge within to-night.' 'Gramercy,' saith Messire Gawain, 'right well shall my name be known or ever I depart from the castle.' The squire goeth his way a great pace, and Messire Gawain rideth softly at a walk for he had yet a long way to go. And he found a chapel that stood between the forest and the castle, and it was builded upon four columns of marble and within was a right fair sepulchre. The chapel had no fence of any kind about it, so that he seeth the coffin within full clearly, and Messire Gawain bideth awhile to look thereon. And the squire is entered into the

The castle and hath made the bridge be lowered and
the door opened. He alighteth and is come
into the hall where was the Widow Lady and
her daughter. Saith the Lady to the squire:
'Wherefore have you returned from doing my
message?' 'Lady, for the comeliest knight
that I have seen ever, and fain would he harbour
within to-night, and he is garnished of all arms
and rideth without company.' 'And what
name hath he?' saith the Lady. 'Lady, he
told me you should know it well or ever he
depart from this castle.' Therewithal the Lady
gan weep for joy and her daughter also, and,
lifting their hands toward heaven, 'Fair Lord
God!' saith the Widow Lady, 'And this be
indeed my son, never tofore have I had joy
that might be likened to this! Now shall I
not be disherited of mine honour, neither shall
I lose my castle whereof they would fain reave
me by wrong, for that no Lord nor champion
have I!'

The Lady Yglais

VII

Thereupon the Widow Lady ariseth up and
her daughter likewise, and they go over the bridge
of the castle and see Messire Gawain that was
yet looking on the coffin within the chapel.
'Now haste!' saith the Lady; 'At the tomb
shall we be well able to see whether it be he!'
They go to the chapel right speedily, and Messire
Gawain seeth them coming and alighteth.
'Lady,' saith he, 'Welcome may you be, you
and your company.' The Lady answereth
never a word until that they are come to the

tomb. When she findeth it not open, she falleth down in a swoon. And Messire Gawain is sore afraid when he seeth it. The Lady cometh back out of her swoon and breaketh out into great lamentation. 'Sir,' saith the damsel to Messire Gawain, 'Welcome may you be! But now sithence my mother supposed that you had been her son and made great joy thereof, and now seeth she plainly that you are not he, whereof is she sore sorrowful, for so soon as he shall return, this coffin behoveth open, nor until that hour shall none know who it is that lieth therein.' The Lady riseth up and taketh Messire Gawain by the hand. 'Sir,' saith she, 'What is your name?' 'Lady,' saith he, 'I am called Gawain, King Arthur's nephew.' 'Sir,' saith she, 'You shall be he that is welcome both for the sake of my son and for your own sake.' The Lady biddeth a squire lead his horse into the castle and carry his shield and spear. Then they enter into the castle and lead Messire Gawain into the hall, and make disarm him. After that, they fetch him water to wash his hands and his face, for he was distained of the rust of his habergeon. The Lady maketh apparel him in a rich robe of silk and gold, and furred of ermine. The Widow Lady cometh forth of her chamber and maketh Messire Gawain sit beside her. 'Sir,' saith she, 'Can you tell me any tidings of my son that I have not seen of this long time past, and of whom at this present am I sore in need?'

Dindrane her daughter

VIII

No tidings of Perceval

'Lady,' saith he, 'No tidings of him know I to tell you, and right heavy am I thereof, for he is the knight of the world that fainest I would see and he be your son as I am told. What name hath he?' 'Sir,' saith she, 'His name in right baptism is Perceval, and a right comely squire was he when he departed hence. Now as at this time is it said that he is the comeliest knight on live and the most hardy and the cleanest of all wickedness. And sore need have I of his hardiment, for what time that he departed hence, he left me in the midst of a great warfare on behalf of the Knight of the Red Shield that he slew. Within the se'nnight thereafter he went away, nor never once have I seen him sithence, albeit a full seven year hath passed already. And now the brother of the knight that he slew and the Lord of the Moors are warring upon me and are fain to reave me of my castle and God counsel me not. For my brothers are too far away from me, and King Pelles of the Lower Folk hath renounced his land for God's sake and entered into a hermitage. But the King of Castle Mortal hath in him as much of wickedness and felony as these twain have in them of good, and enough thereof have they. But neither succour nor help may they give me, for the King of Castle Mortal challengeth my Lord King Fisherman both of the most Holy Graal and of the Lance whereof the point bleedeth every day, albeit God forbid he should ever have them.'

IX

'Lady,' saith Messire Gawain, 'There was at the hostel of King Fisherman a knight before whom the Holy Graal appeared three times, yet never once would he ask whereof it served nor whom it honoured.' 'Sir,' saith the Widow Lady's daughter, 'You say true, and the Best Knight is he of the world. This say I for love of my brother, and I love all knights for the love of him, but by the foolish wit of the knight hath mine uncle King Fisherman fallen into languishment.' 'Sir,' saith the Lady, 'Behoveth all good knights go see the rich King Fisherman. Will you not therefore go?' 'Lady,' saith Messire Gawain, 'Yea, that will I, so speedily as I may, for not elsewhither have I emprised my way.' 'Sir,' saith she, 'Then are you going to see my son, wherefore tell my son, and you see him, of my evil plight and my misease, and King Fisherman my brother. But take heed, Messire Gawain, that you be better mindful than was the knight.' 'Lady,' saith Messire Gawain, 'I shall do as God shall teach me.' In the meanwhile as they were speaking thus together, behold you therewithal the Widow Lady's five knights that were come in from the forest and make bring harts and hinds and wild swine. So they alighted and made great joy of Messire Gawain when they knew who he was.

Of King Fisherman

X

When the meat was ready they sate to eat, and full plenteously were they provided and right well were they served. Thereupon, behold, cometh the squire that had opened the door for Messire Gawain, and kneeleth before the Widow Lady. 'And what tidings?' saith she. 'Lady, there is to be a right great assembly of tourney in the valleys that aforetime were ours. Already have they spread the Welsh booths, and thither are come these two that are warring upon you and great store other knights. And they have ordained that he which shall do best at the assembly shall undertake the garrison of this castle in such sort as that he shall hold it for his own alone against all other.' The Widow Lady beginneth to weep: 'Sir,' saith she to Messire Gawain, 'Now may you understand that the castle is not mine own, sith that these knights say it is theirs as you hear.' 'Certes, Lady,' saith he, 'Herein do they great dishonour and a sin.'

An assembly of tourney

XI

When the table was removed the damsel fell at Messire Gawain's feet, weeping. He raiseth her forthwith and saith to her, 'Damsel, herein do you ill.' 'For God's sake, Sir, take pity on my Lady mother and me!' 'Certes, damsel, great pity have I of you.' 'Sir, now shall it be seen in this strait whether you be good knight, for good is the knighthood that doeth well for God's sake.' The Widow Lady and her daughter go into the chamber, and Messire Gawain's bed was made in the midst of the hall. So he went and lay down as did also the five knights. All the night was

Messire Gawain in much thought. The morrow, *Gawain*
when he was risen, he went to hear mass in a *goeth*
chapel that was within and ate thereafter three *thither*
sops in wine and then armed himself, and at the
same time asked the five knights that were there
in the hall whether they would go see the
assembly. 'Yea, Sir,' say they, 'and you be
going thither.' 'In faith, thither verily will I
go!' saith Messire Gawain. The knights are
armed forthwith, and their horses brought and
Messire Gawain's, and he goeth to take leave
of the Widow Lady and her daughter. But
great joy make they of this that they have heard
say that he will go with their knights to the
assembly.

XII

Messire Gawain and the five knights mounted
and issued forth of the castle and rode a great
gallop before a forest. Messire Gawain looketh
before him about the foreclose of the forest, and
seeth the fairest purlieus that he had seen ever,
and so broad they be that he may not see nor
know the fourth part thereof. They are garnished of tall forests on one hand and on the
other, and there are high rocks in the midst with
wild deer among. 'Sir,' say the knights, 'Lo,
these be the Valleys of Camelot whereof my
Lady and her daughter have been bereft, and
bereft also hath she been of the richest castles
that be in Wales to the number of seven.' 'A
wrong is it and a sin!' saith Messire Gawain.
So far have they ridden that they see the ensigns and the shields there where the assembly

Chaos the Red unhorsed

is to be held, and they see already mounted the more part of the knights all armed and running their horses down the meadow-land. And they see the tents stretched on the one hand and on another. And Messire Gawain bideth, and the five knights under a tree, and see the knights assembling on one hand and on another. One of the five knights that were with him gave him witting of the Lord of the Moors and the brother of the knight of the Red Shield that had to name Chaos the Red. So soon as the tournament was assembled, Messire Gawain and the knights come to the assembly, and Messire Gawain goeth to a Welsh knight and beareth him to the ground, both him and his horse, all in a heap. And the five come after at a great gallop and each overthroweth his own, and greatly pride they themselves of Messire Gawain. Chaos the Red seeth Messire Gawain but knoweth him not. He goeth toward him a full career, and Messire Gawain receiveth him on the point of his spear and hurtleth against him so sore that he all to-brast his collarbone and maketh the spear fly from his fist. And Messire Gawain searcheth the fellowships of one part and the other, and findeth not nor encountereth no knight before him in his way but he putteth him off his horse or woundeth him, either by himself or by one of the five knights, that make right great joy of that they see him do. They show him the Lord of the Moors that was coming with a full great fellowship of folk. He goeth thitherward a great gallop. They mell together either upon other of their spears that they bent and all to-brast in flinders, and hurtle together so stoutly both of their horses and their bodies that the Lord of the Moors loseth his stirrups and hath the hinder saddlebow to-frushed, and falleth down to the ground over his horse croup in such sort that the peak of his helm dinteth a full palm's breadth into the turf. And Messire Gawain taketh the horse that was right rich and good, maugre all of his fellowship, and giveth it to one of the five knights that maketh it be led to Camelot of a squire. Messire Gawain searcheth the ranks on the one hand and on the other, and doeth such feats of arms as never no knight might do the same again. The five knights also showed great hardiment, and did more of arms that day than ever had they done tofore, for not one of them but had overthrown at least a single knight and won his horse. The Lord of the Moors was mounted again on another rich horse and had great shame for that Messire Gawain had overthrown him. He espieth Messire Gawain and goeth toward him a great gallop and thinketh to avenge his shame. They come together either on other with a great shock, and Messire Gawain smiteth him with the truncheon of his spear that he had still left, in the midst of his breast, so that it was all to-splintered. The Lord of the Moors likewise again to-brast his spear upon him. Messire Gawain draweth his sword and flingeth the truncheon to the ground. The Lord of the Moors doth likewise and commandeth his folk not to mell betwixt them twain, for never

The Lord of the Moors

yet had he found no knight that he had not conquered. They deal them great buffets on the helms, either upon other, in such sort that the sparks fly thereout and their swords are blunted. The buffets of Messire Gawain are heavier than the other's, for he dealeth them so mighty and horrible that the blood rayeth out from the Lord of the Moors by the mouth and the nose so that his habergeon is all bloody thereof and he may no more endure. Thereupon he yieldeth him prisoner to Messire Gawain, that is right glad thereof and his five knights likewise. The Lord of the Moors goeth to his tent to alight, and Messire Gawain with him and alighteth. And Messire Gawain taketh the horse and saith to one of the knights, 'Keep this for me.' And all the knights are repaired to their tents, and with one accord say they all that the knight of the Red Shield with the eagle of gold thereon hath done better than we, and they ask the Lord of the Moors whether he accordeth with them, and he saith 'Aye.' 'Sir,' saith he to Messire Gawain, 'You, then, are the warden of this castle of Camelot.' 'Gramercy, lord!' saith Messire Gawain. He calleth the five knights and saith unto them: 'Lords, my will is that you be there on my behalf and that you shall safeguard the same by consent of the knights that are here present.' 'Sir, right gladly do we agree thereto.' 'Sir,' saith Messire Gawain to the Lord of the Moors, 'I give you moreover as my prisoner to the Widow Lady that harboured me last night.' 'Sir,' saith he, 'This have you no right to do. Assembly of tourney is not war. Hence have you no right to imprison my body in castle, for well am I able to pay my ransom here. But tell me, what is your name?' 'I am called Gawain.' 'Ha, Messire Gawain, many a time have I heard tell of you albeit never tofore have I seen you. But sith that the castle of Camelot is in your keeping, I promise you loyally that before a year and a day neither the castle nor none of the Lady's land need fear nought from me nor from any other so far forth as I may hinder him, and hereto do I pledge me in the presence of all these knights that are here. And, so you would have of me gold or silver, thereof will I give you at your will.' 'Sir,' saith Messire Gawain, 'Gramercy! I consent freely to as much as you have said.' Messire Gawain taketh leave and turneth him again toward the castle of Camelot, and sendeth by a squire the horse of the Lord of the Moors to the daughter of the Widow Lady, that made great joy thereof. And the five knights drive before them the horses they have taken booty. Whereof great also was the joy. No need to wonder whether Messire Gawain were well harboured that night at the castle. He recounted to the Lady how the castle was in the keeping of these knights. When it came to morning-tide, Messire Gawain took leave and departed from the castle, but not before he had heard mass, for such was his custom. The Widow Lady and her daughter commend him to God, and the castle remaineth in better keeping than he had found it.

Camelot made safe

BRANCH IV

INCIPIT

Of Marin the Jealous HERE beginneth another branch of the Graal in the name of the Father, and of the Son, and of the Holy Ghost.

TITLE I

And the story is silent here of the mother of the Good Knight, and saith that Messire Gawain goeth so as God and adventure lead him toward the land of the rich King Fisherman. And he entereth into a great forest, all armed, his shield at his neck and his spear in his hand. And he prayeth Our Lord that He counsel him of this holy errand he hath emprised so as that he may honourably achieve it. He rode until that he came at evensong to a hold that was in the midst of the forest. And it was compassed about of a great water, and had about it great clumps of trees so as that scarce with much pains might he espy the hall, that was right large. The river that compassed it about was water royal, for it lost not its right name nor its body as far as the sea. And Messire Gawain bethought him that it was the hold of a worshipful man, and draweth him thitherward to lodge. And as he drew anigh the bridge of the hold, he looketh and seeth a dwarf sitting on a high bench. He leapeth up: **A treacherous dwarf** 'Messire Gawain,' saith he, 'Welcome may you be!' 'Fair, sweet friend,' saith Messire Gawain,-'God give you good adventure! You know me, then?' saith he. 'Well do I know you,' saith the dwarf, 'For I saw you at the tournament. At a better moment could you not have come hither, for my lord is not here. But you will find my lady, the fairest and most gentle and most courteous in the realm of Logres, and as yet is she not of twenty years.' 'Fair friend,' saith Messire Gawain, 'What name hath the lord of the hold?' 'Sir, he is called of Little Gomeret. I will go tell my lady that Messire Gawain is come, the good knight, and bid her make great joy.' Howbeit, Messire Gawain marvelleth much that the dwarf should make him such cheer, for many knaveries hath he found in many places within the bodies of many dwarfs. The dwarf is come into the chamber where the lady was. 'Now, haste, Lady!' saith he, 'Make great joy, for Messire Gawain is come to harbour with you.' 'Certes,' saith she, 'Of this am I right glad and right sorry; glad, for that the good knight will lie here to-night, sorry, for that he is the knight that my lord most hateth in the world. Wherefore he warneth me against him for love of him, for oftentimes hath he told me that never did Messire Gawain keep faith with dame nor damsel but he would have his will of them.' 'Lady,' saith the dwarf, 'It is not true albeit it is so said.'

Marin's fair wife

II

Thereupon Messire Gawain entereth into the courtyard and alighteth, and the lady cometh to meet him and saith to him: 'May you be come to joy and good adventure.' 'Lady,' saith he, 'May you also have honour and good adventure.' The lady taketh him by the hand and leadeth him into the hall and maketh him be seated on a cushion of straw. And a squire leadeth his horse to stable. And the dwarf summoneth two other squires and doeth Messire Gawain be disarmed, and helpeth them right busily, and maketh fetch water to wash his hands and his face. 'Sir,' saith the dwarf, 'Your fists are still all swollen of the buffets you gave and received at the tournament.' Messire Gawain answered him nought. And the dwarf entereth into the chamber and bringeth a scarlet robe furred of ermine and maketh it be done on Messire Gawain. And meat was made ready and the table set, and the lady sate to eat. Many a time looked he upon the lady by reason of her great beauty, and, had he been minded to trust to his heart and his eyes, he would have all to-changed his purpose; but so straitly was his heart bound up, and so quenched the desires thereof, that nought would he allow himself to think upon that might turn to wickedness, for the sake of the high pilgrimage he had emprised. Rather 'gan he withdraw his eyes from looking at the lady, that was held to be of passing great beauty. After meat Messire Gawain's bed was made, and he apparelled himself to lie down. The lady bade him God give him good adventure, and he made answer the like. When the lady was in her chamber, the dwarf said to Messire Gawain: 'Sir, I will lie before you, so as to keep you company until you be asleep.' 'Gramercy,' saith he, 'And God allow me at some time to reward you of the service.' The dwarf laid himself down on a mattress before Messire Gawain, and when he saw that he slept, he ariseth as quietly as he may, and cometh to a boat that was on the river that ran behind the hall, and entereth thereinto and roweth up-stream of the river. And he cometh to a fishery, where was a right fair hall on a little eyot enclosed by a marshy arm of the river. The jealous knight was come thither for disport, and lay in the midst of the hall upon a couch. The dwarf cometh forth of his boat thereinto, and lighteth a great candle in his fist and cometh before the couch. 'What ho, there!' saith the dwarf, 'Are you sleeping?' And the other waketh up sore startled, and asketh what is the matter and wherefore he is come? 'In God's name,' saith he, 'You sleep not so much at your ease as doth Messire Gawain!' 'How know you that?' saith he. 'Well know I,' saith the dwarf, 'For I left him but now in your hall, and methinketh he and your lady are abed together arm to arm.' 'How?' saith he, 'I forbade her she should ever harbour Messire Gawain.' 'In faith,' said the dwarf, 'She hath made him greater cheer than ever saw I her make to none other! But haste you and come, for great fear

The dwarf's deceit

have I lest he carry her away!' 'By my head!' saith the knight; 'I will go not, howsoever it be! But she shall pay for it, even though she go!' 'Then of wrong will it be!' saith the dwarf, 'as methinketh!'

Marin cometh home

III

Messire Gawain lay in the hall that was ware of nought of this. He seeth that day hath broken fair and clear, and ariseth up. The lady cometh to the door of the hall and seeth not the dwarf, whereby well she understandeth his treachery. She saith to Messire Gawain, 'Sir, for God's sake have pity upon me, for the dwarf hath betrayed me! And you withdraw yourself forth of our forest and help not to rescue me from the smart that my lord will make me suffer, great sin will you have thereof. For well know you that of right ought I not to be held guilty toward my lord nor toward any other, for aught that you have done toward me or I toward you.' 'You say true,' saith Messire Gawain. Thereupon is he armed, and taketh leave of the lady and issueth forth of the fair hold and setteth him in an ambush in the forest nigh thereby. Straightway behold the jealous knight where he cometh, he and his dwarf. He entereth into the hall. The lady cometh to meet him. 'Sir,' saith she, 'Welcome may you be!' 'And you,' saith he, 'Shame and evil adventure may you have, as the most disloyal dame on live, for that this night have you harboured in my hostel and in my bed him that most have I warned you against!'

'Sir,' saith she, 'In your hostel did I harbour him, but never hath your bed been shamed by me, nor never shall be!' 'You lie!' saith he, 'like a false woman!' He armeth himself all incontinent and maketh his horse be armed, then maketh the lady go down and despoil her to her shirt, that crieth him mercy right sweetly and weepeth. He mounteth his horse and taketh his shield and his spear, and maketh the lady be taken of the dwarf by her tresses and maketh her be led before him into the forest. And he bideth above a pool where was a spring, and maketh her enter into the water that flowed forth full cold, and gathereth saplings in the forest for rods and beginneth to smite and beat her across upon her back and her breast in such sort that the stream from the spring was all bloody therewithal. And she began to cry out right loud, until at last Messire Gawain heareth her and draweth forth of the ambush wherein he was, and cometh thitherward a great gallop. 'By my faith,' saith the dwarf, 'Look you here where Messire Gawain cometh!' 'By my faith,' saith the knight, 'Now know I well that nought is there here but treachery, and that the matter is well proven!' By this time, Messire Gawain is come, and saith: 'Avoid, Sir knight! Wherefore slay you the best lady and most loyal that ever have I seen? Never tofore have I found lady that hath done me so much honour, and this ought you to be well pleased to know, for neither in her bearing, nor in her speech, nor in herself found I nought save all goodness only. Where-

Marin beateth his wife

fore I pray you of franchise and of love that you forbear your wrath and that you set her forth of the water. And so will I swear on all the sacred hallows in this chapel that never did I beseech her of evil nor wantonness nor never had I no desire thereof.' The knight was full of great wrath when he saw that Messire Gawain had not gone his way thence, and an anguish of jealousy burneth him heart and body and overburdeneth him of folly and outrage, and Messire Gawain that is still before him moveth him to yet further transgression. Natheless, for the fear that he hath of him he speaketh to him: 'Messire Gawain,' saith he, 'I will set her forth thence on one condition, that you joust at me and I at you, and, so you conquer me, quit shall she be of misdoing and of blame, but and if I shall conquer you, she shall be held guilty herein. Such shall be the judgment in this matter.' 'I ask no better,' saith Messire Gawain.

Marin chal- lengeth Gawain

IV

Thereupon, the knight biddeth the dwarf make set the lady forth of the pool of the spring and make her sit in a launde whereas they were to joust. The knight draweth him back the better to take his career, and Messire Gawain cometh as fast as his horse may carry him toward Marin the Jealous. And when Marin seeth him coming, he avoideth his buffet and lowereth his spear and cometh to his wife that was right sore distraught, and wept as she that suffered blameless, and smote her throughout the body and slew her, and then turneth him again so fast as his horse might carry him toward his hold. Messire Gawain seeth the damsel dead and the dwarf that fleeth full speed after his lord. He overtaketh him and trampleth him under his horse's feet so that he bursteth his belly in the midst. Then goeth he toward the hold, for he thinketh to enter therein. But he found the bridge shut up and the gate barred. And Marin crieth out upon him: 'This shame and misadventure hath befallen me along of you, but you shall pay for it yet and I may live.' Messire Gawain hath no mind to argue with him, but rather draweth him back and cometh again to where the lady lay dead, and setteth her on the neck of his horse all bleeding, and then beareth her to a chapel that was without the entrance of the hold. Then he alighted and laid her within the chapel as fairly as most he might, as he that was sore grieved and wrathful thereof. After that, he shut the door of the chapel again as he that was afeared of the body for the wild beasts, and bethought him that one should come thither to set her in her shroud and bury her after that he was departed.

Marin slayeth his wife

V

Thereupon Messire Gawain departeth, sore an-angered, for it seemed him that never had no thing tofore befallen him that weighed so heavy on his heart. And he rideth thoughtful and down-cast through the forest, and seeth a knight coming along the way he came. And in strange fashion came he. He bestrode his

The Knight Coward horse backwards in right outlandish guise, face to tail, and he had his horse's reins right across his breast and the foot of his shield bore he topmost and the chief bottom-most, and his spear upside down and his habergeon and chausses of iron trussed about his neck. He seeth Messire Gawain coming beside the forest, that hath great wonderment of him when he seeth him. Natheless, when they draw nigh, he turneth him not to look at Messire Gawain, but crieth to him aloud: 'Gentle knight, you that come there, for God's sake do me no hurt, for I am the Knight Coward.' 'By God!' saith Messire Gawain, 'You look not like a man to whom any ought to do hurt!' And, but for the heaviness of his heart and the sore wrath that he had, he would have laughed at his bearing with a right good will. 'Sir knight,' saith Messire Gawain, 'nought have you to be afeard of from me!' With that he draweth anigh and looketh on him in the face and the Knight Coward on him. 'Sir,' saith he, 'Welcome may you be!' 'And you likewise!' saith Messire Gawain. 'And whose man are you, Sir knight?' 'The Damsel's man of the Car.' 'Thereof I love you the better,' saith Messire Gawain. 'God be praised thereof,' saith the Knight Coward, 'For now shall I have no fear of you.' 'Nay, truly,' saith Messire Gawain, 'Thereof be well assured!' The Knight Coward seeth Messire Gawain's shield and knoweth it. 'Ha, Sir,' saith he, 'Now know I well who you are. Now will I alight and ride the right way and

set my arms to rights. For you are Messire
Gawain, nor hath none the right to claim this
shield but only you.' The knight alighteth and
setteth his armour to rights, and prayeth Messire
Gawain abide until he be armed. So he abideth
right willingly, and helpeth him withal. Thereupon behold you a knight where he cometh a
great gallop athwart the forest like a tempest,
and he had a shield party black and white.
'Abide, Messire Gawain!' saith he, 'For on
behalf of Marin the Jealous do I defy you, that
hath slain his wife on your account.' 'Sir
knight,' saith Messire Gawain, 'Thereof am I
right heavy of heart, for death had she not
deserved.' 'That availeth not,' saith the
Party Knight, 'For I hold you to answer for
the death. So I conquer you, the wrong is
yours; but, and you conquer me, my lord
holdeth his blame and shame for known, and
will hold you to forfeit and you allow me to
escape hence or live.' 'To this will I not
agree,' saith Messire Gawain, 'For God well
knoweth that no blame have I herein.' 'Ha,
Messire Gawain,' saith the Knight Coward,
'Fight him not as having affiance in me, for of
me will you have neither succour nor help!'
'Heretofore,' saith Messire Gawain, 'have I
achieved adventures without you, and this also,
and God help me, will I yet achieve.' They
come together a full career and break their
lances on their shields, and Messire Gawain
hurtleth against the horse and passeth beyond
and overthroweth him and his horse together.
Then draweth he his sword and runneth upon

The Party Knight

him. And the knight crieth out: 'Hold,
Messire Gawain! Are you minded to slay
me? I yield me conquered, for no mind have
I to die for another's folly, and so I cry you
mercy hereof.' Messire Gawain thinketh that
he will do him no further harm, for that of
right behoveth him do his lord's bidding.
Messire Gawain holdeth his hands, and he doth
him homage on behalf of his lord for his hold
and all of his land, and becometh his man.

The Party Knight yieldeth

VI

Thereupon the knight departeth and Messire
Gawain remaineth there. 'Sir,' saith the
Knight Coward to Messire Gawain, 'I have
no mind to be so hardy as are you; for, so
God help me, had he defied me in such-wise as
he defied you, I should have fled away forthwith, or elsewise I should have fallen at his
feet and cried him of mercy.' 'You wish for
nought but peace,' saith Messire Gawain. 'By
S. James,' saith the Coward, 'Therein are
you quite right, for of war cometh nought but
evil; nor never have I had no hurt nor wound
save some branch of a tree or the like gave it
me, and I see your face all seamed and scarred
in many places. So God help me, of such
hardiesse make I but small account, and every
day I pray God that He defend me. And so
to God I commend you, for I am going after
my Damsel of the Car.' 'Not thus shall you
go,' saith Messire Gawain, 'save you tell me
first wherefore your Damsel of the Car beareth
her arm slung to her neck in such-wise.' 'Sir,

this may I will tell you. With this hand **Of** served she of the most Holy Graal the knight **Marin's** that was in the hostel of King Fisherman that **malice** would not ask whereof the Graal served; for that she held therein the precious vessel whereinto the glorious blood fell drop by drop from the point of the lance, so that none other thing is she minded to hold therein until such time as she shall come back to the holy place where it is. Sir,' saith the Knight Coward, 'Now, so please you, may I well go hence, and see, here is my spear that I give you, for nought is there that I have to do therewithal.' Messire Gawain taketh it, for his own was broken short, and departeth from the knight and commendeth him to God. And he goeth his way a great pace, and Messire Gawain also goeth amidst the forest, and full weary is he and forspent with travail. And he rode until the sun was due to set. And he meeteth a knight that was coming athwart the forest and came toward Messire Gawain a great gallop like as he were smitten through the body, and crieth over all the forest: 'What is your name, Sir knight?' 'My name is Gawain.' 'Ha, Messire Gawain,' saith the other, 'In your service am I wounded thus!' 'How in my service?' saith Messire Gawain. 'Sir, I was minded to bury the damsel that you bare into the chapel, and Marin the Jealous ran upon me and wounded me in many places in such manner as you see. And I had already dug a grave with my sword to bury the body when he seized it from me and abandoned it to the wild beasts. Now go I hence yonder to the chapel of a hermit that is in this forest to confess me, for well know I that I have not long to live for that the wound lieth me so nigh my heart. But I shall die the more easily now that I have found you and shown you the hurt that hath been done me for your sake.' 'Certes,' saith Messire Gawain, 'this grieveth me.'

The Proud Maiden

VII

Therewithal the knights depart asunder, and Messire Gawain rode on until he found in the forest a castle right fair and rich, and met an ancient knight that was issued forth of the castle for disport, and held a bird on his fist. He saluteth Messire Gawain and he him again, and he asked him what castle is this that he seeth show so fair? And he telleth him it is the castle of the Proud Maiden that never deigned ask a knight his name. 'And we, that are her men, durst not do it on her behalf. But right well will you be lodged in the castle, for right courteous is she otherwise and the fairest that ever any may know. Nor never hath she had any lord, nor deigned to love no knight save she heard tell that he was the best knight in the world. And I will go to her with you of courtesy.' 'Gramercy, Sir,' saith Messire Gawain. They enter into the castle both twain together, and alight at the mounting-stage before the hall. The knight taketh Messire Gawain by the hand and leadeth him up, and maketh disarm him, and bringeth him a surcoat of scarlet purfled of vair and maketh him do it on. Then leadeth he the lady of the castle to Messire Gawain, and he riseth up to meet her. 'Lady,' saith he, 'Welcome may you be!' 'And you, Sir, be welcome!' saith she, 'Will you see my chapel?' 'Damsel,' saith he, 'At your pleasure.' And she leadeth him and taketh Messire Gawain by the hand, and he looketh at the chapel and it well seemeth him that never before had he come into none so fair nor so rich, and he seeth four tombs within, the fairest that he had seen ever. And on the right hand side of the chapel were three narrow openings in the wall that were wrought all about with gold and precious stones, and beyond the three openings he seeth great circlets of lighted candles that were before three coffers of hallows that were there, and the smell thereof was sweeter than balm. 'Sir knight,' saith the damsel, 'See you these tombs?' 'Yea, damsel,' saith Messire Gawain. 'These three are made for the three best knights in the world and the fourth for me. The one hath for name Messire Gawain and the second Lancelot of the Lake. Each of them do I love for love's sake, by my faith! And the third hath for name Perceval. Him love I better than the other two. And within these three openings are the hallows set for love of them. And behold what I would do to them and their three heads were therein; and so I might not do it to the three together, yet would I do it to two, or even to one only.' She setteth her hand toward the openings and draweth forth a pin that was fastened into the wall, and a cutting blade of steel droppeth down,

_{Three knights' tombs}

<small>Gawain's tomb</small> of steel sharper than any razor, and closeth up the three openings. 'Even thus will I cut off their heads when they shall set them into those three openings thinking to adore the hallows that are beyond. Afterward will I make take the bodies and set them in the three coffins, and do them be honoured and enshrouded right richly, for joy of them in their life may I never have. And when the end of my life shall be come as God will, even so will I make set me in the fourth coffin, and so shall I have company of the three good knights.' Messire Gawain heard the word, whereof he marvelled right sore, and would right fain that the night were overpassed. They issue forth of the chapel. The damsel maketh Messire Gawain be greatly honoured that night, and there was great company of knights within that served him and helped guard the castle. They show Messire Gawain much worship, but they knew not that it was he, nor did none ask him, for such was the custom of the castle. But well she knew that he oftentimes passed to and fro amidst the forest, and four of the knights that watched the forest and the passers-by had she commanded that and if any of these three knights should pass they should bring him to her without gainsay, and she would increase the land of each for so doing.

VIII

Messire Gawain was in the castle that night until the morrow, and went to hear mass in the chapel or ever he removed thence. Afterward, when he had heard mass and was armed, he took leave of the damsel and issued forth of the castle as he that had no desire to abide there longer. And he entereth into the forest and rideth a long league Welsh and findeth two knights sitting by a narrow pass in the forest. And when they see him coming they leap up on their horses all armed and come against Messire Gawain, shields on sides and spears in fists. 'Bide, Sir knight!' say they, 'And tell us your name without leasing!' 'Lords,' saith he, 'Right willingly! never hath my name been with-holden when it hath been asked for. I am called Gawain, King Arthur's nephew.' 'Nay, then, Sir, welcome may you be! One other demand have we to make of you. Will you come with us to the lady in the world that most desireth you, and will make much joy of you at Castle Orguelleux where she is?' 'Lord,' saith Messire Gawain, 'No leisure have I at this time, for I have emprised my way else-whither.' 'Sir,' say they, 'Needs must you come thither without fail, for in such wise hath she commanded us that we shall take you thither by force an you come not of your own good will.' 'I have told you plainly that thither will I not go,' saith Messire Gawain. With that, they leap forward and take him by the bridle, thinking to lead him away by force. And Messire Gawain hath shame thereof, and draweth his sword and smiteth one of them in such wrath that he cutteth off his arm. And the other letteth the bridle go and turneth him full speed; and his fellow with him that was

Gawain maimeth a knight

maimed. And away go they toward Castle Orguelleux and the Proud Maiden of the castle and show her the mischief that hath befallen them. 'Who hath mis-handled you thus?' saith she. 'Certes, lady, Messire Gawain.' 'Where found you him?' 'Lady,' say they, 'In the forest, where he came toward us a full gallop, and was minded to pass by the narrows of the way, when we bade him abide and come to you. But come he would not. We offered him force, and he smote my fellow's arm off.' She biddeth a horn be sounded incontinent, and the knights of the castle arm, and she commandeth them follow Messire Gawain, and saith that she will increase the land and the charge of him that shall bring him to her. They were a good fifteen knights armed. Just as they were about to issue out of the castle, behold you forthwith two keepers of the forest where they come, both twain of them smitten through the body. The damsel and the knights ask who hath done this to them, and they say it was Messire Gawain that did it, for that they would have brought him to the castle. 'Is he far away?' saith the damsel. 'Yea,' say they, 'Four great leagues Welsh.' 'Wherefore the greater folly would it be to follow him,' saith one of the sixteen knights, 'For nought should we increase thereby save only our own shame and hurt, and my Lady hath lost him through her own default, for well know we that he it was that lay within, for that he beareth a shield sinople with a golden eagle.' 'Yea,' saith the wounded knight, 'Without fail.' 'Is this then

Gawain escapeth

he?' saith the damsel. 'I know him well now that I have lost him by my pride and by my outrage; nor never more will knight lie in my hostel sith that he will be estranged for that I ask not his name. But it is too late! Herein have I failed of this one for ever and ever save God bring him back to me, and through this one shall I lose the other two!'

A brachet questeth

IX

Herewithal cometh to a stay the pursuit of Messire Gawain, that goeth his way and prayeth God that He send him true counsel of that he hath emprised, and that He allow him to come into some place where he may hear true witting of the hostel of King Fisherman. And while he was thus thinking, he heareth a brachet questing, and he cometh toward him a great pace. When he is come anigh Messire Gawain he setteth his nose to the ground and findeth a track of blood through a grassy way in the forest, and when Messire Gawain was minded to leave the way where the track of blood was, the brachet came over against him and quested. Messire Gawain is minded not to abandon the track, wherefore he followeth the brachet a great pace until he cometh to a marish in the midst of the forest, and seeth there in the marish a house, ancient and decayed. He passeth with the brachet over the bridge, that was right feeble, and there was a great water under it, and cometh to the hall, that was wasted and old. And the brachet leaveth of his questing. Messire Gawain seeth in the midst

A knight slain by Lancelot of the house a knight that was stricken right through the breast unto the heart and there lay dead. A damsel was issuing forth of the chamber and bare the winding-sheet wherein to enshroud him. 'Damsel,' saith Messire Gawain, 'Good adventure may you have!' The damsel that was weeping right tenderly, saith to him: 'Sir, I will answer you not.' She cometh toward the dead knight, thinking that his wounds should have begun to bleed afresh, but they did not. 'Sir,' saith she to Messire Gawain, 'Welcome may you be!' 'Damsel,' saith he, 'God grant you greater joy than you have!' And the damsel saith to the brachet: 'It was not this one I sent you back to fetch, but him that slew this knight.' 'Know you then, damsel, who hath slain him?' saith Messire Gawain. 'Yea,' saith she, 'well! Lancelot of the Lake slew him in this forest, on whom God grant me vengeance, and on all them of King Arthur's court, for sore mischief and great hurt have they wrought us! But, please God, right well shall this knight yet be avenged, for a right fair son hath he whose sister am I, and so hath he many good friends withal.' 'Damsel, to God I commend you!' saith Messire Gawain. With that, he issueth forth of the Waste Manor and betaketh him back to the way he had abandoned, and prayeth God grant he may find Lancelot of the Lake.

BRANCH V

INCIPIT

HERE beginneth again another branch of the Graal in the name of the Father, and of the Son, and of the Holy Ghost.

Gawain findeth a hermit

TITLE I

Messire Gawain goeth his way and evening draweth on; and on his right hand was there a narrow pathway that seemed him to be haunted of folk. Thitherward goeth he, for that he seeth the sun waxeth low, and findeth in the thick of the forest a great chapel, and without was a right fair manor. Before the chapel was an orchard enclosed of a wooden fence that was scarce so high as a tall man. A hermit that seemed him a right worshipful man was leaning against the fence, and looked into the orchard and made great cheer from time to time. He seeth Messire Gawain, and cometh to meet him, and Messire Gawain alighteth. 'Sir,' saith the hermit, 'Welcome may you be.' 'God grant you the joy of Paradise,' saith Messire Gawain. The hermit maketh his horse be stabled of a squire, and then taketh him by the hand and maketh him sit beside him to look on the orchard.

A boy rideth a lion 'Sir,' saith the hermit, 'Now may you see that whereof I was making cheer.' Messire Gawain looketh therewithin and seeth two damsels and a squire and a child that were guarding a lion. 'Sir,' saith the hermit, 'Here see you my joy, which is this child. Saw you ever so fair a child of his age?' 'Never,' saith Messire Gawain. They go into the orchard to sit, for the evening was fair and calm. He maketh disarm him, and thereupon the damsel bringeth him a surcoat of right rich silk furred of ermine. And Messire Gawain looketh at the child that rode upon the lion right fainly. 'Sir,' saith the hermit, 'None durst guard him or be master over him save this child only, and yet the lad is not more than six years of age. Sir, he is of right noble lineage, albeit he is the son of the most cruel man and most felon that is. Marin the Jealous is his father, that slew his wife on account of Messire Gawain. Never sithence that his mother was dead would not the lad be with his father, for well knoweth he that he slew her of wrong. And I am his uncle, so I make him be tended here of these damsels and these two squires, but no one thing is there that he so much desireth to see as Messire Gawain. For after his father's death ought he of right to be Messire Gawain's man. Sir, if any tidings you know of him, tell us them.' 'By my faith, Sir,' saith he, 'Tidings true can I give you. Lo, there is his shield and his spear, and himself shall you have this night for guest.' 'Fair sir, are you he?' saith the hermit. 'So men call me,' saith Messire Gawain, 'And the lady saw I slain in the forest, whereof was I sore an-angered.'

Meliot of Logres

II

'Fair nephew,' saith the hermit, 'See here your desire. Come to him and make him cheer.' The lad alighteth of the lion and smiteth him with a whip and leadeth him to the den and maketh the door so that he may not issue forth, and cometh to Messire Gawain, and Messire Gawain receiveth him between his arms. 'Sir,' saith the child, 'Welcome may you be!' 'God give you growth of honour!' saith Messire Gawain. He kisseth him and maketh cheer with him right sweetly. 'Sir,' saith the hermit, 'He will be of right your man, wherefore ought you to counsel him and help him, for through you came his mother by her death, and right sore need will he have of your succour.' The child kneeleth before him and holdeth up his joined hands. 'Look, Sir,' saith the hermit, 'Is he not right pitiful? He offereth you his homage.' And Messire Gawain setteth his hands within his own: 'Certes,' saith Messire Gawain, 'Both your honour and your homage receive I gladly, and my succour and my counsel shall you have so often as you shall have need thereof. But fain would I know your name?' 'Sir, I am called Meliot of Logres.' 'Sir,' saith the hermit, 'He saith true, for his mother was daughter of a rich earl of the kingdom of Logres.'

III

A squire of Perceval's

Messire Gawain was well harboured the night and lay in a right fair house and right rich. In the morning, when Messire Gawain had heard mass, the hermit asked him, 'Whitherward go you?' and he said, 'Toward the land of King Fisherman, and God allow me.' 'Messire Gawain,' saith the hermit, 'Now God grant you speed your business better than did the other knight that was there before you, through whom are all the lands fallen into sorrow, and the good King Fisherman languisheth thereof.' 'Sir,' saith Messire Gawain, 'God grant me herein to do His pleasure.' Thereupon he taketh his leave and goeth his way, and the hermit commendeth him to God. And Messire Gawain rideth on his journeys until he hath left far behind the forest of the hermitage, and findeth the fairest land in the world and the fairest meadowlands that ever had he seen, and it lasted a good couple of great leagues Welsh. And he seeth a high forest before him, and meeteth a squire that came from that quarter, and seeth that he is sore downcast and right simple. 'Fair friend,' saith Messire Gawain, 'Whence come you?' 'Sir,' saith he, 'I come from yonder forest down below.' 'Whose man are you?' saith Messire Gawain. 'I belong to the worshipful man that owneth the forest.' 'You seem not over joyful,' saith Messire Gawain. 'Sir, I have right to be otherwise,' saith the squire, 'For he that loseth his good lord ought not to be joyful.' 'And

who is your lord?' 'The best in the world.'
'Is he dead?' saith Messire Gawain. 'Nay,
of a truth, for that would be right sore grief to
the world, but in joy hath he not been this long
time past.' 'And what name hath he?'
'They call him Parlui there where he is.'
'And where then, is he, may I know?' 'In
no wise, Sir, of me; but so much may I well
tell you that he is in this forest, but I ought not
to learn you of the place more at large, nor
ought I to do any one thing that may be against
my master's will.' Messire Gawain seeth that
the squire is of passing comeliness and seeth
him forthwith bow his head toward the ground
and the tears fall from his eyes. Thereupon
he asketh what aileth him. 'Sir,' saith he,
'Never may I have joy until such time as I be
entered into a hermitage to save my soul. For
the greatest sin that any man may do have I
wrought; for I have slain my mother that was
a Queen, for this only that she told me I should
not be King after my father's death, for that
she would make me monk or clerk, and that
my other brother, who is younger-born than I,
should have the kingdom. When my father
knew that I had slain my mother, he withdrew
himself into this forest, and made a hermitage
and renounced his kingdom. I have no will to
hold the land for the great disloyalty that I
have wrought, and therefore am I resolved that
it is meeter I should set my body in banishment
than my father.' 'And what is your name?'
saith Messire Gawain. 'Sir, my name is Joseus,
and I am of the lineage of Joseph of Abarimacie.

Joseus mourneth

A hermit tendeth Perceval

King Pelles is my father, that is in this forest, and King Fisherman my uncle, and the King of Castle Mortal, and the Widow Lady of Camelot my aunt, and the Good Knight Par-lui-fet is of this lineage as near akin as I.'

IV

With that, the squire departeth and taketh leave of Messire Gawain, and he commendeth him to God and hath great pity of him, and entereth into the forest and goeth great pace, and findeth the stream of a spring that ran with a great rushing, and nigh thereunto was a way that was much haunted. He abandoneth his high-way, and goeth all along the stream from the spring that lasteth a long league plenary, until that he espieth a right fair house and right fair chapel well enclosed within a hedge of wood. He looketh from without the entrance under a little tree and seeth there sitting one of the seemliest men that he had ever seen of his age. And he was clad as a hermit, his head white and no hair on his face, and he held his hand to his chin, and made a squire hold a destrier right fair and strong and tall, and a shield with a sun thereon; and he was looking at a habergeon and chausses of iron that he had made bring before him. And when he seeth Messire Gawain he dresseth him over against him and saith: 'Fair sir,' saith he, 'Ride gently and make no noise, for no need have we of worse than that we have.' And Messire Gawain draweth rein, and the worshipful man saith to him: 'Sir, for God's sake take it not

of discourtesy; for right fainly would I have **Perceval**
besought you to harbour had I not good cause **sore sick**
to excuse me, but a knight lieth within yonder
sick, that is held for the best knight in the
world. Wherefore fain would I he should
have no knight come within this close, for and
if he should rise, as sick as he is, none might
prevent him nor hold him back, but presently he
should arm him and mount on his horse and
joust at you or any other; and so he were here,
well might we be the worse thereof. And
therefore do I keep him so close and quiet
within yonder, for that I would not have him
see you nor none other, for and he were so soon
to die, sore loss would it be to the world.'
'Sir,' saith Messire Gawain, 'What name hath
he?' 'Sir,' saith he, 'He hath made him of
himself, and therefore do I call him Par-lui-fet,
of dearness and love.' 'Sir,' saith Messire
Gawain, 'May it not be in any wise that I
may see him?' 'Sir,' saith the hermit, 'I
have told you plainly that nowise may it not be.
No strange man shall not see him within yonder
until such time as he be whole and of good
cheer.' 'Sir,' saith Messire Gawain, 'Will
you in nowise do nought for me whatsoever I
may say?' 'Certes, sir, no one thing is there
in the world that I would tell him, save he
spake first to me.' Hereof is Messire Gawain
right sorrowful that he may not speak to the
knight. 'Sir,' saith he to the hermit, 'Of what
age is the knight, and of what lineage?' 'Of
the lineage of Joseph of Abarimacie the Good
Soldier.'

Gawain rideth on

V

Thereupon behold you a damsel that cometh to the door of the chapel and calleth very low to the hermit, and the hermit riseth up and taketh leave of Messire Gawain, and shutteth the door of the chapel; and the squire leadeth away the destrier and beareth the arms within door and shutteth the postern door of the house. And Messire abideth without and knoweth not of a truth whether it be the son of the Widow Lady, for many good men there be of one lineage. He departeth all abashed and entereth again into the forest. The history telleth not all the journeys that he made. Rather, I tell you in brief words that he wandered so far by lands and kingdoms that he found a right fair land and a rich, and a castle seated in the midst thereof. Thitherward goeth he and draweth nigh the castle and seeth it compassed about of high walls, and he seeth the entrance of the castle far without. He looketh and seeth a lion chained that lay in the midst of the entrance to the gate, and the chain was fixed in the wall. And on either side of the gate he seeth two serjeants of beaten copper that were fixed to the wall, and by engine shot forth quarrels from their cross-bows with great force and great wrath. Messire Gawain durst not come anigh the gate for that he seeth the lion and these folk. He looketh above on the top of the wall and seeth a sort of folk that seemed him to be of holy life, and saw there priests clad in albs and knights bald and ancient that were clad in ancient seeming garments. And in each crenel of the wall was a cross and a chapel. Above the wall, hard by an issue from a great hall that was in the castle, was another chapel, and above the chapel was a tall cross, and on either side of this cross another that was somewhat lower, and on the top of each cross was a golden eagle. The priests and the knights were upon the walls and knelt toward this chapel, and looked up to heaven and made great joy, and well it seemed him that they beheld God in Heaven with His Mother. Messire Gawain looketh at them from afar, for he durst not come anigh the castle for these that shoot their arrows so strongly that none armour might defend him. Way seeth he none to right nor left save he go back again. He knoweth not what to do. He looketh before him and seeth a priest issue forth of the gateway. 'Fair sir,' saith Messire Gawain, 'Welcome may you be!' 'Good adventure to you also,' saith the good man, 'What is your pleasure?' 'Sir,' saith Messire Gawain, 'So please you, I would fain ask you to tell me what castle is this?' 'It is,' saith he, 'the entrance to the land of the rich King Fisherman, and within yonder are they beginning the service of the Most Holy Graal.' 'Allow me then,' saith Messire Gawain, 'that I may pass on further, for toward the land of King Fisherman have I emprised my way.' 'Sir,' saith the priest, 'I tell you of a truth that you may not enter the castle nor come nigher unto the Holy Graal, save you bring the sword wherewith S. John was beheaded.' 'What?' saith

The Castle of Inquest

Gawain swappeth horses Messire Gawain, 'Shall I be evilly entreated and I bring it not?' 'So much may you well believe me herein,' saith the priest, 'And I tell you moreover that he who hath it is the fellest misbelieving King that lives. But so you bring the sword, this entrance will be free to you, and great joy will be made of you in all places wherein King Fisherman hath power.' 'Then must I needs go back again,' saith Messire Gawain, 'Whereof I have right to be sore sorrowful.' 'So ought you not to be,' saith the priest, 'For, so you bring the sword and conquer it for us, then will it be well known that you are worthy to behold the Holy Graal. But take heed you remember him who would not ask whereof it served.' Thereupon Messire Gawain departeth so sorrowful and full of thought that he remembereth not to ask in what land he may find the sword nor the name of the King that hath it. But he will know tidings thereof when God pleaseth.

VI

The history telleth us and witnesseth that he rode so far that he came to the side of a little hill, and the day was right fair and clear. He looketh in front of him before a chapel and seeth a tall burgess sitting on a great destrier that was right rich and fair. The burgess espieth Messire Gawain and cometh over against him, and saluteth him right courteously and Messire Gawain him. 'Sir,' saith Messire Gawain, 'God give you joy.' 'Sir,' saith the goodman, 'Right sorrowful am I of this that you

have a horse so lean and spare of flesh. Better **and**
would it become so worshipful man as you seem **pledgeth**
to be that he were better horsed.' 'Sir,' saith **his word**
Messire Gawain, 'I may not now amend it,
whereof am I sorry; another shall I have
when it shall please God.' 'Fair sir,' saith
the burgess, 'Whither are you bound to go?'
'I go seek the sword wherewith the head of
S. John Baptist was cut off.' 'Ha, sir,' saith
the burgess, 'You are running too sore a peril.
A King hath it that believeth not in God, and
is sore fell and cruel. He is named Gurgalain,
and many knights have passed hereby that went
thither for the sword, but never thence have
they returned. But, and you are willing to
pledge me your word that so God grant you
to conquer the sword, you will return hither and
show it me on your return, I will give you this
destrier, which is right rich, for your own.'
'Will you?' saith Messire Gawain, 'Then are
you right courteous, for you know me not.'
'Certes, sir,' saith he, 'So worshipful man seem
you to be, that you will hold well to this that
you have covenanted with me.' 'And to this
do I pledge you my word,' saith Messire
Gawain, 'that, so God allow me to conquer it,
I will show it to you on my return.'

VII

Thereupon, the burgess alighteth and mount‑
eth upon Messire Gawain's horse, and Messire
Gawain upon his, and taketh leave of the burgess
and goeth his way and entereth into a right
great forest beyond the city, and rideth until

sundown and findeth neither castle nor city. And he findeth a meadow in the midst of the forest, right broad, and it ran on beyond, like as there were the stream of a spring in the midst. He looketh toward the foot of the meadow close by the forest, and seeth a right large tent, whereof the cords were of silk and the pegs of ivory fixed in the ground, and the tops of the poles of gold and upon each was a golden eagle. The tent was white round about, and the hanging above was of the richest silk, the same as red samite. Thitherward goeth Messire Gawain and alighteth before the door of the tent, and smiteth off the bridle of his horse, and letteth him feed on the grass, and leaneth his spear and his shield without the tent, and looketh narrowly within and seeth a right rich couch of silk and gold, and below was a cloth unfolded as it were a feather-bed, and above a coverlid of ermine and vair without any gold, and at the head of the couch two pillows so rich that fairer none ever saw, and such sweet smell gave they forth that it seemed the tent was sprinkled of balm. And round about the couch were rich silken cloths spread on the ground. And at the head of the couch on the one side and the other were two seats of ivory, and upon them were two cushions stuffed with straw, right rich, and at the foot of the couch, above the bed, two candlesticks of gold wherein were two tall waxen tapers. A table was set in the midst of the tent, that was all of ivory banded of gold, with rich precious stones, and upon the table was the napkin spread and the basin of

A fair tent

silver and the knife with an ivory handle and the rich set of golden vessels. Messire Gawain seeth the rich couch and setteth him down thereon all armed in the midst, and marvelleth him wherefore the tent is so richly apparelled and yet more that therein he seeth not a soul. Howbeit, he was minded to disarm himself.

Another dwarf

VIII

Thereupon, behold you, a dwarf that entereth the tent and saluteth Messire Gawain. Then he kneeleth before him and would fain disarm him. Then Messire Gawain remembereth him of the dwarf through whom the lady was slain. 'Fair sweet friend, withdraw yourself further from me, for as at this time I have no mind to disarm.' 'Sir,' saith the dwarf, 'Without misgiving may you do so, for until to-morrow have you no occasion to be on your guard, and never were you more richly lodged than to-night you shall be, nor more honourably.' With that Messire Gawain beginneth to disarm him, and the dwarf helpeth him. And when he was disarmed, he setteth his arms nigh the couch and his spear and sword and shield lying within the tent, and the dwarf taketh a basin of silver and a white napkin, and maketh Messire Gawain wash his hands and his face. Afterward, he unfasteneth a right fair coffer, and draweth forth a robe of cloth of gold furred of ermine and maketh Messire Gawain be clad therewithal. 'Sir,' saith the dwarf, 'Be not troubled as touching your destrier, for you will have him again when you rise in the morning.

The damsels of the tent I will lead him close hereby to be better at ease, and then will I return to you.' And Messire Gawain giveth him leave. Thereupon, behold you, two squires that bear in the wine and set the meats upon the table and make Messire Gawain sit to eat, and they have great torches lighted on a tall cresset of gold and depart swiftly. Whilst Messire Gawain was eating, behold you, thereupon, two damsels that come into the tent and salute him right courteously. And he maketh answer, the fairest he may. 'Sir,' say the damsels, 'God grant you force and power to-morrow to destroy the evil custom of this tent.' 'Is there then any evil custom herein, damsel?' saith he. 'Yea, sir, a right foul custom, whereof much it grieveth me, but well meseemeth that you are the knight to amend it by the help of God.'

IX

Therewith he riseth from the table, and one of the squires was apparelled to take away the cloths. And the two damsels take him by the hand and lead him without the tent, and they set them down in the midst of the meadow. 'Sir,' saith the elder damsel, 'What is your name?' 'Damsel,' saith he, 'Gawain is my name.' 'Thereof do we love you the better, for well we know that the evil custom of the tent shall be done away on condition that you choose to-night the one of us two that most shall please you.' 'Damsel, gramercy,' saith he. Thereupon he riseth up, for he was weary, and draweth him toward the couch, and the damsels help him and wait upon his going to bed. And when he was lien down, they seated themselves before him and lighted the taper and leant over the couch and proffered him much service. Messire Gawain answered them naught save 'Gramercy,' for he was minded to sleep and take his rest. 'By God,' saith the one to the other, 'And this were Messire Gawain, King Arthur's nephew, he would speak to us after another sort, and more of disport should we find in him than in this one. But this is a counterfeit Gawain, and the honour we have done him hath been ill bestowed. Who careth? To-morrow shall he pay his reckoning.'

Gawain will not hear

X

Thereupon, lo you, the dwarf where he cometh. 'Fair friend,' say they, 'Keep good watch over this knight that he flee not away, for he goeth a-cadging from hostel to hostel and maketh him be called Messire Gawain, but Messire Gawain meseemeth is he not. For, and it were he, and we had been minded to watch with him two nights, he would have wished it to be three or four.' 'Damsel,' saith the dwarf, 'He may not flee away save he go afoot, for his horse is in my keeping.' And Messire Gawain heareth well enough that which the damsels say, but he answereth them never a word. Thereupon they depart, and say: God give him an ill night, for an evil knight and a vanquished and recreant, and command the dwarf that he move not on any occasion. Messire Gawain slept right little the

An evil night, and so soon as he saw the day, arose and
custom found his arms ready and his horse that had
been led all ready saddled before the tent. He
armed himself as swiftly as he might, and the
dwarf helpeth him and saith to him: 'Sir, you
have not done service to our damsels as they
would fain you should, wherefore they make sore
complaint of you.' 'That grieveth me,' saith
Messire Gawain, 'if that I have deserved it.'
'It is great pity,' saith the dwarf, 'when knight
so comely as be you is so churlish as they say.'
'They may say their pleasure,' saith he, 'for
it is their right. I know not to whom to
render thanks for the good lodging that I have
had save to God, and if I shall see the lord of
the tent or the lady I shall con them much
thanks thereof.'

XI

Thereupon, lo you, where two knights come
in front of the tent on their horses, all armed,
and see Messire Gawain that was mounted and
had his shield on his neck and his spear in his
fist, as he that thinketh to go without doing
aught further. And the knights come before
him: 'Sir,' say they, 'Pay for your lodging!
Last night did we put ourselves to misease on
your account and left you the tent and all that
is therein at your pleasure, and now you are
fain to go in this fashion.' 'What pleaseth it
you that I should do?' saith Messire Gawain.
'It is meet I should requite you of my victual
and the honour of the tent.' Thereupon, lo
you, where the two damsels come that were of

right great beauty. 'Sir Knight,' say they, **Gawain** 'Now shall we see whether you be King **slayeth** Arthur's nephew!' 'By my faith,' saith the **two** dwarf, 'Methinketh this is not he that shall **knights** do away the evil custom whereby we lose the coming hither of knights! Albeit if he may do it, I will forego mine ill will toward him.' Messire Gawain thus heard himself mocked by day as well as by night and had great shame thereof. He seeth that he may not depart without a fight. One of the knights drew to backward and was alighted; the other was upon his horse all armed, his shield on his neck and grasping his spear in his fist. And he cometh toward Messire Gawain full career and Messire Gawain toward him, and smiteth him so wrathfully that he pierceth his shield and pinneth his shield to his arm and his arm to his rib and thrusteth his spear into his body, and hurtleth against him so sore that he beareth him to the ground, him and his horse together at the first blow. 'By my head! Look at Messire Gawain the counterfeit! Better doth he to-day than he did last night!' He draweth back his spear, and pulleth forth his sword and runneth upon him, when the knight crieth him mercy and saith that he holdeth himself vanquished. Messire Gawain bethinketh him what he shall do and whether the damsels are looking at him. 'Sir knight,' saith the elder, 'Need you not fear the other knight until such time as this one be slain, nor will the evil custom be done away so long as this one is on live. For he is the lord of the other and

A sturdy because of the shameful custom hath no knight
strife come hither this right long space.' 'Hearken
now,' saith the knight, 'the great disloyalty of
her! Nought in the world is there she loved
so well in seeming as did she me, and now
hath she adjudged me my death!' 'Again
I tell you plainly,' saith she, 'that never will
it be done away unless he slay you.' Thereupon Messire Gawain lifteth the skirt of his
habergeon and thrusteth his sword into his
body. Thereupon, lo you, the other knight,
right angry and sorrowful and full of wrath
for his fellow that he seeth dead, and
cometh in great rage to Messire Gawain
and Messire Gawain to him, and so stoutly
they mell together that they pierce the shields
and pierce the habergeons and break the flesh
of the ribs with the points of their spears, and
the bodies of the knights and their horses
hurtle together so stiffly that saddle-bows are
to-frushed and stirrups loosened and girths to-
brast and fewtres splintered and spears snapped
short, and the knights drop to the ground with
such a shock that the blood flieth forth at mouth
and nose. In the fall that the knight made,
Messire Gawain brake his collar-bone in the
hurtle. Thereupon the dwarf crieth out:
'Damsel, your counterfeit Gawain doth it
well!' 'Our Gawain shall he be,' say they,
'so none take him from us!' Messire Gawain
draweth from over the knight and cometh
toward his horse, and right fain would he have
let the knight live had it not been for the
damsels. For the knight crieth him mercy

and Messire Gawain had right great pity of him. Howbeit the damsels cry to him; 'And you slay him not, the evil custom will not be overthrown.' 'Sir,' saith the younger damsel, 'And you would slay him, smite him in the sole of his foot with your sword, otherwise will he not die yet.' 'Damsel,' saith the knight, 'Your love of me is turned to shame! Never more ought knight to set affiance nor love on damsel. But God keep the other that they be not such as you!' Messire Gawain marvelleth at this that the damsel saith to him, and draweth him back, and hath great pity of the knight, and cometh to the other side whither the horses were gone, and taketh the saddle of the knight that was dead and setteth it on his own horse and draweth him away. And the wounded knight was remounted, for the dwarf had helped him, and fleeth toward the forest a great gallop. And the damsels cry out, 'Messire Gawain, your pity will be our death this day! For the Knight without Pity is gone for succour, and if he escape, we shall be dead and you also!'

[sidenote: Light love soon lost]

XII

Thereupon Messire Gawain leapeth on his horse and taketh a spear that was leaning against the tent and followeth the knight in such sort that he smiteth him to the ground. Afterward he saith to him: 'No further may you go!' 'That grieveth me,' saith the knight, 'For before night should I have been avenged of you and of the damsels.' And Messire Gawain draweth his sword and thrusteth it into the sole of his foot a full palm's breadth, and the knight stretcheth himself forth and dieth. And Messire Gawain returneth back, and the damsels make great joy of him and tell him that never otherwise could the evil custom have been done away. For, and he had gone his way, all would have been to begin over again, for he is of such kind seeing that he was of the kindred of Achilles, and that all his ancestors might never otherwise die. And Messire Gawain alighteth, and the damsels would have searched the wound in his side, and he telleth them that he taketh no heed thereof. 'Sir,' say they, 'Again do we proffer you our service, for well we know that you are a good knight. Take for your lady-love which of us you will.' 'Gramercy, damsel,' saith Messire Gawain, 'Your love do I refuse not and to God do I commend you.' 'How?' say the damsels, 'Will you go your way thus? Certes, meeter were it to-day for you to sojourn in this tent and be at ease.' 'It may not be,' saith he, 'for leisure have I none to abide here.' 'Let him go!' saith the younger, 'for the falsest knight is he of the world.' 'By my head,' saith the elder, 'it grieveth me that he goeth, for his stay would have pleased me well.' Therewithal Messire Gawain departeth and is remounted on his horse. Then he entereth into the forest.

[marginal note: Achilles' kin]

BRANCH VI

INCIPIT

ANOTHER branch that Josephus telleth us recounteth and witnesseth of the Holy Graal, and here beginneth for us in the name of the Father, and of the Son, and of the Holy Ghost.

The King of Wales

TITLE I

Messire Gawain rode until he came to a forest, and seeth a land right fair and rich in a great enclosure of wall, and round the land and country-side within, the wall stretched right far away. Thitherward he cometh and seeth but one entrance thereinto, and he seeth the fairest land that ever he beheld and the best garnished and the fairest orchards. The country was not more than four leagues Welsh in length, and in the midst thereof was a tower on a high rock. And on the top was a crane that kept watch over it and cried when any strange man came into the country. Messire Gawain rode amidst the land and the crane cried out so loud that the King of Wales heard it, that was lord of the land. Thereupon, behold you, two knights that come after Messire Gawain and say

Gawain is tricked to him: 'Hold, Sir Knight, and come speak with the king of this country, for no strange knight passeth through his land but he seeth him.' 'Lords,' saith Messire Gawain, 'I knew not of the custom. Willingly will I go.' They led him thither to the hall where the King was, and Messire Gawain alighteth and setteth his shield and his spear leaning against a mounting stage and goeth up into the hall. The King maketh great joy of him and asketh him whither he would go? 'Sir,' saith Messire Gawain, 'Into a country where I was never.' 'Well I know,' saith the king, 'where it is, for that you are passing through my land. You are going to the country of King Gurgalain to conquer the sword wherewith S. John was beheaded.'

II

'Sir,' saith Messire Gawain, 'You say true. God grant me that I may have it!' 'That may not be so hastily,' saith the King, 'For you shall not go forth of my land before a year.' 'Ha, Sir,' saith Messire Gawain, 'For God's sake, mercy!' 'None other mercy is here,' saith the King. Straightway he maketh Messire Gawain be disarmed and afterward maketh bring a robe wherewith to apparel him, and showeth him much honour. But ill is he at ease, wherefore he saith to him: 'Sir, wherefore are you fain to hold me here within so long?' 'For this, that I know well you will have the sword and will not return by me.' 'Sir,' saith Messire Gawain, 'I pledge you my word that, so God give me to conquer it, I will return by you.' 'And I will allow you to depart from me at your will. For nought is there that I so much desire to see.' He lay the night therewithin, and on the morrow departed thence and issued forth of the land right glad and joyful. And he goeth toward the land of King Gurgalain. And he entereth into a noisome forest at the lower part and findeth at the right hour of noon a fountain that was enclosed of marble, and it was overshadowed of the forest like as it were with leaves down below, and it had rich pillars of marble all round about with fillets of gold and set with precious stones. Against the master-pillar hung a vessel of gold by a silver chain, and in the midst of the fountain was an image as deftly wrought as if it had been alive. When Messire appeared at the fountain, the image set itself in the water and was hidden therewith. Messire Gawain goeth down, and would fain have taken hold on the vessel of gold when a voice crieth out to him: 'You are not the Good Knight unto whom is served thereof and who thereby is made whole.' Messire Gawain draweth him back and seeth a clerk come to the fountain that was young of age and clad in white garments, and he had a stole on his arm and held a little square vessel of gold, and cometh to the little vessel that was hanging on the marble pillar and looketh therein, and then rinseth out the other little golden vessel that he held, and then setteth the one that he held in the place of the other.

A wondrous fountain

A miracle

III

Therewith, behold, three damsels that come of right great beauty, and they had white garments and their heads were covered with white cloths, and they carried, one, bread in a little golden vessel, and the other wine in a little ivory vessel, and the third flesh in one of silver. And they come to the vessel of gold that hung against the pillar and set therein that which they have brought, and afterward they make the sign of the cross over the pillar and come back again. But on their going back, it seemed to Messire Gawain that only one was there. Messire Gawain much marvelled him of this miracle. He goeth after the clerk that carried the other vessel of gold, and saith to him: 'Fair Sir, speak to me.' 'What is your pleasure?' saith the clerk. 'Whither carry you this golden vessel and that which is therein?' 'To the hermits,' saith he, 'that are in this forest, and to the Good Knight that lieth sick in the house of his uncle King Hermit.' 'Is it far from hence?' saith Messire Gawain. 'Yea, Sir,' saith the clerk, 'to yourself. But I shall be there sooner than will you.' 'By God,' saith Messire Gawain, 'I would fain I were there now, so that I might see him and speak to him.' 'That believe I well,' saith the clerk, 'But now is the place not here.' Messire Gawain taketh leave and goeth his way and rideth until he findeth a hermitage and seeth the hermit therewithout. He was old and bald and of good life. 'Sir,' saith he to Messire

Gawain, 'Whither go you?' 'To the land of King
King Gurgalain, Sir; is this the way?' 'Yea,' Gurgalain
saith the hermit, 'But many knights have passed
hereby that hither have never returned.' 'Is
it far?' saith he. 'He and his land are hard
by, but far away is the castle wherein is the
sword.' Messire Gawain lay the night therewithin. On the morrow when he had heard
mass, he departed and rode until he cometh to
the land of King Gurgalain, and heareth the
folk of the land making dole right sore. And
he meeteth a knight that cometh a great pace to
a castle.

IV

'Sir,' saith Messire Gawain, 'Wherefore
make the folk of this castle such dole, and they
of all this land and all this country? For I
hear them weep and beat their palms together
on every side.' 'Sir,' saith he, 'I will tell
you. King Gurgalain had one only son of
whom he hath been bereft by a Giant that hath
done him many mischiefs and wasted much of
his land. Now hath the King let everywhere
be cried that to him that shall bring back his
son and slay the Giant he will give the fairest
sword of the world, the which sword he hath,
and of all his treasure so much as he may be
fain to take. As at this time, he findeth no
knight so hardy that he durst go; and much
more blameth he his own law than the law of
the Christians, and he saith that if any Christian
should come into his land, he would receive
him.' Right joyous is Messire Gawain of

A priceless sword

After these tidings, and departeth from the castle and rideth on until he cometh to the castle of King Gurgalain. The tidings come to the King that there is a Christian come into his castle. The King maketh great joy thereof, and maketh him come before him and asketh him of his name and of what land he is. 'Sir,' saith he, 'My name is Gawain and I am of the land of King Arthur.' 'You are,' saith he, 'of the land of the Good Knight. But of mine own land may I find none that durst give counsel in a matter I have on hand. But if you be of such valour that you be willing to undertake to counsel me herein, right well will I reward you. A Giant hath carried off my son whom I loved greatly, and so you be willing to set your body in jeopardy for my son, I will give you the richest sword that was ever forged, whereby the head of S. John was cut off. Every day at right noon is it bloody, for that at that hour the good man had his head cut off.' The King made fetch him the sword, and in the first place showeth him the scabbard that was loaded of precious stones and the mountings were of silk with buttons of gold, and the hilt in likewise, and the pommel of a most holy sacred stone that Enax, a high emperor of Rome, made be set thereon. Then the King draweth it forth of the scabbard, and the sword came forth thereof all bloody, for it was the hour of noon. And he made hold it before Messire Gawain until the hour was past, and thereafter the sword becometh as clear as an emerald and as green. And Messire looketh

at it and coveteth it much more than ever he **A cruel**
did before, and he seeth that it is as long as **Giant**
another sword, albeit, when it is sheathed in the
scabbard, neither scabbard nor sword seemeth
of two spans length.

V

'Sir Knight,' saith the King, 'This sword
will I give you, and another thing will I do
whereof you shall have joy.' 'Sir,' saith
Messire Gawain, 'And I will do your need, if
God please and His sweet Mother.' Thereupon he teacheth him the way whereby the
Giant went, and the place where he had his
repair, and Messire Gawain goeth his way
thitherward and commendeth himself to God.
The country folk pray for him according to
their believe that he may back repair with life
and health, for that he goeth in great peril. He
hath ridden until that he cometh to a great high
mountain that lay round about a land that the
Giant had all laid waste, and the enclosure of
the mountain went round about for a good three
leagues Welsh, and therewithin was the Giant,
so great and cruel and horrible that he feared
no man in the world, and for a long time had
he not been sought out by any knight, for none
durst won in that quarter. And the pass of the
mountain whereby he went to his hold was so
strait that no horse might get through; wherefore behoveth Messire Gawain leave his horse
and his shield and spear and to pass beyond the
mountain by sheer force, for the way was like a
cut between sharp rocks. He is come to level

Gawain slayeth the Giant

ground and looketh before him and seeth a hold that the Giant had on the top of a rock, and espieth the Giant and the lad where they were sitting on the level ground under a tree. Messire Gawain was armed and had his sword girt on, and goeth his way thitherward. And the Giant seeth him coming and leapeth up and taketh in hand a great axe that was at his side, and cometh toward Messire Gawain all girded for the fight and thinketh to smite him a two-handed stroke right amidst the head. But Messire Gawain swerveth aside and bestirreth him with his sword and dealeth him a blow such that he cut off his arm, axe and all. And the Giant returneth backward when he feeleth himself wounded, and taketh the King's son by the neck with his other hand and grippeth him so straitly that he strangleth and slayeth him. Then he cometh back to Messire Gawain and falleth upon him and grippeth him sore strait by the flanks, and lifteth him three foot high off the ground and thinketh to carry him to his hold that was within the rock. And as he goeth thither he falleth, Messire Gawain and all, and he lieth undermost. Howbeit he thinketh to rise, but cannot, for Messire Gawain sendeth him his sword right through his heart and beyond. Afterward, he cut off the head and cometh there where the King's child lay dead, whereof is he right sorrowful. And he beareth him on his neck, and taketh the Giant's head in his hand and returneth there where he had left his horse and shield and spear, and mounteth and cometh back and bringeth the King's son before the King and the head of the Giant hanging.

Gurgalain cooketh strange meat

VI

The King and all they of the castle come to meet him with right great joy, but when they see the young man dead, their great joy is turned into right great dole thereby. And Messire Gawain alighteth before the castle and presenteth to the King his son and the head of the Giant. 'Certes,' saith he, 'might I have presented him to you on live, much more joyful should I have been thereof.' 'This believe I well,' saith the King, 'Howbeit, of so much as you have done am I well pleased, and your guerdon shall you have.' And he looketh at his son and lamenteth him right sweetly, and all they of the castle after him. Thereafter he maketh light a great show of torches in the midst of the city, and causeth a great fire to be made, and his son be set thereon in a brazen vessel all full of water, and maketh him be cooked and sodden over this fire, and maketh the Giant's head be hanged at the gate.

VII

When his son was well cooked, he maketh him be cut up as small as he may, and biddeth send for all the high men of his land and giveth thereof to each so long as there was any left. After that, he maketh bring the sword and giveth it to Messire Gawain, and Messire Gawain thanketh him much thereof. 'More yet will I do for you,' saith the King. He biddeth send for all the men of his land to come

<small>The King of Wales false</small>

to his hall and castle. 'Sir,' saith he, 'I am fain to baptize me.' 'God be praised thereof,' saith Messire Gawain. The King biddeth send for a hermit of the forest, and maketh himself be baptized, and he had the name of Archis in right baptism; and of all them that were not willing to believe in God, he commanded Messire Gawain that he should cut off their heads.

VIII

In such wise was this King baptized that was the lord of Albanie, by the miracle of God and the knighthood of Messire Gawain, that departeth from the castle with right great joy and rideth until he is come into the land of the King of Wales and bethought him he would go fulfil his pledge. He alighted before the hall, and the King made right great cheer when he saw him come. And Messire Gawain hath told him: 'I come to redeem my pledge. Behold, here is the sword.' And the King taketh it in his hand and looketh thereon right fainly, and afterward maketh great joy thereof and setteth it in his treasury and saith: 'Now have I done my desire.' 'Sir,' saith Messire Gawain, 'Then have you betrayed me.' 'By my head,' saith the King, 'That have I not, for I am of the lineage of him that beheaded S. John, wherefore have I a better right to it than you.' 'Sir,' say the knights to the King, 'Right loyal and courteous knight is Messire Gawain, wherefore yield him that which he hath conquered, for sore blame will you have of evil-treating him.' 'I will yield it,' saith the King, **The** 'on such condition that the first damsel that **crafty** maketh request of him, what thing soever she **burgess** may require and whatsoever it be shall not be denied of him.' And Messire Gawain agreeth thereto, and of this agreement thereafter did he suffer much shame and anguish and was blamed of many knights. And the King yielded him the sword. He lay the night therewithin, and on the morrow so soon as he might, he departed and rode until he came without the city where the burgess gave him the horse in exchange for his own. And he remembered him of his covenant, and abideth a long space and leaneth him on the hilt of his sword until the burgess cometh. Therewithal made they great joy the one of the other, and Messire showeth him the sword, and the burgess taketh it and smiteth his horse with his spurs and goeth a great gallop toward the city. And Messire Gawain goeth after a great pace and crieth out that he doth great treachery. 'Come not after me into the city,' saith the burgess, 'for the folk have a commune.' Howbeit, he followeth after into the city for that he might not overtake him before, and therein he meeteth a great procession of priests and clerks that bore crosses and censers. And Messire Gawain alighteth on account of the procession, and seeth the burgess that hath gone into the church and the procession after. 'Lords,' saith Messire Gawain, 'Make yield me the sword whereof this burgess that hath entered your church hath plundered me.' 'Sir,' say the priests, 'Well know we

The Castle of the Ball

that it is the sword wherewith S. John was beheaded, wherefore the burgess hath brought it to us to set with our hallows in yonder, and saith that it was given him.' 'Ha, lords!' saith Messire Gawain, 'Not so! I have but shown it to him to fulfil my pledge. And he hath carried it off by treachery.' Afterward he telleth them as it had befallen him, and the priests make the burgess give it up, and with great joy Messire Gawain departeth and remounteth his horse and issueth forth of the city. He hath scarce gone far before he meeteth a knight that came all armed, as fast as his horse could carry him, spear in rest. 'Sir,' saith he to Messire Gawain, 'I have come to help you. We were told that you had been evil-entreated in the city, and I am of the castle that succoureth all strange knights that pass hereby whensoever they have need thereof.' 'Sir,' saith Messire Gawain, 'Blessed be the castle! I plain me not of the trespass for that right hath been done me. And how is the castle named?' 'Sir, they call it the Castle of the Ball. Will you return back thither with me, since you are delivered, and lodge there the night with Messire, that is a right worshipful man and of good conditions?' Therewith they go together to the castle, that was right fair and well-seeming. They enter in, and when they were within, the Lord, that sate on a mounting-stage of marble, had two right fair daughters, and he made them play before him with a ball of gold, and looked at them right fainly. He seeth Messire Gawain alight and cometh to meet him and maketh him great cheer. Afterward, he biddeth his two daughters lead him into the hall.

<small>The dwarf's brother</small>

IX

When he was disarmed, the one brought him a right rich robe, and after meat the two maidens sit beside him and make him right great cheer. Thereupon behold you, a dwarf that issueth forth of a chamber, and he holdeth a scourge. And he cometh to the damsels and smiteth them over their faces and their heads. 'Rise up,' saith he, 'ye fools, ill-taught! Ye make cheer to him whom you ought to hate! For this is Messire Gawain, King Arthur's nephew, by whom was your uncle slain!' Thereupon they rise, all ashamed, and go into the chamber, and Messire Gawain remaineth there sore abashed. But their father comforteth him and saith: 'Sir, be not troubled for aught that he saith, for the dwarf is our master; he chastiseth and teacheth my daughters, and he is wroth for that you have slain his brother, whom you slew the day that Marin slew his wife on your account, whereof we are right sorrowful in this castle.' 'So also am I,' saith Messire Gawain, 'But no blame of her death have I nor she, as God knoweth of very truth.'

X

Messire Gawain lay the night at the castle, and departed on the morrow, and rode on his journeys until he cometh to the castle at the entrance to the land of the rich King Fisher-

Gawain returneth man, where he seeth that the lion is not at the entrance nor were the serjeants of copper shooting. And he seeth in great procession the priests and them of the castle coming to meet him, and he alighteth, and a squire was apparelled ready, that took his armour and his horse, and he showeth the sword to them that were come to meet him. It was the hour of noon. He draweth the sword, and seeth it all bloody, and they bow down and worship it, and sing *Te Deum laudamus*. With such joy was Messire Gawain received at the castle, and he set the sword back in his scabbard, and kept it right anigh him, and made it not known in all the places where he lodged that it was such. The priests and knights of the castle make right great joy, and pray him right instantly that so God should lead him to the castle of King Fisherman, and the Graal should appear before him, he would not be so forgetful as the other knights. And he made answer that he would do that which God should teach him.

XI

'Messire Gawain,' saith the master of the priests, that was right ancient: 'Great need have you to take rest, for meseemeth you have had much travail.' 'Sir, many things have I seen whereof I am sore abashed, nor know I what castle this may be.' 'Sir,' saith the priest, 'This castle is the Castle of Inquest, for nought you shall ask whereof it shall not tell you the meaning, by the witness of Joseph, the good clerk and good hermit through whom we

have it, and he knoweth it by annunciation of **Riddles**
the Holy Ghost.' 'By my faith,' saith Messire **darkly**
Gawain, 'I am much abashed of the three **revealed**
damsels that were at the court of King Arthur.
Two of them carried, the one the head of a
king and the other of a queen, and they had in
a car an hundred and fifty heads of knights
whereof some were sealed in gold, other in
silver, and the rest in lead.' 'True,' saith the
priest, 'For as by the queen was the king betrayed
and killed, and the knights whereof the heads
were in the car, so saith she truth as Joseph
witnesseth to us, for he saith of remembrance
that by envy was Adam betrayed, and all the
people that were after him and the people that
are yet to come shall have dole thereof for
ever more. And for that Adam was the first
man is he called King, for he was our earthly
father, and his wife Queen. And the heads
of the knights sealed in gold signify the new
law, and the heads sealed in silver the old, and
the heads sealed in lead the false law of the
Sarrazins. Of these three manner of folk is
the world stablished.' 'Sir,' saith Messire
Gawain, 'I marvel of the castle of the Black
Hermit, there where the heads were all taken
from her, and the Damsel told me that the
Good Knight should cast them all forth when
he should come. And the other folk that are
therewithin are longing for him.' 'Well know
you,' saith the priest, 'that on account of the
apple that Eve gave Adam to eat, all went to
hell alike, the good as well as the evil, and to
cast His people forth from hell did God become

<small>More riddles</small> man, and cast these souls forth from hell of His bounty and of His puissance. And to this doth Joseph make us allusion by the castle of the Black Hermit, which signifieth hell, and the Good Knight that shall thence cast forth them that are within. And I tell you that the Black Hermit is Lucifer, that is Lord of hell in like manner as he fain would have been Lord of Paradise. Sir,' saith the priest, ' By this significance is he fain to draw the good hermits on behalf of the new law wherein the most part are not well learned, wherefore he would fain make allusion by ensample.' 'By God,' saith Messire Gawain, ' I marvel much of the Damsel that was all bald, and said that never should she have her hair again until such time as the Good Knight should have achieved the Holy Graal.' ' Sir,' saith the good man, ' Each day full bald behoveth her to be, ever since bald she became when the good King fell into languishment on account of the knight whom he harboured that made not the demand. The bald damsel signifieth Joseu Josephus, that was bald before the crucifixion of Our Lord, nor never had his hair again until such time as He had redeemed His people by His blood and by His death. The car that she leadeth after her signifieth the wheel of fortune, for like as the car goeth on the wheels, doth she lay the burden of the world on the two damsels that follow her; and this you may see well, for the fairest followeth afoot and the other was on a sorry hackney, and they were poorly clad, whereas the third had costlier attire. The shield

whereon was the red cross, that she left at and the court of King Arthur, signifieth the most darker holy shield of the rood that never none durst lift save God alone.' Messire Gawain heareth these significances and much pleaseth him thereof, and thinketh him that none durst set his hand to nor lift the shield that hung in the King's hall, as he had heard tell in many places; wherefore day by day were they waiting for the Good Knight that should come for the shield.

XII

'Sir,' saith Messire Gawain, 'By this that you tell me you do me to wit that whereof I was abashed, but I have been right sorrowful of a lady that a knight slew on my account though no blame had she therein, nor had I.' 'Sir,' saith the priest, 'Right great significance was there in her death, for Josephus witnesseth us that the old law was destroyed by the stroke of a sword without recover, and to destroy the old law did Our Lord suffer Himself to be smitten in the side of a spear. By this stroke was the old law destroyed, and by His crucifixion. The lady signifieth the old law. Would you ask more of me?' saith the priest. 'Sir,' saith Messire Gawain, 'I met a knight in the forest that rode behind before and carried his arms upside down. And he said that he was the Knight Coward, and his habergeon carried he on his neck, and so soon as he saw me he set his arms to rights and rode like any other knight.' 'The law was turned to the worse,' saith the priest, 'before Our Lord's crucifixion,

_{Yet more riddles} and so soon as He was crucified, was again restored to right.' 'Even yet have I not asked you of all,' saith Messire Gawain, 'For a knight came and jousted with me party of black and white, and challenged me of the death of the lady on behalf of her husband, and told me and I should vanquish him that he and his men would be my men. I did vanquish him and he did me homage.' 'It is right,' saith the priest, 'On account of the old law that was destroyed were all they that remained therein made subject, and shall be for ever more. Wish you to enquire of aught further?' saith the priest. 'I marvel me right sore,' saith Messire Gawain, 'of a child that rode a lion in a hermitage, and none durst come nigh the lion save the child only, and he was not of more than six years, and the lion was right fell. The child was the son of the lady that was slain on my account.' 'Right well have you spoken,' saith the priest, 'in reminding me thereof. The child signifieth the Saviour of the world that was born under the old law and was circumcised, and the lion whereon he rode signifieth the world and the people that are therein, and beasts and birds that none may govern save by virtue of Him alone.' 'God!' saith Messire Gawain, 'How great joy have I at heart of that you tell me! Sir, I found a fountain in a forest, the fairest that was ever seen, and an image had it within that hid itself when it saw me, and a clerk brought a golden vessel and took another golden vessel that hung at the column that was there, and set his own in place

thereof. Afterward, came three damsels and filled the vessel with that they had brought thither, and straightway meseemed that but one was there.' 'Sir,' saith the priest, 'I will tell you no more thereof than you have heard, and therewithal ought you to hold yourself well apaid, for behoveth not discover the secrets of the Saviour, and them also to whom they are committed behoveth keep them covertly.'

The Secret of the Graal

XIII

'Sir,' saith Messire Gawain, 'I would fain ask you of a King. When I had brought him his son back dead, he made him be cooked and thereafter made him be eaten of all the folk of his land.' 'Sir,' saith the priest, 'Already had he leant his heart upon Jesus Christ, and would fain make sacrifice of his flesh and blood to Our Lord, and for this did he make all those of his land eat thereof, and would fain that their thoughts should be even such as his own. And therefore was all evil belief uprooted from his land, so that none remained therein.' 'Blessed be the hour,' saith Messire Gawain, 'that I came herewithin!' 'Mine be it!' saith the priest. Messire Gawain lay therewithin the night, and right well lodged was he. The morrow, when he had heard mass, he departed and went forth of the castle when he had taken leave. And he findeth the fairest land of the world and the fairest meadow-grounds that were ever seen, and the fairest rivers and forests garnished of wild deer and hermitages. And he rideth until he cometh one day as evening was about to draw on, to the house of a hermit, and the house was so low that his horse might not enter therein. And his chapel was scarce taller, and the good man had never issued therefrom of forty years past. The Hermit putteth his head out of the window when he seeth Messire Gawain and saith, 'Sir, welcome may you be,' saith he. 'Sir, God give you joy, Will you give me lodging to-night?' saith Messire Gawain. 'Sir, herewithin none harboureth save the Lord God alone, for earthly man hath never entered herewithin but me this forty year, but see, here in front is the castle wherein the good knights are lodged.' 'What is the castle?' 'Sir, the good King Fisherman's, that is surrounded with great waters and plenteous in all things good, so the lord were in joy. But behoveth them harbour none there save good knights only.' 'God grant,' saith Messire Gawain, 'that I may come therein!'

The Castle of the Graal

XIV

When he knoweth that he is nigh the castle, he alighteth and confesseth him to the hermit, and avoweth all his sins and repenteth him thereof right truly. 'Sir,' saith the hermit, 'Now forget not, so God be willing to allow you, to ask that which the other knight forgat, and be not afeard for aught you may see at the entrance of the castle, but ride on without misgiving and adore the holy chapel you will see appear in the castle, there where the flame of the Holy Spirit descendeth each day for the most Holy Graal and the point of the lance that is served there.' 'Sir,' saith Messire Gawain, 'God teach me to do His will!' He taketh leave, and goeth his way and rideth until the valley appeareth wherein the castle is seated garnished of all things good, and he seeth appear the most holy chapel. He alighteth, and then setteth him on his knees and boweth him down and adoreth right sweetly. Thereafter he remounteth and rideth until he findeth a sepulchre right rich, and it had a cover over, and it lay very nigh the castle, and it seemed to be within a little burial ground that was enclosed all round about, nor were any other tombs therein. A voice crieth to him as he passeth the burial-ground: 'Touch not the sepulchre, for you are not the Good Knight through whom shall it be known who lieth therein.' Messire Gawain passeth beyond when he had heard the voice and draweth nigh the entrance of the castle, and seeth that three bridges are there, right great and right horrible to pass. And three great waters run below, and him seemeth that the first bridge is a bowshot in length and in breadth not more than a foot. Strait seemeth the bridge and the water deep and swift and wide. He knoweth not what he may do, for it seemeth him that none may pass it, neither afoot nor on horse.

Three bridges

XV

Thereupon, lo you, a knight that issueth forth of the castle and cometh as far as the head of the bridge, that was called the Bridge of the Eel, and shouteth aloud: 'Sir knight, pass

The Eel Bridge quickly before it shall be already night, for they of the castle are awaiting us.' 'Ha,' saith Messire Gawain, 'Fair sir, but teach me how I may pass hereby.' 'Certes, Sir Knight, no passage know I to this entrance other than this, and if you desire to come to the castle, pass on without misgiving.' Messire Gawain hath shame for that he hath stayed so long, and forthinketh him of this that the Hermit told him, that of no mortal thing need he be troubled at the entrance of the castle, and therewithal that he is truly confessed of his sins, wherefore behoveth him be the less adread of death. He crosseth and blesseth himself and commendeth himself to God as he that thinketh to die, and so smiteth his horse with his spurs and findeth the bridge wide and large as soon as he goeth forward, for by this passing were proven most of the knights that were fain to enter therein. Much marvelled he that he found the bridge so wide that had seemed him so narrow. And when he had passed beyond, the bridge, that was a drawbridge, lifted itself by engine behind him, for the water below ran too swiftly for other bridge to be made. The knight draweth himself back beyond the great bridge and Messire Gawain cometh nigh to pass it, and this seemed him as long as the other. And he seeth the water below, that was not less swift nor less deep, and, so far as he could judge, the bridge was of ice, feeble and thin, and of a great height above the water, and he looked at it with much marvelling, yet natheless not for that would he any the more hold back from passing on toward the entrance. He goeth forward and commendeth himself to God, and cometh in the midst thereof and seeth that the bridge was the fairest and richest and strongest he had ever beheld, and the abutments thereof were all full of images. When he was beyond the bridge, it lifted itself up behind him as the other had done, and he looketh before him and seeth not the knight, and is come to the third bridge and nought was he adread for anything he might see. And it was not less rich than the other, and had columns of marble all round about, and upon each a knop so rich that it seemed to be of gold. After that, he beholdeth the gate over against him, and seeth Our Lord there figured even as He was set upon the rood, and His Mother of the one side and S. John of the other, whereof the images were all of gold, with rich precious stones that flashed like fire. And on the right hand he seeth an angel, passing fair, that pointed with his finger to the chapel where was the Holy Graal, and on his breast had he a precious stone, and letters written above his head that told how the lord of the castle was the like pure and clean of all evil-seeming as was this stone.

The gateway

XVI

Thereafter at the entrance of the gate he seeth a lion right great and horrible, and he was upright upon his feet. So soon as he seeth Messire Gawain, he croucheth to the ground, and Messire Gawain passeth the en-

The chess-board trance without gainsay and cometh to the castle, and alighteth afoot, and setteth his shield and his spear against the wall of the hall, and mounteth up a flight of marble steps and cometh into a hall right fair and rich, and here and there in divers places was it painted with golden images. In the midst thereof he findeth a couch right fair and rich and high, and at the foot of this couch was a chess-board right fair and rich, with an orle of gold all full of precious stones, and the pieces were of gold and silver and were not upon the board. Meanwhile, as Messire Gawain was looking at the beauty of the chess-board and the hall, behold you two knights that issue forth of a chamber and come to him. 'Sir,' say the knights, 'Welcome may you be.' 'God give you joy and good adventure,' saith Messire Gawain. They make him sit upon the couch and after that make him be disarmed. They bring him, in two basins of gold, water to wash his face and hands. After that, come two damsels that bring him a rich robe of silk and cloth of gold. Then they make him do on the same. Then say the two damsels to him, 'Take in good part whatsoever may be done to you therewithin, for this is the hostel of good knights and loyal.' 'Damsels,' saith Messire Gawain, 'So will I do. Gramercy of your service.' He seeth well that albeit the night were dark, within was so great brightness of light without candles that it was marvel. And it seemed him the sun shone there. Wherefore marvelled he right sore whence so great light should come.

XVII

When Messire Gawain was clad in the rich robe, right comely was he to behold, and well seemed he to be a knight of great valour. 'Sir,' say the knights, 'May it please you come see the Lord of this castle?' 'Right gladly will I see him,' saith he, 'For I would fain present him with a rich sword.' They lead him into the chamber where lay King Fisherman, and it seemed as it were all strown and sprinkled of balm, and it was all strown with green herbs and reeds. And King Fisherman lay on a bed hung on cords whereof the stays were of ivory; and therein was a mattress of straw whereon he lay, and above, a coverlid of sables whereof the cloth was right rich. And he had a cap of sables on his head covered with a red samite of silk, and a golden cross, and under his head was a pillow all smelling sweet of balm, and at the four corners of the pillow were four stones that gave out a right great brightness of light; and over against him was a pillar of copper whereon sate an eagle that held a cross of gold wherein was a piece of the true cross whereon God was set, as long as was the cross itself, the which the good man adored. And in four tall candlesticks of gold were four tall wax tapers set as often as was need. Messire Gawain cometh before the King and saluteth him. And the King maketh him right great cheer, and biddeth him be welcome. 'Sir,' saith Messire Gawain, 'I present you with the sword whereof John was

King Fisherman

beheaded.' 'Gramercy,' saith the King: 'Certes, I knew well that you would bring it, for neither you nor other might have come in hither without the sword, and if you had not been of great valour you would not have conquered it.' He taketh the sword and setteth it to his mouth and his face and so kisseth it right sweetly and maketh right great joy thereof. And a damsel cometh to sit at the head of the bed, to whom he giveth the sword in keeping. Two others sit at his feet that look at him right sweetly. 'What is your name?' saith the King. 'Sir, my name is Gawain.' 'Ha, Messire Gawain,' saith he, 'This brightness of light that shineth there within cometh to us of God for love of you. For every time that a knight cometh hither to harbour within this castle it appeareth as brightly as you see it now. And greater cheer would I make you than I do were I able to help myself, but I am fallen into languishment from the hour that the knight of whom you have heard tell harboured herewithin. On account of one single word he delayed to speak, did this languishment come upon me. Wherefore I pray you for God's sake that you remember to speak it, for right glad should you be and you may restore me my health. And see here is the daughter of my sister that hath been plundered of her land and disherited in such wise that never can she have it again save through her brother only whom she goeth to seek; and we have been told that he is the Best Knight of the world, but we can learn no true tidings of him.' 'Sir,' saith the damsel to her uncle the King, 'Thank Messire Gawain of the honour he did to my lady-mother when he came to her hostel. He stablished our land again in peace, and conquered the keeping of the castle for a year, and set my lady-mother's five knights there with us to keep it. The year hath now passed, wherefore will the war be now renewed against us and God succour us not, and I find not my brother whom we have lost so long.' 'Damsel,' saith Messire Gawain, 'I helped you so far as I might, and so would I again and I were there. And fainer am I to see your brother than all the knights of the world. But no true tidings may I hear of him, save so much, that I was at a hermitage where was a King hermit, and he bade me make no noise for that the Best Knight of the world lay sick therewithin, and he told me that his name was Par-lui-fet. I saw his horse being led by a squire before the chapel, and his arms and shield whereon was a sun figured.' 'Sir,' saith the damsel, 'My brother's name is not Par-lui-fet, but Perlesvax in right baptism, and it is said of them that have seen him that never comelier knight was known.' 'Certes,' saith the King, 'Never saw I comelier than he that came in hither nor better like to be good knight, and I know of a truth that such he is, for otherwise never might he have entered hereinto. But good reward of harbouring him had I not, for I may help neither myself nor other. For God's sake, Messire Gawain, hold me in remembrance this night, for great affiance have I in your

Dindrane and Gawain

Of the valour.' 'Certes, Sir, please God, nought
feast will I do within yonder, whereof I may be
blamed of right.'

XVIII

Thereupon Messire Gawain was led into the
hall and findeth twelve ancient knights, all bald,
albeit they seemed not to be so old as they
were, for each was of an hundred year of age
or more and yet none of them seemed as though
he were forty. They have set Messire Gawain
to eat at a right rich table of ivory and seat
themselves all round about him. 'Sir,' saith
the Master of the Knights, 'Remember you of
that the good King hath prayed of you and told
you this night as you have heard.' 'Sir,' saith
Messire Gawain, 'God remember it!' With
that bring they larded meats of venison and
wild-boar's flesh and other in great plenty,
and on the table was rich array of vessels of
silver and great cups of gold with their covers,
and the rich candlesticks where the great
candles were burning, albeit their brightness
was hidden of the great light that appeared
within.

XIX

Thereon, lo you, two damsels that issue forth
of a chapel, whereof the one holdeth in her
hands the most Holy Graal, and the other the
Lance whereof the point bleedeth thereinto.
And the one goeth beside the other in the
midst of the hall where the knights and Messire
Gawain sat at meat, and so sweet a smell and so

holy came to them therefrom that they forgat to eat. Messire Gawain looketh at the Graal, and it seemed him that a chalice was therein, albeit none there was as at this time, and he seeth the point of the lance whence the red blood ran thereinto, and it seemeth him he seeth two angels that bear two candlesticks of gold filled with candles. And the damsels pass before Messire Gawain, and go into another chapel. And Messire Gawain is thoughtful, and so great a joy cometh to him that nought remembereth he in his thinking save of God only. The knights are all daunted and sorrowful in their hearts, and look at Messire Gawain. Thereupon behold you the damsels that issue forth of the chamber and come again before Messire Gawain, and him seemeth that he seeth three there where before he had seen but two, and seemeth him that in the midst of the Graal he seeth the figure of a child. The Master of the Knights beckoneth to Messire Gawain. Messire Gawain looketh before him and seeth three drops of blood fall upon the table. He was all abashed to look at them and spake no word.

The Graal appeareth

XX

Therewith the damsels pass forth and the knights are all adread and look one at the other. Howbeit Messire Gawain may not withdraw his eyes from the three drops of blood, and when he would fain kiss them they vanish away, whereof he is right sorrowful, for he may not set his hand nor aught that of him is

Gawain forgetteth to speak to touch thereof. Therewithal behold you the two damsels that come again before the table and seemeth to Messire Gawain that there are three, and he looketh up and it seemeth him to be the Graal all in flesh, and he seeth above, as him thinketh, a King crowned, nailed upon a rood, and the spear was still fast in his side. Messire Gawain seeth it and hath great pity thereof, and of nought doth he remember him save of the pain that this King suffereth. And the Master of the Knights summoneth him again by word of mouth, and telleth him that if he delayeth longer, never more will he recover it. Messire Gawain is silent, as he that heareth not the knight speak, and looketh upward. But the damsels go back into the chapel and carry back the most Holy Graal and the Lance, and the knights make the tablecloths be taken away and rise from meat and go into another hall and leave Messire Gawain all alone. And he looketh all around and seeth the doors all shut and made fast, and looketh to the foot of the hall and seeth two candlesticks with many candles burning round about the chess-board, and he seeth that the pieces are set, whereof the one sort are silver and the other gold. Messire Gawain sitteth at the game, and they of gold played against him and mated him twice. At the third time, when he thought to revenge himself and saw that he had the worse, he swept the pieces off the board. And a damsel issued forth of a chamber and made a squire take the chess-board and the pieces and so carry them away. And Messire Gawain, that was way-worn of

his wanderings to come thither where he now **Gawain**
hath come, slept upon the couch until the **departeth**
morrow when it was day, and he heard a horn
sound right shrill.

XXI

Thereupon he armeth him and would fain go
to take leave of King Fisherman, but he findeth
the doors bolted so that he may not get forth.
And right fair service seeth he done in a chapel,
and right sorrowful is he for that he may not
hear the mass. A damsel cometh into the hall
and saith to him: 'Sir, now may you hear the
service and the joy that is made on account of
the sword you presented to the good King, and
right glad at heart ought you to have been if
you had been within the chapel. But you lost
entering therein on account of a right little word.
For the place of the chapel is so hallowed of the
holy relics that are therein that man nor priest
may never enter therein from the Saturday at
noon until the Monday after mass.' And he
heard the sweetest voices and the fairest services
that were ever done in chapel. Messire Gawain
answereth her not a word so is he abashed.
Howbeit the damsel saith to him: 'Sir, God
be guardian of your body, for methinketh that
it was not of your own default that you would
not speak the word whereof this castle would
have been in joy.' With that the damsel
departeth and Messire Gawain heareth the horn
sound a second time and a voice warning him
aloud: 'He that is from without, let him go
hence! for the bridges are lowered and the

The Forest Perilous gate open, and the lion is in his den. And thereafter behoveth the bridge be lifted again on account of the King of the Castle Mortal, that warreth against this castle, and therefore of this thing shall he die.'

XXII

Thereupon Messire Gawain issueth forth of the hall and findeth his horse all made ready at the mounting-stage, together with his arms. He goeth forth and findeth the bridges broad and long, and goeth his way a great pace beside a great river that runneth in the midst of the valley. And he seeth in a great forest a mighty rain and tempest, and so strong a thunder-storm ariseth in the forest that it seemeth like all the trees should be uprooted. So great is the rain and the tempest that it compelleth him set his shield over his horse's head lest he be drowned of the abundance of rain. In this mis-ease rideth he down beside the river that runneth in the forest until he seeth in a launde across the river a knight and a damsel right gaily appointed riding at pleasure, and the knight carrieth a bird on his fist, and the damsel hath a garland of flowers on her head. Two brachets follow the knight. The sun shineth right fair on the meadow and the air is right clear and fresh. Messire Gawain marvelleth much of this, that it raineth so heavily on his way, whereas, in the meadow where the knight and the damsel are riding, the sun shineth clear and the weather is bright and calm. And he seeth them ride joyously. He can ask them

naught for they are too far away. Messire **A castle**
Gawain looketh about and seeth on the other **of joy**
side the river a squire nearer to him than is
the knight. 'Fair friend,' saith Messire
Gawain, 'How is this that it raineth upon me
on this side the river, but on the other raineth
it not at all?' 'Sir,' saith the squire, 'This
have you deserved, for such is the custom of
the forest.' 'Will this tempest that is over me
last for ever?' saith Messire Gawain. 'At
the first bridge you come to will it be stayed
upon you,' saith the squire.

XXIII

Therewith the squire departeth, and the
tempest rageth incontinent until he is come to
the bridge; and he rideth beyond and cometh
to the meadow, and the storm is stayed so that
he setteth his shield to rights again upon his
neck. And he seeth before him a castle where
was a great company of folk that were making
great cheer. He rideth until he cometh to the
castle and seeth right great throng of folk,
knights and dames and damsels. Messire
Gawain alighteth, but findeth in the castle
none that is willing to take his reins, so busied
are they making merry. Messire Gawain
presenteth himself on the one side and the
other, but all of them avoid him, and he seeth
that he maketh but an ill stay therewithin for
himself, wherefore he departeth from the castle
and meeteth a knight at the gate. 'Sir,' saith
he, 'What castle is this?' 'And see you not,'
saith the knight, 'that it is a castle of joy?'

The Poor Knight 'By my faith,' saith Messire Gawain, 'They of the castle be not over-courteous, for all this time hath none come to take my reins.' 'Not for this lose they their courtesy,' saith the knight, 'For this is no more than you have deserved. They take you to be as slothful of deed as you are of word, and they saw that you were come through the Forest Perilous whereby pass all the discomfited, as well appeareth by your arms and your horse.' Therewith the knight departeth, and Messire Gawain hath ridden a great space sorrowful and sore abashed, until he cometh to a land parched and poor and barren of all comfort, and therein findeth he a poor castle, whereinto he cometh and seeth it much wasted, but that within was there a hall that seemed haunted of folk. And Messire Gawain cometh thitherward and alighteth, and a knight cometh down the steps of the hall right poorly clad. 'Sir,' saith the knight to Messire Gawain, 'Welcome may you be!' After that, he taketh him by the hand and leadeth him upward to the hall, that was all waste. Therewithal issue two damsels from a chamber, right poorly clad, that were of passing great beauty, and make great cheer to Messire Gawain. So, when he was fain to disarm, behold you thereupon a knight that entereth into the hall, and he was smitten with the broken end of a lance through his body. He seeth Messire Gawain whom he knoweth. 'Now haste!' saith he, 'and disarm you not! Right joyful am I that I have found you! I come from this forest wherein have I left

Lancelot fighting with four knights, whereof one is dead, and they think that it is you, and they are of kindred to the knight that you slew at the tent where you destroyed the evil custom. I was fain to help Lancelot, when one of the knights smote me as you may see.' Messire Gawain goeth down from the hall and mounteth all armed upon his horse.

Gawain helpeth Lancelot

XXIV

'Sir,' saith the knight of the hall, 'I would go help you to my power, but I may not issue forth of the castle until such time as it be replenished of the folk that are wont to come therein and until my land be again given up to me through the valour of the Good Knight.' Messire Gawain departeth from the castle as fast as horse may carry him, and entereth the forest and followeth the track of the blood along the way the knight had come, and rideth so far in the forest as that he heareth the noise of swords, and seeth in the midst of the launde Lancelot and the three knights, and the fourth dead on the ground. But one of the knights had drawn him aback, for he might abide the combat no longer, for the knight that brought the tidings to Messire Gawain had sore wounded him. The two knights beset Lancelot full sore, and right weary was he of the buffets that he had given and received. Messire Gawain cometh to one of the knights and smiteth him right through the body and maketh him and his horse roll over all of a heap.

The Poor Knight's hostel

XXV

When Lancelot perceiveth Messire Gawain, much joy maketh he thereof. In the meanwhile as the one held the other, the fourth knight fled full speed through the midst of the forest, and he that the knight had wounded fell dead. They take their horses, and Messire Gawain telleth Lancelot he hath the most poverty-stricken host that ever he hath seen, and the fairest damsels known, but that right poorly are they clad. 'Shall we therefore take them of our booty?' 'I agree,' saith Lancelot, 'But sore grieveth me of the knight that hath thus escaped us.' 'Take no heed!' saith Messire Gawain, 'We shall do well enough herein.' Thereupon they return back toward the poor knight's hostel and alight before the hall, and the Poor Knight cometh to meet them, and the two damsels, and they deliver to them the three horses of the three knights that were dead. The knight hath great joy thereof, and telleth them that now is he a rich man and that betimes will his sisters be better clad than are they now, as well as himself.

XXVI

Thereupon come they into the hall. The knight maketh one of his own squires stable the horses and the two damsels help disarm Lancelot and Messire Gawain. 'Lords,' saith the knight, 'So God help me, nought have I to lend you wherewith to clothe you, for robe have I none save mine own jerkin.' Lancelot hath great pity thereof and Messire Gawain, and the two damsels take off their kirtles that were made like surcoats of cloth that covered their poor shirts, and their jackets that were all to-torn and ragged and worn, and present them to the knights to clothe them. They were fain not to refuse, lest the damsels should think they held them not in honour, and did on the two kirtles right poor as they were. The damsels had great joy thereof that so good knights should deign wear garments so poor. 'Lords,' saith the Poor Knight, 'The knight that brought the tidings hither, and was stricken through of a lance-shaft, is dead and lieth on a bier in a chapel within the castle, and he confessed himself right well to a hermit and bade salute you both, and was right fain you should see him after that he were dead, and he prayed me instantly that I would ask you to be to-morrow at his burial, for better knights than be ye might not be thereat, so he told me.' 'Certes,' saith Lancelot, 'A good knight was he, and much mischief is it of his death; and sore grieveth me that I know not his name nor of what country he was.' 'Sir,' saith Messire Gawain, 'He said that you should yet know it well.' The two good knights lay the night at the castle, and the Poor Knight lodged them as well as he might. When it cometh to morning, they go to the chapel to hear mass and to be at the burial of the body. After that they take leave of the Poor Knight and the two damsels and depart from the castle all armed. 'Messire Gawain,' saith Lancelot, 'They know not at

The Poor Knight

Gawain and Lancelot court what hath become of you, and they hold you for dead as they suppose.' 'By my faith,' saith Messire Gawain, 'thitherward will I go, for I have had sore travail, and there will I abide until some will shall come to me to go seek adventure.' He recounteth to Lancelot how the Graal hath appeared to him at the court of King Fisherman: 'And even as it was there before me, I forgat to ask how it served and of what.' 'Ha, Sir,' saith Lancelot, 'Have you then been there?' 'Yea,' saith he, 'And thereof am I right sorry and glad: glad for the great holiness I have seen, sorry for that I asked not that whereof King Fisherman prayed me right sweetly.' 'Sir,' saith Lancelot, 'Right sorely ill have you wrought, nor is there nought whereof I have so great desire as I have to go to his castle.' 'By my faith,' saith Messire Gawain, 'Much shamed was I there, but this doth somewhat recomfort me, that the Best Knight was there before me that gat blame thereof in like manner as I.' Lancelot departeth from Messire Gawain, and they take leave either of other. They issue forth of a forest, and each taketh his own way without saying a word.

BRANCH VII

TITLE I

HERE the story is silent of Messire Gawain **Of** and beginneth to speak of Lancelot, that **Lancelot** entereth into a forest and rideth with right great ado and meeteth a knight in the midst of the forest that was coming full speed and was armed of all arms. 'Sir,' saith he to Lancelot, 'Whence come you?' 'Sir,' saith Lancelot, 'I come from the neighbourhood of King Arthur's court.' 'Ha, Sir, can you tell me tidings of a knight that beareth a green shield such as I bear? If so, he is my brother.' 'What name hath he?' saith Lancelot. 'Sir,' saith he, 'His name is Gladoens, and he is a good knight and a hardy, and he hath a white horse right strong and swift.' 'Be there other knights in your country that bear such arms as your shield and his besides you and he?' 'Certes, Sir, none.' 'And wherefore do you ask?' saith Lancelot. 'For this, that a certain man hath reft him of one of his castles for that he was not there. Howbeit, I know well that he will have it again through his good knighthood.' 'Is he so good knight?' saith Lancelot. 'Certes, Sir, yea! He is the best of the Isles of the Moors.' 'Sir, of your mercy, lower your coif.' He quickly thereon lowereth his coif, and Lancelot looketh at him in the face. 'Certes, Sir Knight,' saith he, 'you very much resemble him.' 'Ha,

Sir,' saith the knight, 'Know you then any tidings of him?' 'Certes, Sir,' saith he, 'Yea! and true tidings may I well say, for he rode at my side five leagues Welsh, nor never saw I one man so like another as are you to him.' 'Good right hath he to resemble me,' saith the knight, 'for we are twins, but he was born first and hath more sense and knighthood than I; nor in all the Isles of the Moors is there damsel that hath so much worth and beauty as she of whom he is loved of right true love, and more she desireth to see him than aught else that liveth, for she hath not seen him of more than a year, wherefore hath she gone seek her prize, my brother, by all the forests of the world. Sir,' saith the knight, 'Let me go seek my brother, and tell me where I may find him.' 'Certes,' saith Lancelot, 'I will tell you though it grieve me sore.' 'Wherefore?' saith the knight, 'Hath he done you any mis-deed?' 'In no wise,' saith Lancelot, 'Rather hath he done so much for me that I love you thereof and offer you my service.' 'Sir,' saith the knight, 'I am going my way, but for God's sake tell me where I shall find my brother.' 'Sir,' saith Lancelot, 'I will tell you. This morning did I bid his body farewell and help to bury him.' 'Ha, Sir,' saith the knight, 'Do you tell me true?' 'Certes,' saith Lancelot, 'True it is that I tell you.' 'Is he slain then, my brother?' saith the knight. 'Yea, and of succouring me,' saith Lancelot. 'Ha, sir,' saith the knight, 'For God's sake tell me nought that is not right.' 'By God, Sir,' saith he, 'Sore grieved

am I to tell it you, for never loved I knight so *of Rock*
much in so brief a time as loved I him. He *Gladoens*
helped to save me from death, and therefore will
I do for you according to that he did for me.'
'Sir,' saith the knight, 'If he be dead, a great
grief is it to myself, for I have lost my comfort
and my life and my land without recovery.'
'Sir,' saith Lancelot, 'He helped me to save
my life, and yours will I help to save henceforth
for ever and so be that I shall know of your
jeopardy.' The knight heareth that his brother
is dead and well believeth Lancelot, and beginneth to make dole thereof the greatest that was
ever heard. And Lancelot saith to him, 'Sir
Knight, let be this dole, for none recovery is
there; but my body do I offer you and my
knighthood in any place you please, where I
may save your honour.' 'Sir,' saith the knight,
'With good will receive I your help and your
love, sith that you deign to offer me the same,
and now have I sorer need of them than ever.
Sir,' saith the knight, 'Sith that my brother is
dead, I will return back and bear with my
wrong, though well would he have amended it
had he been on live.' 'By my head,' saith
Lancelot, 'I will go with you, that so may I
reward you of that he hath done for me. He
delivered his body to the death for me, and in
like manner freely would I fain set mine own
in jeopardy for love of you and of him.'

II

'Sir,' saith the knight, 'Right good will do
I owe you of this that you say to me, so your

Castle of deeds be but the same herein.' 'Yea, so help
Gladoens me God,' saith Lancelot, 'The same shall they be, if God lend me the power.' With that, they go on their way together, and the knight comforteth him much of that which Lancelot hath said to him, but of the death of his brother was he right sorrowful. And they ride until they come to the land of the Moors; then espy they a castle upon a rock, and below was a broad meadow-land. 'Sir,' saith the Knight of the Green Shield to Lancelot, 'This castle was my brother's and is now mine, and much it misliketh me that it hath fallen to me on this wise. And the knight that reft it of my brother is of so great hardihood that he feareth no knight on live, and you will presently see him issue forth of this castle so soon as he shall perceive you. Lancelot and the knight ride until they draw nigh the castle. And the knight looketh in the way before him, and seeth a squire coming on a hackney, that was carrying before him a wild boar dead. The Knight of the Green Shield asketh him whose man he is, and the squire maketh answer: 'I am man of the Lord of the Rock Gladoens, that cometh there behind, and my lord cometh all armed, he and others, for the brother of Gladoens hath defied him on behalf of his brother, but right little recketh my lord of his defiance.'

III

Lancelot heareth how he that is coming is the enemy of him to whom had he been alive, his love most was due. The Knight of the

Green Shield pointed him out so soon as he saw him. 'Sir,' saith he to Lancelot, 'Behold him by whom I am disherited, and yet worse would he do to me and he knew that my brother were dead.' Lancelot, without saying more, so soon as he had espied the Knight of the Rock, smiteth his horse with his spurs and cometh toward him. The Lord of the Rock, that was proud and hardy, seeth Lancelot coming and smiteth with his spurs the horse whereon he sitteth. They come with so swift an onset either upon other that they break their spears upon their shields, and hurtle together so sore that the Knight of the Rock Gladoens falleth over the croup of his horse. Lancelot draweth his sword and cometh above him, and he crieth him mercy and asketh him wherefore he wisheth to slay him? Lancelot saith for the sake of Gladoens from whom he hath reft his land and his castle. 'And what is that to you?' saith the knight. 'Behoveth his brother challenge me thereof.' 'As much it behoveth me as his brother,' saith Lancelot. 'Wherefore you?' 'For this,' saith Lancelot, 'That as much as he did for me will I do to you.' He cutteth off his head and giveth it incontinent to the Knight of the Green Shield. 'Now tell me,' saith Lancelot, 'Sith that he is dead, is he purged of that whereof you appeached him?' 'Sir,' saith the knight, 'I hold him rightly quit thereof, for, sith that he is dead, all claim on behalf of his kindred is abated by his death.' 'And I pledge you my faith loyally,' saith Lancelot, 'as I am a knight, that never shall

Lancelot slayeth the lord

The Castle you be in peril nor in jeopardy of aught wherein I may help you, so I be in place and free, but my help shall you have for evermore, for that your brother staked his life to help me.'

IV

Lancelot and the knight lay the night at the Rock Gladoens, and the Knight of the Green Shield had his land at his pleasure, and all were obedient to him. And the upright and loyal were right glad, albeit when they heard the tidings of Gladoens' death they were right sorrowful thereof. Lancelot departed from the castle on the morrow, and the knight remained therein, sorrowful for his brother that he had lost, and glad for the land that he had gotten again. Lancelot goeth back right amidst the forest and rideth the day long, and meeteth a knight that was coming, groaning sore. And he was stooping over the fore saddle-bow for the pain that he had. He meeteth Lancelot and saith to him: 'Sir, for God's sake, turn back, for you will find there the most cruel pass in the world there where I have been wounded through the body. Wherefore I beseech you not go thither.' 'What pass is it then?' saith Lancelot. 'Sir,' saith he, 'It is the pass of the Castle of Beards, and it hath the name of this, that every knight that passeth thereby must either leave his beard there or challenge the same, and in such sort have I challenged my beard that meseemeth I shall die thereof.' 'By my head,' saith Lancelot, 'I hold not this of cowardize, sith that

you were hardy to set your life in jeopardy to
challenge your beard, but now would you argue
me of cowardize when you would have me turn
back. Rather would I be smitten through the
body with honour, so and I had not my death
thereof, than lose with shame a single hair of
my beard.' 'Sir,' saith the knight, 'May God
preserve you, for the castle is far more cruel
than you think, and God guide the knight that
may destroy the evil custom of the castle, for
right shameful is the custom to strange knights
that pass thereby.'

of Beards

V

Lancelot departeth from the knight and
cometh toward the castle. Just as he had
passed over a great bridge, he looketh about
and seeth two knights come all armed to the
entrance of the castle, and they made hold
their horses before them, and their shields and
spears are before them leaning against the wall.
Lancelot looketh at the gateway of the castle
and seeth the great door all covered with beards
fastened thereon, and heads of knights in great
plenty hung thereby. So, as he was about to
enter the gate, two knights issue therefrom
over against him. 'Sir,' saith the one, 'Abide
and pay your toll!' 'Do knights, then, pay
toll here?' saith Lancelot. 'Yea!' say the
knights, 'All they that have beards, and they
that have none are quit. Sir, now pay us
yours, for a right great beard it is, and thereof
have we sore need.' 'For what?' saith
Lancelot. 'I will tell you,' saith the knight.

<small>Lancelot saveth his beard</small> 'There be hermits in this forest that make hair-shirts thereof.' 'By my head,' saith Lancelot, 'Never shall they have hair-shirt of mine, so I may help it.' 'That shall they,' say the knights, 'Of yours as of the other, or dearly shall you pay therefor!'

VI

Right wroth waxeth Sir Lancelot, and cometh to the knight, and smiteth him with his spear amidst the breast with such a thrust that it passeth half an ell beyond, and overthroweth him and his horse together. The other knight seeth his fellow wounded to the death, and cometh towards him with a great sweep and breaketh his spear upon his shield. Howbeit, Lancelot beareth him to the ground right over his horse-croup and maketh him fall so heavily that he breaketh one of his legs. The tidings are come to the Lady of the Castle that a knight hath come to the pass that hath slain one of her knights and wounded the other. The Lady is come thither and bringeth two of her damsels with her. She seeth Lancelot that is fain to slay the knight that lieth wounded on the ground. 'Sir,' saith the Lady to Lancelot, 'Withdraw yourself back and slay him not, but alight and speak to me in safety.' 'Lady,' saith one of the maidens, 'I know him well. This is Lancelot of the Lake, the most courteous knight that is in the court of King Arthur.' He alighteth and cometh before the Lady. 'Lady,' saith he, 'what is your pleasure?' 'I desire,' saith she, 'that you come to my hostel to harbour, and that you make me amends of the shame you have done me.' **A foul service**

VII

'Lady,' saith Lancelot, 'Shame have I never done you nor shall do, but the knights took in hand too shameful a business when they were minded to take the beards of stranger knights by force.' 'Sir,' saith she, 'I will forego my ill-will on condition that you harbour herewithin to-night.' 'Lady,' saith Lancelot, 'I desire not your ill-will, wherefore will I gladly do your pleasure.' He setteth him within the castle and maketh his horse be led in after him, and the Lady hath the dead knight brought into the chapel and buried. The other she biddeth be disarmed and clothed and commandeth that his wounds be searched. Then maketh she Lancelot be disarmed and clad right richly in a good robe, and telleth him that she knoweth well who he is. 'Lady,' saith Lancelot, 'It is well for me.' Thereupon they sit to eat, and the first course is brought in by knights in chains that had their noses cut off; the second by knights in chains that had their eyes put out; wherefore they were led in by squires. The third course was brought in by knights that had but one hand and were in chains. After that, came other knights that had each but one foot and brought in the fourth course. At the fifth course came knights right fair and tall, and each brought a naked sword in his hand and presented their heads to the Lady.

The Lady wooeth Lancelot

VIII

Lancelot beheld the martyrdom of these knights, and sore misliking had he of the services of such folk. They are risen from meat and the lady goeth to her chamber and sitteth on a couch. 'Lancelot,' saith the Lady, 'you have seen the justice and the lordship of my castle. All these knights have been conquered at the passing of my door.' 'Lady,' saith Lancelot, 'foul mischance hath befallen them.' 'The like mischance would have befallen you had you not been knight so good. And greatly have I desired to see you this long time past. And I will make you lord of this castle and myself.' 'Lady,' saith he, 'the lordship of this castle hold I of yourself without mesne, and to you have I neither wish nor right to refuse it. Rather am I willing to be at your service.' 'Then,' saith she, 'you will abide with me in this castle, for more do I love you than any other knight that liveth.' 'Lady,' saith Lancelot, 'Gramercy, but in no castle may I abide more than one night until I have been thither whither behoveth me to go.' 'Whither are you bound?' saith she. 'Lady,' saith he, 'to the Castle of Souls.' 'Well know I the castle,' saith she. 'The King hath the name Fisherman, and lieth in languishment on account of two knights that have been at his castle and made not good demand. Would you fain go thither?' saith the Lady. 'Yea,' saith Lancelot. 'Then pledge me your faith that you will return by me to speak to me, so the

Graal shall appear to you, and you ask whereof **The**
it serveth.' 'Yea, truly,' saith Lancelot, 'were **Grave-**
you beyond sea!' 'Sir,' saith one of the **yard**
damsels, 'So much may you well promise, for **Perilous**
the Graal appeareth not to no knight so wanton
as be ye. For you love the Queen Guenievre,
the wife of your lord, King Arthur, nor so long
as this love lieth at your heart may you never
behold the Graal.'

IX

Lancelot heard the damsel and blushed of
despite. 'Ha, Lancelot,' saith the Lady, 'Love
you other than me?' 'Lady,' saith he, 'the
damsel may say her pleasure.' Lancelot lay
the night at the castle, and right wroth was he
of the damsel that calleth the love of him and
the Queen disloyal. And the morrow when he
had heard mass, he took leave of the Lady of
the Castle, and she besought him over and over
to keep his covenant, and he said that so would
he do without fail. Therewithal he issueth forth
of the castle and entereth into a tall and ancient
forest, and rideth the day long until he cometh
to the outskirt of the forest, and seeth a tall cross
at the entrance of a burying-ground enclosed all
round about with a hedge of thorns. And the
way lay through the burying-ground. Lancelot
entered therein and the night was come. He
seeth the grave-yard full of tombs and sepulchres.
He looketh behind and seeth a chapel wherein
were candles burning. Thitherward goeth he,
and passeth beyond without saying aught more
by the side of a dwarf that was digging a grave

Lancelot in the chapel in the ground. 'Lancelot,' saith the dwarf, 'you are right not to salute me, for you are the man of all the world that most I hate; and God grant me vengeance of your body. So will He what time you are stricken down here within!' Lancelot heard the dwarf, but deigned not to answer him of nought. He is come to the chapel, and alighteth and maketh fast the bridle of his horse to a tree, and leaneth his shield and spear without. After that he entereth into the chapel, and findeth a damsel laying out a knight in his winding-sheet. As soon as Lancelot was entered therewithin the wounds of the knight were swollen up and began to bleed afresh. 'Ha, Sir Knight, now see I plainly that you slew him that I am wrapping in his winding-sheet!'

X

Thereupon, behold you, two knights that are carrying other two knights dead. They alight and then set them in the chapel. And the dwarf crieth out to them: 'Now shall it be seen how you avenge your friends of the enemy that fell upon you!' The knight that had fled from the forest when Messire Gawain came thither where the three lay dead, was come therewithin and knew Lancelot, whereupon saith he: 'Our mortal enemy are you, for by you were these three knights slain.' 'Well had they deserved it,' saith Lancelot, 'and in this chapel am I in no peril of you, wherefore as at this time will I depart not hence, for I know not the ways of the forest.' He was in the

chapel until the day broke, when he issued forth
thereof, and sore it weighed upon him that his
horse was still fasting. He taketh his arms
and is mounted. The dwarf crieth out aloud:
'What aileth you?' saith he to the two knights,
'Will you let your mortal enemy go thus?'
With that the two knights mount their horses
and go to the two issues of the grave-yard,
thinking that Lancelot is fain to flee therefrom;
but no desire hath he thereof, wherefore he
cometh to the knight that was guarding the
entrance whereby he had to issue out, and
smiteth him so stiffly that he thrusteth the point
of his spear right through his body. The other
knight that was guarding the other entrance,
that had fled out of the forest before, had no
mind to avenge his fellow, and fled incontinent
so fast as he might. And Lancelot taketh the
horse of the knight he had slain and driveth
him before him, for he thinketh that some knight
may haply have need thereof. He rideth on
until he cometh to a hermitage in the forest
where he alighteth and hath his horses stabled,
and the Hermit giveth them of the best he
hath. And Lancelot heard mass, and afterward ate a little and fell asleep. Thereafter,
behold you, a knight that cometh to the Hermit
and seeth Lancelot that was about to mount.
'Sir,' saith he, 'Whither go you?' 'Sir
Knight,' saith Lancelot, 'thither shall I go
where God may please; but you, whitherward
are you bound to go?' 'Sir, I go to see one
of my brethren and my two sisters, for I have
been told that he hath fallen on such mishap as

The Poor Knight's brother

The Waste City that he is called the Poor Knight, whereof am I sore sorrowful.' 'Certes,' saith Lancelot, 'Poor he is, the more the pity! Howbeit, will you do him a message from me?' 'Sir,' saith the knight, 'Right willingly!' 'Will you present him with this horse on my behalf, and tell him how Lancelot that harboured with him hath sent it?' 'Sir,' saith the knight, 'Right great thanks, and blessed may you be, for he that doth a kindness to a worshipful man loseth it not.' 'Salute the two damsels for me,' saith Lancelot. 'Sir, right willingly!' The knight delivereth the horse to his squire, and taketh leave of Lancelot.

XI

Thereupon, Lancelot departeth from the hermitage and rideth on until he cometh forth of the forest, and findeth a waste land, a country broad and long wherein wonned neither beast nor bird, for the land was so poor and parched that no victual was to be found therein. Lancelot looketh before him and seeth a city appear far away. Thither rideth he full speed and seeth that the city is so great that it seemeth him to encompass a whole country. He seeth the walls that are falling all around, and the gates ruined with age. He entereth within and findeth the city all void of folk, and seeth the great palaces fallen down and waste, and the great grave-yards full of sepulchres, and the tall churches all lying waste, and the markets and exchanges all empty. He rideth amidst the streets and findeth a great palace that seemeth him to be better and more ancient than all the others. He bideth awhile before it and heareth within how knights and ladies are making great dole. And they say to a knight: 'Ha, God, sore grief and pity is this of you, that you must needs die in such manner, and that your death may not be respited! Sore hatred ought we to bear toward him that hath adjudged you such a death.' The knights and ladies swoon over him as he departeth. Lancelot hath heard all this and much marvelleth he thereof, but nought thereof may he see.

A knight desireth death

XII

Thereupon, lo you, the knight that cometh down into the midst of the hall, clad in a short red jerkin; and he was girt with a rich girdle of gold, and had a rich clasp at his neck wherein were many rich stones, and on his head had he a great cap of gold, and he held a great axe. The knight was of great comeliness and young of age. Lancelot seeth him coming, and looketh upon him right fainly when he seeth him appear. And the knight saith to him, 'Sir, alight!' 'Certes,' saith Lancelot, 'Willingly.' He alighteth and maketh his horse fast to a ring of silver that was on the mounting-stage, and putteth his shield from his neck and his spear from his hand. 'Sir,' saith he to the knight, 'What is your pleasure?' 'Sir, needs must you cut me off my head with this axe, for of this weapon hath my death been adjudged, but and you will not, I will cut off your own therewith.' 'Hold, Sir,' saith

Lancelot, 'What is this you tell me?' 'Sir,' saith the knight, 'You must needs do even as I say, sith that you are come into this city.' 'Sir,' saith Lancelot, 'Right foolish were he that in such a jeopardy should not do the best for himself, but blamed shall I be thereof and I shall slay you when you have done me no wrong.' 'Certes,' saith the Knight, 'In no otherwise may you go hence.' 'Fair Sir,' saith Lancelot, 'So gentle are you and so well nurtured, how cometh it that you take your death so graciously? You know well that I shall kill you before you shall kill me, sith that so it is.' 'This know I well for true,' saith the Knight, 'But you will promise me before I die, that you will return into this city within a year from this, and that you will set your head in the same jeopardy without challenge, as I have set mine.' 'By my head,' saith Lancelot, 'Needeth no argument that I shall choose respite of death to dying here on the spot. But I marvel me of this that you are so fairly apparelled to receive your death.'

Lancelot pledgeth his head

XIII

'Sir,' saith the Knight, 'He that would go before the Saviour of the World ought of right to apparel him as fairly as he may. I am by confession purged of all wickedness and of all the misdeeds that ever I have committed, and do repent me truly thereof, wherefore at this moment am I fain to die.' Therewithal he holdeth forth the axe, and Lancelot taketh it and seeth that it is right keen and well whetted.

'Sir,' saith the Knight, 'Hold up your hand toward the minster that you see yonder.' 'Sir,' saith Lancelot, 'Willingly.' 'Thus, then, will you swear to me upon the holy relics that are within this minster, that on this day year at the hour that you shall have slain me, or before, you yourself will come back here and place your head in the very same peril as I shall have placed mine, without default?' 'Thus,' saith Lancelot, 'do I swear and give you thereto my pledge.' With that, the Knight kneeleth and stretcheth his neck as much as he may, and Lancelot taketh the axe in his hands, and then saith to him, 'Sir Knight, for God's sake, have mercy on yourself!' 'Let cut off my head!' saith the Knight, 'For otherwise may I not have mercy upon you!' 'In God's name,' saith Lancelot, 'fain would I deny you.' With that, he swingeth the axe and cutteth off the head with such a sweep that he maketh it fly seven foot high from the body. The Knight fell to the ground when his head was cut off, and Lancelot flung down the axe, and thinketh that he will make but an ill stay there for himself. He cometh to his horse, and taketh his arms and mounteth and looketh behind him, but seeth neither the body of the Knight nor the head, neither knoweth he what hath become of them all, save only that he heard much dole and a great cry far off in the city of knights and ladies, saying that he shall be avenged, please God, at the term set, or before. Lancelot hath heard and understood all that the knights say and the ladies, and issueth forth of the city.

Lancelot slayeth the knight

BRANCH VIII

INCIPIT

Perceval's recovery   OF the most Holy Graal here beginneth another branch in such wise as the authority witnesseth and Joseph that made recoverance thereof, in the name of the Father, and of the Son, and of the Holy Ghost.

TITLE I

This high history and profitable witnesseth us that the son of the Widow Lady sojourned still with his uncle King Pelles in the hermitage, and, through distress of the evil that he had had since he came forth of the house of King Fisherman, was he confessed to his uncle and told him of what lineage he was, and that his name was Perceval. But the good Hermit the good King had given him the name of Parluifet, for that he was made of himself. King Hermit was one day gone into the forest, and the good knight Parluifet felt himself sounder of health and lustier than he wont to be. He heard the birds sing in the forest, and his heart began to swell of knighthood, and he minded him of the adventures he wont to find in the forest and of the damsels and knights that he wont to meet, and never was he so fain of arms as was he at that time, for that he had been sojourning so long within doors. He felt courage in his heart and lustiness in his limbs and fainness in his thought. Right soon armeth he himself and setteth the saddle on his horse and mounteth forthwith. He prayeth God give him adventure that he may meet good knight, setteth himself forth of his uncle's hermitage and entereth into the forest that was broad and shady. He rideth until he cometh into a launde that was right spacious, and seeth a leafy tree that was at the head of the launde. He alighteth in the shadow, and thinketh to himself that two knights might joust on this bit of ground fair and well, for the place was right broad. And, even as he was thinking on this wise, he heard a horse neigh full loud in the forest three times, and right glad was he thereof and said: 'Ha, God, of your sweetness grant that there be a knight with that horse, so may I prove whether there be any force or valour or knighthood in me. For I know not now what strength I may have, nor even whether my heart be sound and my limbs whole. For on a knight that hath neither hardihood nor valour in himself, may not another knight that hath more force in him reasonably prove his mettle, for many a time have I heard say that one is better than other. And for this pray I to the Saviour and this be a knight that cometh there, that he may have strength and hardihood and mettle to defend his body against mine own, for great desire have I to run upon him. Grant now that he slay me not, nor I him!'

Perceval would fain fight

Perceval runneth upon Lancelot

II

Therewithal, he looketh before him, and seeth the knight issue from the forest and enter into the launde. The knight was armed and had at his neck a white shield with a cross of gold. He carried his lance low, and sate upon a great destrier and rode at a swift pace. As soon as Perceval seeth him, he steadieth him in his stirrups and setteth spear in rest and smiteth his horse with his spurs, right joyous, and goeth toward the knight a great gallop. Then he crieth: 'Sir Knight, cover you of your shield to guard you as I do of mine to defend my body, for you do I defy on this side slaying, and our Lord God grant that I find you so good knight as shall try what hardihood of heart I may have, for I am not such as I have been aforetime, and better may one learn of a good knight than of a bad.' With that he smiteth the knight upon his shield with such a sweep that he maketh him lose one of his stirrups and pierceth his shield above the boss, and passeth beyond full speed. And the knight marvelleth much, and maketh demand, saying, 'Fair Sir, what misdeed have I done you?' Perceval is silent, and hath no great joy of this that he hath not overthrown the knight, but not so easy was he to overthrow, for he was one of the knights of the world that could most of defence of arms. He goeth toward Perceval as fast as his horse may carry him and Perceval toward him. They mell together upon their shields right stiffly, so that they pierce and batter them with the points of their spears. And **Both are** Perceval thrusteth his spear into the flesh two **wounded** finger-breadths, and the knight doth not amiss, for he passeth his spear right through his arm so that the shafts of the lances were splintered. They hurtle together either against other at the passing so mightily, that the flinders of iron from the mail of their habergeons stick into their foreheads and faces, and the blood leapeth forth by mouth and nose so that their habergeons were all bloody. They drew their swords with a right great sweep. The knight of the white shield holdeth Perceval's rein and saith: 'Gladly would I know who you are and wherefore you hate me, for you have wounded me right sore, and sturdy knight have I found you and of great strength.' Perceval saith not a word to him and runneth again upon him sword drawn, and the knight upon him, and right great buffets either giveth other on the helm, so that their eyes all sparkle of stars and the forest resoundeth of the clashing of their swords. Right tough was the battle and right horrible, for good knights were both twain. But the blood that ran down from their wounds at last slackened their sinews, albeit the passing great wrath that the one had against the other, and the passing great heat of their will, had so enchafed them they scarce remembered the wounds that they had, and still dealt each other great buffets without sparing.

III

King Hermit cometh from labouring in the forest and findeth not his nephew in the

King Hermit hermitage, whereof is he right sorrowful, and he mounteth on a white mule that he had therewithin. She was starred in the midst of her forehead with a red cross. Josephus the good clerk witnesseth us that this same mule had belonged to Joseph of Abarimacie at the time he was Pilate's soldier, and that he bequeathed her to King Pelles. King Hermit departeth from the hermitage and prayeth God grant him to find his nephew. He goeth through the forest and rideth until he draweth nigh the launde where the two knights were. He heareth the strokes of the swords, and cometh towards them full speed and setteth him between the twain to forbid them. 'Ha, sir,' saith he to the Knight of the White Shield, 'Right great ill do you to combat against this knight that hath lain sick this long time in this forest, and right sorely have you wounded him.' 'Sir,' saith the knight, 'As much hath he done by me, and never would I have run upon him now had he not challenged me, and he is not minded to tell me who he is nor whence ariseth his hatred of me.' 'Fair Sir,' saith the Hermit, 'And you, who are you?' 'Sir,' saith the knight, 'I will tell you. I am the son of King Ban of Benoic.' 'Ha, fair nephew,' saith King Hermit to Perceval, 'See here your cousin, for King Ban of Benoic was your father's cousin-german. Make him right great cheer!' He maketh them take off their helmets and lower their ventails, and then kiss one another, afterward he leadeth them to his hermitage. They alight together. He calleth

his own squire that waited upon him, and made A wise
them be disarmed right tenderly. There was leech
a damsel within that was cousin-german to
King Pelles and had tended Perceval within in
his sickness. She washeth their wounds right
sweetly and cleanseth them of the blood. And
they see that Lancelot is sorer wounded than
Perceval. 'Damsel,' saith the Hermit, 'How
seemeth you?' 'Sir,' saith she, 'Needs must
this knight sojourn here, for his wound is in a
right perilous place.' 'Hath he danger of
death?' 'Sir,' saith she, 'In no wise of this
wound, but behoveth him take good heed
thereto.' 'God be praised!' saith he, 'And
of my nephew how seemeth you?' 'Sir, the
wound that he hath will be soon healed. He
will have none ill thereof.'

IV

The damsel, that was right cunning of leech-
craft, tended the wounds of the knights, and
made them whole as best she might, and King
Hermit himself gave counsel therein. But and
Perceval had borne his shield that was there
within, of sinople with a white hart, Lancelot
would have known him well, nor would there
have been any quarrel between them, for he had
heard tell of this shield at the court of King
Arthur. The authority of this story recordeth
that the two knights are in hermitage, and that
Perceval is well-nigh whole; but Lancelot
hath sore pain of his wound and is still **far**
from his healing.

BRANCH IX

TITLE I

Clamados of the Shadows   NOW the story is silent about the two knights for a little time, and speaketh of the squire that Messire Gawain meeteth in the midst of the forest, that told him he went seek the son of the Widow Lady that had slain his father. And the squire saith that he will go to avenge him, wherefore cometh he to the court of King Arthur, for that he had heard tell how all good knights repaired thither. And he seeth the shield hang on the column in the midst of the hall that the Damsel of the Car had brought thither. The squire knoweth it well, and kneeleth before the King and saluteth him, and the King returneth his salute and asketh who he is. 'Sir,' saith he, 'I am the son of the Knight of the Red Shield of the Forest of Shadows, that was slain of the Knight that ought to bear the shield that hangeth on this column, wherefore would I right gladly hear tidings of him.' 'As gladly would I,' saith the King, 'so that no evil came to him thereof, for he is the knight of the world that I most desire.' 'Sir,' saith the Squire, 'Well behoveth me to hate him for that he slew my father. He that ought to bear this shield was squire when he slew him, wherefore am I the more sorrowful for that I thought to be avenged upon him squire. But this I may not do, wherefore I pray you for God's sake that you will make me knight, for the like favour are you accustomed to grant to others.' 'What is your name, fair friend?' saith the King. 'Sir,' saith he, 'I am called Clamados of the Shadows.' Messire Gawain that had repaired to court, was in the hall, and said to the King: 'If this squire be enemy of the Good Knight that ought to bear this shield, behoveth you not set forward his mortal enemy but rather set him back, for he is the Best Knight of the world and the most chaste that liveth in the world and of the most holy lineage, and therefore have you sojourned right long time in this castle to await his coming. I say not this for the hindering of the squire's advancement, but that you may do nought whereof the Good Knight may have cause of complaint against you.' 'Messire Gawain,' saith Queen Guenievre, 'well know I that you love my Lord's honour, but sore blame will he have if he make not this one knight, for so much hath he never refused to do for any; nor yet will the Good Knight have any misliking thereof, for greater shame should he have, and greater despite of the hatred of a squire than of a knight; for never yet was good knight that was not prudent and well-advised and slow to take offence. Wherefore I tell you that he will assuredly listen to reason, and I commend my Lord the rather that he make him knight, for much blame would he have of gainsaying him.' 'Lady,' saith Messire Gawain, 'So you are content, I

knighted by Arthur

am happy.' The King made him knight right richly, and when he was clad in the robes, they of the court declare and witness that never this long time past had they seen at the court knight of greater comeliness. He sojourned therein long time, and was much honoured of the King and all the barons. He was every day on the watch for the Good Knight that should come for the shield, but the hour and the place were not as yet.

The damsels of the Car

II

When he saw that he did not come, he took leave of the King and the Queen and all them of the court, and departed, thinking him that he would go prove his knighthood in some place until he should have heard tidings of his mortal enemy. He rideth amidst the great forests bearing a red shield like as did his father, and he was all armed as for defending of his body. And a long space of time he rideth, until one day he cometh to the head of a forest, and he espied his way that ran between two mountains and saw that he had to pass along the midst of the valley that lay at a great depth. He looketh before him and seeth a tree far away from him, and underneath were three damsels alighted, and one prayed God right heartily aloud that He would send them betimes a knight that durst convoy them through this strait pass.

III

Clamados heareth the damsel and cometh thitherward. When they espied him, great joy

have they thereof and rise up to meet him. **Clamados**
'Sir,' say they, 'Welcome may you be!' **con-**
'Damsels,' saith he, 'Good adventure may you **voyeth**
have! And whom await you here?' saith he. **them**
'We await,' saith the Mistress of the damsels,
'some knight that shall clear this pass, for no
knight durst pass hereby.' 'What is the pass,
then, damsel?' saith he. 'It is the one of a
lion, and a lion, moreover, so fell and horrible
that never was none seen more cruel. And
there is a knight with the lion between the two
mountains that is right good knight and hardy
and comely. Howbeit none durst pass without
great company of folk. But the knight that
hath repair with the lion is seldom there, for so
he were there we need fear no danger, for much
courtesy is there in him and valour.' And the
knight looketh and seeth in the shadow of the
forest three fair stags harnessed to a car. 'Ha,'
saith he, 'You are the Damsel of the Car,
wherefore may you well tell me tidings of the
knight of whom I am in quest.' 'Who is he?'
saith the Damsel. 'It is he that should bear a
shield banded argent and azure with a red cross.'
'Of him am I likewise in quest,' saith the
Damsel; 'please God, we shall hear tidings of
him betimes.' 'Damsel,' saith the knight,
'that would I. And for that you are in quest
of him as am I likewise, I will convoy you
beyond this pass.' The Damsel maketh her
Car go on before, and the damsels go before the
knight; and so enter they into the field of the
lion, and right fair land found they therewithin.
Clamados looketh and seeth the hall within an

Clamados killeth the lion enclosure and seeth the lion that lay at the entrance of the gateway. As soon as he espieth Clamados and the damsels, he cometh toward them full speed, mouth open and ears pricked up. 'Sir,' saith the Damsel, 'and you defend not your horse on foot, he is dead at the first onset.'

IV

Clamados is alighted to his feet, by her counsel, and holdeth his spear in his fist, and the lion rampeth toward him all in a fury. Clamados receiveth him on the point of his spear, and smiteth him therewith so stoutly that it passeth a fathom beyond his neck. He draweth back his spear without breaking it, and thinketh to smite him again. But the lion cheateth him, and raising himself on his two hinder feet, setteth his fore feet on his shoulders, then huggeth him toward him like as one man doth another. But the grip was sore grievous, for he rendeth his habergeon in twain and so teareth away as much flesh as he can claw hold on.

V

When Clamados felt himself wounded, he redoubled his hardihood, and grippeth the lion so straitly to him that he wringeth a huge roar out of him, and then flingeth him to the ground beneath him. Then he draweth his sword and thrusteth it to the heart right through the breast. The lion roareth so loud that all the mountains resound thereof. Clamados cutteth off his head

and goeth to hang it at the door of the hall.
Then he cometh back to his horse and mounteth
the best he may. And the Damsel saith to
him, 'Sir, you are sore wounded.' 'Damsel,'
said he, 'Please God, I shall take no hurt
thereof.' Thereupon, behold you a squire that
issueth forth of the hall and cometh after him
full speed. 'Hold, Sir Knight,' saith he; 'Foul
wrong have you wrought, for you have slain the
lion of the most courteous knight that may be
known, and the fairest and most valiant of this
kingdom, and in his despite have you hung the
head at his door! Right passing great outrage
have you done hereby!' 'Fair sweet friend,'
saith Clamados, 'it may well be that the lord
is right courteous, but the lion was rascal and
would have slain me and them that were passing
by. And your lord loved him so much he
should have chained him up, for better liketh
me that I slew him than that he should slay
me.' 'Sir,' saith the squire, 'There is no road
this way, for it is a forbidden land whereof
certain would fain reave my lord, and it was
against the coming of his enemies that the lion
was allowed forth unchained.' 'And what
name hath your lord, fair friend?' saith
Clamados. 'Sir, he is called Meliot of Logres,
and he is gone in quest of Messire Gawain, of
whom he holdeth the land, for right dear is he
to him.' 'Messire Gawain,' saith Clamados,
'left I at the court of King Arthur, but behoveth
him depart thence or ever I return thither.'
'By my head,' saith the squire, 'Fain would I
you might meet them both twain, if only my

*of Meliot
of Logres*

lord knew that you had slain him his lion.' 'Fair friend,' saith Clamados, 'And he be as courteous as you say, no misliking will he have of me thereof, for I slew him in defending mine own body, and God forbid I should meet any that would do me evil therefor.'

<blockquote>The Tents</blockquote>

VI

Thereupon the knight and the damsels depart and pass the narrow strait in the lion's field, and ride on until they draw nigh a right rich castle seated in a meadowland surrounded of great waters and high forests, and the castle was always void of folk. And they were fain to turn thitherward, but they met a squire that told them that in the castle was not a soul, albeit and they would ride forward they would find great plenty of folk. So far forward have they ridden that they are come to the head of a forest and see great foison of tents stretched right in the midst of a launde, and they were compassed round of a great white sheet that seemed from afar to be a long white wall with crenels, and it was a good league Welsh in length. They came to the entrance of the tents and heard great joy within, and when they had entered they saw dames and damsels, whereof was great plenty, and of right passing great beauty were they. Clamados alighteth, that was right sore wounded. The Damsel of the Car was received with right great joy. Two of the damsels come to Clamados, of whom make they right great joy. Afterward they lead him to a tent and made disarm him. Then they washed his wounds right sweetly and tenderly. Then they brought him a right rich robe and made him be apparelled therein, and led him before the ladies of the tents, that made right great joy of him.

The Queen of the Tents

VII

'Lady,' saith the Damsel of the Car, 'This knight hath saved my life, for he hath slain the lion on account of which many folk durst not come to you, wherefore make great joy of him.' 'Greater joy may I not make, than I do, nor the damsels that are herein, for we await the coming of the Good Knight that is healed, from day to day. And now is there nought in the world I more desire to see.' 'Lady,' saith Clamados, 'Who is this Good Knight?' 'The son of the Widow Lady of the Valleys of Camelot,' saith she. 'Tell me, Lady, do you say that he will come hither presently?' 'So methinketh,' saith she. 'Lady, I also shall have great joy thereof, and God grant he come betimes!' 'Sir Knight,' saith she, 'What is your name?' 'Lady,' saith he, 'I am called Clamados, and I am son of the lord of the Forest of Shadows.' She throweth her arms on his neck and kisseth and embraceth him right sweetly, and saith: 'Marvel not that I make you joy thereof, for you are the son of my sister-in-law, nor have I any friend nor blood-kindred so nigh as are you, and fain would I you should be lord of all my land and of me, as is right and reason.' The damsels of the tents make right great joy of him when

Perceval setteth forth they know the tidings that he is so nigh of kin to the Lady of the Tents. And he sojourned therewithin until that he was whole and heal, awaiting the coming of the knight of whom he had heard the tidings. And the damsels marvel them much that he cometh not, for the damsel that had tended him was therewithin and telleth them that he was healed of his arm, but that Lancelot is not yet whole, wherefore he is still within the hermitage.

VIII

This high history witnesseth us and recordeth that Joseph, who maketh remembrance thereof, was the first priest that sacrificed the body of Our Lord, and forsomuch ought one to believe the words that come of him. You have heard tell how Perceval was of the lineage of Joseph of Abarimacie, whom God so greatly loved for that he took down His body hanging on the cross, which he would not should lie in the prison there where Pilate had set it. For the highness of the lineage whereof the Good Knight was descended ought one willingly to hear brought to mind and recorded the words that are of him. The story telleth us that he was departed of the hermitage all sound and whole, albeit he hath left Lancelot, for that his wound was not yet healed, but he hath promised him that he will come back to him so soon as he may. He rideth amidst a forest, all armed, and cometh toward evensong to the issue of the forest and seeth a castle before him right fair and well seated, and goeth thitherward for lodging, for the sun was set. He entereth into the castle and alighteth. The lord cometh to meet him that was a tall knight and a red, and had a felon look, and his face scarred in many places; and knight was there none therewithin save only himself and his household.

<small>Chaos the Red</small>

IX

When he seeth Perceval alighted, he runneth to bar the door, and Perceval cometh over against him. For all greeting, the knight saluteth him thus: 'Now shall you have,' saith he, 'such guerdon as you have deserved. Never again shall you depart hence, for my mortal enemy are you, and right hardy are you thus to throw yourself upon me, for you slew my brother the Lord of the Shadows, and Chaos the Red am I that war upon your mother, and this castle have I reft of her. In like manner will I wring the life out of you or ever you depart hence!' 'Already,' saith Perceval, 'have I thrown myself on this your hostel to lodge with you, wherefore to blame would you be to do me evil. But lodge me this night as behoveth one knight do for another, and on the morrow at departing let each do the best he may.' 'By my head!' saith Chaos the Red, 'Mortal enemy of mine will I never harbour here save I harbour him dead.' He runneth to the hall above, and armeth himself as swiftly as he may, and taketh his sword all naked in his hand and cometh back to the place where Perceval was, right full of anguish of heart for this that he said, that he would war upon his mother and

Perceval slayeth Chaos had reft her of this castle. He flung his spear to the ground, and goeth toward him on foot and dealeth him a huge buffet above the helmet upon the coif of his habergeon, such that he cleaveth the mail and cutteth off two fingers'- breadth of the flesh in such sort that he made him reel three times round.

X

When Chaos the Red felt himself wounded, he was sore grieved thereof, and cometh toward Perceval and striketh him a great buffet above in the midst of his helmet, so that he made the sparks fly and his neck stoop and his eyes sparkle of stars. And the blow slippeth down on to the shield, so that it is cleft right down to the boss. Perceval felt his neck stiff and heavy, and feeleth that the knight is sturdy and of great might. He cometh back towards him, and thinketh to strike him above in the midst of his head, but Chaos swerved aside from him: howbeit Perceval reached him and caught his right arm and cutteth it sheer from his side, sword and all, and sendeth it flying to the ground, and Chaos runneth upon him, thinking to grapple him with his left arm, but his force was waning; nathless right gladly would he have avenged himself and he might. Howbeit, Perceval setteth on him again that loved him not in his heart, and smiteth him again above on the head, and dealeth him such a buffet as maketh his brains be all to-scattered abroad. His household and servants were at the windows of the hall. When they see that their lord is nigh to the death, they cry to Perceval: 'Sir, you have slain the hardiest knight in the kingdom of Logres, and him that was most redoubted of his enemies; but we can do no otherwise; we know well that this castle is your mother's and ought to be yours. We challenge it not; wherefore may you do your will of whatsoever there is in the castle; but allow us to go to our lord that there lieth dead, and take away the body and set it in some seemly place for the sake of his good knighthood, and for that it behoveth us so to do.' 'Readily do I grant it you,' saith Perceval. They bear the body to a chapel, then they disarm him and wind him in his shroud. After that, they lead Perceval into the hall and disarm him and say to him: 'Sir, you may be well assured that there be none but us twain herewithin and two damsels, and the doors are barred, and behold, here are the keys which we deliver up to you.' 'And I command you,' saith Perceval, 'that you go straightway to my mother, and tell her that she shall see me betimes and I may get done, and so salute her and tell her I am sound and whole. And what is the name of this castle?' 'Sir, it hath for name the Key of Wales, for it is the gateway of the land.'

XI

Perceval lay the night in the castle he had reconquered for his mother, and the morrow, when he was armed, he departed. These promised that they would keep the castle loyally and would deliver it up to his mother at her will. He rode until he came to the tents where the damsels were, and drew rein and listened. But there was not so great joy as when the damsel that rode like a knight and led the Car came thither with Clamados. Great dole heard he that was made, and beating of palms. Wherefore he bethought him what folk they might be. Natheless he was not minded to draw back without entering. He alighted in the midst of the tents and set down his shield and his spear, and seeth the damsels wringing their hands and tearing their hair, and much marvelleth he wherefore it may be. A damsel cometh forward that had set forth from the castle where he had slain the knight: 'Sir, to your shame and ill adventure may you have come hither!' Perceval looketh at her and marvelleth much of that she saith, and she crieth out: 'Lady, behold here him that hath slain the best knight of your lineage! And you, Clamados, that are within there, he hath slain your father and your uncle! Now shall it be seen what you will do!' The Damsel of the Car cometh thitherward and knoweth Perceval by the shield that he bare of sinople with a white hart. 'Sir,' saith she, 'Welcome may you be! Let who will make dole, I will make joy of your coming!'

XII

Therewith, the Damsel leadeth him into a tent and maketh him sit on a right rich couch; afterward she maketh him be disarmed of her two damsels and clad in a right rich robe. Then she leadeth him to the Queen of the Tents that was still making great dole. 'Lady,' saith the Damsel of the Car, 'Stint your sorrow, for behold, here is the Good Knight on whose account were the tents here pitched, and on whose account no less have you been making this great joy right up to this very day!' 'Ha,' saith she, 'Is this then the son of the Widow Lady?' 'Yea, certes,' saith the Damsel. 'Ha,' saith the Lady, 'He hath slain me the best knight of all my kin, and the one that protected me from mine enemies.' 'Lady,' saith the Damsel, 'This one will be better able to protect and defend us, for the Best Knight is he of the world and the comeliest.' The Queen taketh him by the hand and maketh him sit beside her. 'Sir,' saith she, 'Howsoever the adventure may have befallen, my heart biddeth me make joy of your coming.' 'Lady,' saith he, 'Gramercy! Chaos would fain have slain me within his castle, and I defended myself to my power.' The Queen looketh at him amidst his face, and is taken with a love of him so passing strong and fervent that she goeth nigh to fall upon him. 'Sir,' saith she, 'And you will grant me your love, I will pardon you of all the death of Chaos the Red.' 'Lady,' saith he, 'Your love am I right fain to deserve, and mine you have.' 'Sir,' saith she, 'How may I perceive that you love me?' 'Lady,' saith he, 'I will tell you. There is no knight in the world that shall desire to do you a wrong, but I will help you against him to my power.' 'Such love,' saith she, 'is the common love that knight ought to bear to lady. Would you

The Queen loveth him

Clamados is wrath do as much for another?' 'Lady,' saith he, 'It well may be, but more readily shall a man give help in one place than in another.' The Queen would fain that Perceval should pledge himself to her further than he did, and the more she looketh at him the better he pleaseth her, and the more is she taken with him and the more desirous of his love. But Perceval never once thought of loving her or another in such wise. He was glad to look upon her, for that she was of passing great beauty, but never spake he nought to her whereby she might perceive that he loved her of inward love. But in no wise might she refrain her heart, nor withdraw her eyes, nor lose her desire. The damsels looked upon her with wonder that so soon had she forgotten her mourning.

XIII

Thereupon, behold you Clamados, that had been told that this was the knight that, as yet only squire, had slain his father and put Chaos his uncle to death. He cometh into the tent and seeth him sitting beside the Queen, that looked at him right sweetly. 'Lady,' saith he, 'Great shame do you to yourself, in that you have seated at your side your own mortal enemy and mine. Never again henceforth ought any to have affiance in your love nor in your help.' 'Clamados,' saith the Queen, 'The knight hath thrown himself upon me suddenly. Wherefore ought I do him no evil, rather behoveth me lodge him and keep his body in safety. Nought, moreover, hath he done whereof he might be

adjudged of murder nor of treason.' 'Lady,' **Clamados**
saith Clamados, 'He slew my father in the **accuseth**
Lonely Forest without defiance, and treacher- **Perceval**
ously cast a javelin at him and smote him
through the body, wherefore shall I never be
at ease until I have avenged him. Therefore
do I appeal and pray you to do me my right,
not as being of your kindred, but as stranger.
For right willing am I that kinship shall avail
me nought herein.' Perceval looketh at the
knight and seeth that he is of right goodly
complexion of body and right comely of face.
'Fair Sir,' saith he, 'As of treason I would that
you hold me quit, for never toward your father
nor toward other have had I never a mind to do
treason, and God defend me from such shame,
and grant me strength to clear myself of any
blame thereof.' Clamados cometh forward to
proffer his gage. 'By my head,' saith the
Queen, 'Not this day shall gage be received
herein. But to-morrow will come day, and
counsel therewith, and then shall right be done
to each.' Clamados is moved of right great
wrath, but the Queen of the Tents showeth
Perceval the most honour she may, whereof is
Clamados right heavy, and saith that never ought
any to put his trust in woman. But wrongly
he blameth her therein, for she did it of the
passing great love she hath for Perceval, inasmuch
as well she knoweth that he is the Best Knight
of the world and the comeliest. But it only
irketh her the more that she may not find in him
any sign of special liking toward herself neither
in deed nor word, whereof is she beyond measure

sorrowful. The knights and damsels lay the night in the tents until the morrow, and went to hear mass in a chapel that was in the midst of the tents.

Meliot challengeth Clamados

XIV

When mass was sung, straightway behold you, a knight that cometh all armed, bearing a white shield at his neck. He alighteth in the midst of the tents and cometh before the Queen all armed, and saith: 'Lady, I plain me of a knight that is there within that hath slain my lion, and if you do me not right herein, I will harass you as much or more than I will him, and will harm you in every wise I may. Wherefore I pray and require you, for the love of Messire Gawain, whose man I am, that you do me right herein.' 'What is the knight's name?' saith the Queen. 'Lady,' saith he, 'He is called Clamados of the Shadows, and methinketh I see him yonder, for I knew him when he was squire.' 'And what is your name?' saith the Queen. 'Lady, I am called Meliot of Logres.' 'Clamados,' saith the Queen, 'Hear you what this knight saith?' 'Yea, Lady,' saith he; 'But again I require that you do me right of the knight that slew my father and my uncle.' 'Lady,' saith Meliot, 'I would fain go. I know not toward whom the knight proffereth his gage, but him do I appeal of felony for my lion that he hath slain.' He taketh in his hand the skirt of his habergeon: 'Lady, behold here the gage I offer you.'

XV

The Queen alloweth battle

'Clamados,' saith the Queen, 'Hear you then not that which this knight saith?' 'Lady,' saith he, 'I hear him well. Truth it is that I slew his lion, but not until after he had fallen upon me, and made the wounds whereof I have been healed herewithin. But well you know that the knight who came hither last night hath done me greater wrong than have I done this other. Wherefore would I pray you that I may take vengeance of him first.' 'You hear,' saith she, 'how this knight that hath come hither all armed is fain to go back forthwith. Quit you, therefore, of him first, and then will we take thought of the other.' 'Lady, gramercy!' saith Meliot, 'and Messire Gawain will take it in right good part, for this knight hath slain my lion that defended me from all my enemies. Nor is it true that the entrance to your tent was deserted on account of my lion; and in despite of me hath he hung the head at my gate.' 'As of the lion,' saith the Queen, 'you have no quarrel against him and he slew him in defending his body, but as of the despite he did you as you say, when in nought had you done him any wrong, it shall not be that right shall be denied you in my court, and if you desire to deliver battle, no blame shall you have thereof.'

XVI

Clamados maketh arm him and mounteth on his horse, and he seemeth right hardy of his arms and valorous. He cometh right in the

Both are wounded midst of the tent, where the ground was fair and level, and found Meliot of Logres all armed upon his horse, and a right comely knight was he and a deliver. And the ladies and damsels were round about the tilting-ground. 'Sir,' saith the Queen to Perceval, 'I will that you keep the field for these knights.' 'Lady,' saith he, 'At your pleasure.' Meliot moveth toward Clamados right swiftly and Clamados toward him, and they melled together on their shields in such sort that they pierced them and cleft the mail of their habergeons asunder with the points of their spears, and the twain are both wounded so that the blood rayeth forth of their bodies. The knights draw asunder to take their career, for their spears were broken short, and they come back the one toward the other with a great rush, and smite each other on the breast with their spears so stiffly that there is none but should have been pierced within the flesh, for the habergeons might protect them not. They hurtle against each other so strongly that knights and horses fall together to the ground all in a heap. The Queen and the damsels have great pity of the two knights, for they see that they are both so passing sore wounded. The two knights rise to their feet and hold their swords naked and run the one on the other right wrathfully, with such force as they had left. 'Sir,' saith the Queen to Perceval, 'Go part these two knights asunder that one slay not the other, for they are sore wounded.' Perceval goeth to part them and cometh to Meliot of Logres. 'Sir,' saith he, 'With-

draw yourself back; you have done enough.' **Perceval must abide**
Clamados felt that he was sore wounded in two
places, and that the wound he had in his breast
was right great. He draweth himself back.
The Queen is come thither. 'Fair nephew,'
saith she, 'Are you badly wounded?' 'Yea,
Lady,' saith Clamados. 'Certes,' saith the
Queen, 'This grieveth me, but never yet saw I
knight and he were desirous of fighting, but
came at some time by mischance. A man may
not always stand on all his rights.' She made
him be carried on his shield into a tent, and
made search his wounds, and saw that of one
had he no need to fear, but that the other was
right sore perilous.

XVII

'Lady,' saith Clamados, 'Once more do I
pray and require you that you allow not the
knight that slew my father to issue forth from
hence, save he deliver good hostage that he
will come back when I shall be healed.' 'So
will I do, sith that it is your pleasure.' The
Queen cometh to the other knight that was
wounded, for that he declareth himself Messire
Gawain's man, and maketh search his wounds,
and they say that he hath not been hurt so sore
as is Clamados. She commandeth them to
tend him and wait upon him right well-willingly.
'Sir,' saith she to Perceval, 'Behoveth you
abide here until such time as my nephew be
heal, for you know well that whereof he
plaineth against you, nor would I that you
should depart hence without clearing you of the

The blame.' 'Lady, no wish have I to depart with-
Damsel out your leave, but rather shall I be ready to
becometh
surety clear myself of blame whensoever and where-
soever time and place may be. But herewithin
may I make not so long sojourn. Natheless
to this will I pledge my word, that I will
return thither within a term of fifteen days from
the time he shall be whole.' 'Sir,' saith the
Damsel of the Car, 'I will remain here in
hostage for you.' 'But do you pray him,' saith
the Queen, 'that he remain herewithin with us.'

XVIII

'Lady,' saith Perceval, 'I may not, for I
left Lancelot wounded right sore in my uncle's
hermitage.' 'Sir,' saith the Queen, 'I would
fain that remaining here might have pleased
you as well as it would me.' 'Lady,' saith
he, 'None ought it to displease to be with you,
but every man behoveth keep his word as well
as he may, and none ought to lie to so good a
knight as he.' 'You promise me, then,' saith
the Queen, 'that you will return hither the
soonest you may, or at the least, within the
term appointed after you shall have learnt that
Clamados is healed, to defend you of the treason
that he layeth upon you?' 'Lady,' saith he,
'And if he die, shall I be quit?' 'Yea, truly,
Sir, and so be that you have no will to come
for love of me. For right well should I love
your coming.' 'Lady,' saith he, 'Never shall
be the day my services shall fail you, so I be
in place, and you in need thereof.' He taketh

leave and departeth, armed. The Damsel of the Car commendeth him to God, and Perceval departeth full speed and rideth so far on his journeys that he cometh to his uncle's hermitage and entereth in, thinking to find Lancelot. But his uncle telleth him that he hath departed all sound and all heal of his wound, as of all other malady, as him thinketh.

Perceval returneth

BRANCH X

INCIPIT

Lancelot and the Vavasour

ANOTHER branch of the Graal again beginneth in the name of the Father, and of the Son, and of the Holy Ghost.

TITLE I

And the story is here silent of Perceval, and saith that Lancelot goeth his way and rideth by a forest until he findeth a castle amidst his way at the head of a launde, and seeth at the gateway of the castle an old knight and two damsels sitting on a bridge. Thitherward goeth he, and the knight and damsels rise up to meet him, and Lancelot alighteth. 'Sir,' saith the Vavasour, 'Welcome may you be.' The damsels make great joy of him and lead him into the castle. 'Sir,' saith the Vavasour, 'Sore need had we of your coming.' He maketh him go up into the hall above and be disarmed of his arms. 'Sir,' saith the Vavasour, 'Now may you see great pity of these two damsels that are my daughters. A certain man would reave them of this castle for that no aid nor succour have they save of me alone. And little enough can I do, for I am old and feeble, and my kin also are of no avail, insomuch that hitherto have I been able to find no knight that durst defend me from the knight that is fain to

reave this castle from me. And you seem to **Lancelot**
be of so great valiance that you will defend me **maketh**
well herein to-morrow, for the truce cometh to **promise**
an end to-night.' 'How?' saith Lancelot,
'I have but scarce come in hither to lodge,
and you desire me so soon already to engage
myself in battle?' 'Sir,' saith the Vavasour,
'Herein may it well be proven whether there
be within you as much valour as there seemeth
from without to be. For, and you make good
the claim of these two damsels that are my
daughters to the fiefs that are of right their
own, you will win thereby the love of God
as well as praise of the world.' They fall at
his feet weeping, and pray him of mercy that
they may not be disherited. And he raiseth
them forthwith, as one that hath great pity
thereof. 'Damsels,' saith he, 'I will aid you
to my power. But I would fain that the term
be not long.' 'Sir,' say they, 'To-morrow is
the day, and to-morrow, so we have no knight
to meet him that challengeth this castle, we
shall have lost it. And our father is an old
knight, and hath no longer lustihood nor force
whereby he might defend it for us, and all
of our lineage are fallen and decayed. This
hatred hath fallen on us on account of Messire
Gawain, whom we harboured.' Lancelot lay
there the night within the castle and was right
well lodged and worshipfully entreated. And
on the morrow he armed himself when he had
heard mass, and leant at the windows of the
hall and seeth the gate shut and barred, and
heareth a horn sound without the gate three

times right loud. 'Sir,' saith the Vavasour, 'The knight is come, and thinketh that within here is no defence.' 'By my head,' saith Lancelot, 'but there is, please God!' The knight bloweth another blast of his horn. 'Hearken, Sir,' saith the Vavasour, 'It is nigh noon, and he thinketh him that none will issue hence to meet him.'

A horn soundeth

II

Lancelot cometh down below and findeth his horse saddled and is mounted as soon. The damsels are at his stirrup, and pray him for God's sake remember to defend the honour that is theirs of the castle, for, save only he so doth, they must flee like beggars into other lands. Thereupon the Knight soundeth his horn again. Lancelot, when he heareth the blast, hath no mind to abide longer, and forthwith issueth out of the castle all armed, lance in hand and shield at his neck. He seeth the knight at the head of the bridge, all armed under a tree. Thitherward cometh Lancelot full speed. The knight seeth him coming, and crieth to him. 'Sir Knight,' saith he, 'What demand you? Come you hither to do me evil?' 'Yea,' saith Lancelot, 'for that evil are you fain to do to this castle; wherefore on behalf of the Vavasour and his daughters do I defy you.' He moveth against the knight and smiteth him on the shield with his spear and the knight him. But Lancelot pierceth his shield for him with his sword, and smiteth him so stiffly that he pinneth his arm to his side, and hurtleth against him so passing stoutly that he thrusteth him to the ground, him and his horse, and runneth over him, sword drawn. 'Ha,' saith the knight to Lancelot. 'Withdraw a little from over me, and slay me not, and tell me your name, of your mercy.' 'What have you to do with my name?' saith Lancelot. 'Sir,' saith he, 'Gladly would I know it, for a right good knight seem you to be, and so have I well proven in the first encounter.' 'Sir,' saith he, 'I am called Lancelot of the Lake. And what is your name?' 'Sir,' saith he, 'I am called Marin of the castle of Gomeret. So am I father of Meliot of Logres. I pray you, by that you most love in the world, that you slay me not.' 'So will I do,' saith Lancelot, 'and you renounce not your feud against this castle.' 'By my faith,' saith the knight, 'Thus do I renounce it, and I pledge myself that thenceforth for ever shall it have no disturbance of me.' 'Your pledge,' saith Lancelot, 'will I not accept save you come in thither.' 'Sir,' saith the knight, 'You have sore wounded me in such sort that I cannot mount but with right great pain.' Lancelot helpeth him until he was mounted again on his horse, and leadeth him into the castle with him, and maketh him present his sword to the Vavasour and his daughters, and yield up his shield and his arms, and afterward swear upon hallows that never again will he make war upon them. Lancelot thereupon receiveth his pledge to forego all claim to the castle and Marin turneth him back to Gomeret.

Marin the Jealous

The Vavasour and his daughters abide in great joy.

The Burning City

III

The story saith that Lancelot went his way by strange lands and by forests to seek adventure, and rode until he found a plain land lying without a city that seemed to be of right great lordship. As he was riding by the plain land, he looketh toward the forest and seeth the plain fair and wide and the land right level. He rideth all the plain, and looketh toward the city and seeth great plenty of folk issuing forth thereof. And with them was there much noise of bag-pipes and flutes and viols and many instruments of music, and they came along the way wherein was Lancelot riding. When the foremost came up to him, they halted and redoubled their joy. 'Sir,' say they, 'Welcome may you be!' 'Lords,' saith Lancelot, 'Whom come ye to meet with such joy?' 'Sir,' say they, 'They that come behind there will tell you clearly that whereof we are in need.'

IV

Thereupon behold you the provosts and the lords of the city, and they come over against Lancelot. 'Sir,' say they, 'All this joy is made along of you, and all these instruments of music are moved to joy and sound of gladness for your coming.' 'But wherefore for me?' saith Lancelot. 'That shall you know well betimes,' say they. 'This city began to burn and to melt in one of the houses from the

very same hour that our king was dead, nor **A parlous**
might the fire be quenched, nor never will **kingship**
be quenched until such time as we have a
king that shall be lord of the city and
of the honour thereunto belonging, and on
New Year's Day behoveth him to be crowned
in the midst of the fire, and then shall the fire
be quenched, for otherwise may it never be
put out nor extinguished. Wherefore have we
come to meet you to give you the royalty, for
we have been told that you are a good knight.'
'Lords,' saith Lancelot, 'Of such a kingdom
have I no need, and God defend me from it.'
'Sir,' say they, 'You may not be defended
thereof, for you come into this land at hazard,
and great grief would it be that so good land as
you see this is were burnt and melted away by
the default of one single man, and the lordship
is right great, and this will be right great
worship to yourself, that on New Year's Day
you should be crowned in the fire and thus save
this city and this great people, and thereof shall
you have great praise.'

V

Much marvelleth Lancelot of this that they
say. They come round about him on all sides
and lead him into the city. The ladies and
damsels are mounted to the windows of the
great houses and make great joy, and say the
one to another, 'Look at the new king here that
they are leading in. Now will he quench the
fire on New Year's Day.' 'Lord!' say the
most part, 'What great pity is it of so comely

Lancelot refuseth a crown

a knight that he shall end on such-wise!' 'Be still!' say the others. 'Rather should there be great joy that so fair city as is this should be saved by his death, for prayer will be made throughout all the kingdom for his soul for ever!' Therewith they lead him to the palace with right great joy and say that they will crown him. Lancelot found the palace all strown with rushes and hung about with curtains of rich cloths of silk, and the lords of the city all apparelled to do him homage. But he refuseth right stoutly, and saith that their king nor their lord will he never be in no such sort. Thereupon behold you a dwarf that entereth into the city, leading one of the fairest dames that be in any kingdom, and asketh whereof this joy and this murmuring may be. They tell him they are fain to make the knight king, but that he is not minded to allow them, and they tell him the whole manner of the fire.

VI

The dwarf and the damsel are alighted, then they mount up to the palace. The dwarf calleth the provosts of the city and the greater lords. 'Lords,' saith he, 'Sith that this knight is not willing to be king, I will be so willingly, and I will govern the city at your pleasure and do whatsoever you have devised to do.' 'In faith, sith that the knight refuseth this honour and you desire to have it, willingly will we grant it you, and he may go his way and his road, for herein do we declare him wholly quit.' Therewithal they set the crown on the dwarf's head, and Lancelot maketh great joy thereof. He taketh his leave, and they commend him to God, and so remounteth he on his horse and goeth his way through the midst of the city all armed. The dames and damsels say that he would not be king for that he had no mind to die so soon. When he came forth of the city right well pleased was he. He entereth a great forest and rideth on till daylight began to fail, and seeth before him a hermitage newly stablished, for the house and the chapel were all builded new. He cometh thitherward and alighteth to lodge. The hermit, that was young without beard or other hair on his face, issued from his chapel. 'Sir,' saith he to Lancelot, 'You are he that is welcome.' 'And you, sir, good adventure to you,' saith Lancelot. 'Never have I seen hermit so young as you.' 'Sir, of this only do I repent me, that I came not hither ere now.'

The young hermit

VII

Therewith he maketh his horse be stabled, and leadeth him into his hermitage, and so maketh disarm him and setteth him at ease as much as he may. 'Sir,' saith the hermit, 'Can you tell me any tidings of a knight that hath lain sick of a long time in the house of a hermit?' 'Sir,' saith Lancelot, 'It is no long time agone sithence I saw him in the house of the good King Hermit, that hath tended me and healed me right sweetly of the wounds that the knight gave me.' 'And is the knight healed, then?' saith the hermit. 'Yea, Sir,' saith Lancelot, 'Whereof is right great joy. And wherefore do you ask me?' 'Well ought I to ask it,' saith the hermit, 'For my father is King Pelles, and his mother is my father's own sister.' 'Ha, Sir, then is the King Hermit your father?' 'Yea, Sir, certes.' 'Thereof do I love you the better,' saith Lancelot, 'For never found I any man that hath done me so much of love as hath he. And what, Sir, is your name?' 'Sir,' saith he, 'My name is Joseus, and yours, what?' 'Sir,' saith he, 'I am called Lancelot of the Lake.' 'Sir,' saith the hermit, 'Right close are we akin, I and you.' 'By my head,' saith Lancelot, 'Hereof am I right glad at heart.' Lancelot looketh and seeth in the hermit's house shield and spear, javelins and habergeon. 'Sir,' saith Lancelot, 'What do you with these arms?' 'Sir,' saith he, 'This forest is right lonely, and this hermitage is far from any folk, and none are there herewithin save me and my squire. So, when robbers come hither, we defend ourselves therewith.' 'But hermits, methought, never assaulted nor wounded nor slew?' 'Sir,' saith the hermit, 'God forbid I should wound any man or slay!' 'And how, then, do you defend yourselves?' saith Lancelot. 'Sir, I will tell you thereof. When robbers come to us, we arm ourselves accordingly. If I may catch hold of any in my hands, he cannot escape me. Our squire is so well-grown and hardy that he slayeth him forthwith or handleth him in such sort that he may never help himself after.' 'By my head,' saith Lancelot, 'Were you not hermit, you would be valiant throughout.' 'By my head,' saith the squire, 'You say true, for methinketh there is none so strong nor so hardy as he in all the kingdom of Logres.' The hermit lodged Lancelot the night the best he could.

Four robber knights

VIII

When as they were in their first sleep, come four robber-knights of the forest that knew how a knight was lodged therewithin, and had coveted his horse and his arms. The hermit that was in his chapel saw them first, and awoke his squire and made bring his arms all secretly; then he made his squire arm. 'Sir,' saith the squire, 'Shall I waken the knight?' 'In no-wise,' saith the hermit, 'until such time as we shall know wherefore.' He maketh open the door of the chapel and taketh a great coil of rope, and they issue forth, he and his squire, and they perceived the robbers in the stable where Lancelot's horse was. The hermit crieth out: the squire cometh forward and thereupon beareth one to the ground with his spear. The hermit seizeth him and bindeth him to a tree so strait that he may not move. The other three think to defend them and to rescue their fellow. Lancelot leapeth up all startled when he heareth the noise and armeth himself as quickly as he may, albeit not so quickly but that or ever he come, the hermit hath taken the other three and bound them with the fourth. But of them were some that were wounded right sore. 'Sir,' saith the

Lancelot hangeth the knights

hermit to Lancelot, 'It grieveth me that you have been awakened.' 'Rather,' saith Lancelot, 'have you done me great wrong for that you ought to have awakened me sooner.' 'Sir,' saith the hermit, 'We have assaults such as this often enough.' The four robbers cry mercy of Lancelot that he will pray the hermit to have pity upon them. And Lancelot saith God help not him that shall have pity on thieves! As soon as it was daylight, Lancelot and the squire lead them into the forest, their hands all tied behind their backs, and have hanged them in a waste place far away from the hermitage. Lancelot cometh back again and taketh leave of Joseus the young hermit, and saith it is great loss to the world that he is not knight. 'Sir,' saith the squire, 'To me is it great joy, for many a man should suffer thereby.' Lancelot is mounted, and Joseus commendeth him to God, praying him much that he salute his father and cousin on his behalf, and Messire Gawain likewise that he met in the forest what time he came all weeping to the hermitage.

IX

Lancelot hath set him forth again upon his way, and rideth by the high forests and findeth holds and hermitages enough, but the story maketh not remembrance of all the hostels wherein he harboured him. So far hath he ridden that he is come forth of the forest and findeth a right fair meadow-land all loaded with flowers, and a river ran in the midst thereof that was right fair and broad, and there was forest on the one side and the other, and the meadow lands were wide and far betwixt the river and the forest. Lancelot looketh on the river before him and seeth a man rowing a great boat, and seeth within the boat two knights, white and bald, and a damsel, as it seemed him, that held in her lap the head of a knight that lay upon a mattress of straw and was covered with a coverlid of marten's fur, and another damsel sate at his feet. There was a knight within in the midst of the boat that was fishing with an angle, the rod whereof seemeth of gold, and right great fish he took. A little cock-boat followed the boat, wherein he set the fish he took. Lancelot cometh anigh the bank the swiftest he may, and so saluteth the knights and damsels, and they return his salute right sweetly. 'Lords,' saith Lancelot, 'is there no castle nigh at hand nor no harbour?' 'Yea, Sir,' say they, 'Beyond that mountain, right fair and rich, and this river runneth thither all round about it.' 'Lords, whose castle is it?' 'Sir,' say they, 'It is King Fisherman's, and the good knights lodge there when he is in this country; but such knights have been harboured there as that the lord of the land hath had good right to plain him thereof.' The knights go rowing along the river, and Lancelot rideth until he cometh to the foot of the mountain and findeth a hermitage beside a spring, and bethinketh him, since it behoveth him to go to so high a hostel and so rich, where the Holy Graal appeareth, he will confess him to the good man. He alighteth and confesseth to the good man, and

The Castle of the Graal

Lancelot's confession rehearseth all his sins, and saith that of all thereof doth he repent him save only one, and the hermit asketh him what it is whereof he is unwilling to repent. 'Sir,' saith Lancelot, 'It seemeth to me the fairest sin and the sweetest that ever I committed.' 'Fair Sir,' saith the hermit, 'Sin is sweet to do, but right bitter be the wages thereof; neither is there any sin that is fair nor seemly, albeit there be some sins more dreadfuller than other.' 'Sir,' saith Lancelot, 'This sin will I reveal to you of my lips, but of my heart may I never repent me thereof. I love my Lady, which is the Queen, more than aught else that liveth, and albeit one of the best kings on live hath her to wife. The affection seemeth me so good and so high that I cannot let go thereof, for, so rooted is it in my heart that thence may it nevermore depart, and the best knighthood that is in me cometh to me only of her affection.' 'Alas!' saith the hermit, 'Sinner of mortal sin, what is this that you have spoken? Never may no knighthood come of such wantonness that shall not cost you right dear! A traitor are you toward our earthly lord, and a murderer toward Our Saviour. Of the seven deadly sins, you are labouring under the one whereof the delights are the falsest of any, wherefore right dearly shall you aby thereof, save you repent you forthwith.' 'Sir,' saith Lancelot, 'Never the more do I desire to cast it from me.' 'As much,' saith the hermit, 'is that as to say that you ought long since to have cast it from you and renounced it. For so long as you maintain it, so long are you an enemy of the Saviour!' 'Ha, Sir,' saith Lancelot, 'She hath in her such beauty and worth and wisdom and courtesy and nobleness that never ought she to be forgotten of any that hath loved her!'

The hermit pleadeth with him

X

'The more of beauty and worth she hath in her,' saith the hermit, 'so much the more blame hath she of that she doeth, and you likewise. For of that which is of little worth is the loss not so great as of that which is much worth. And this is a Queen, blessed and anointed, that was thus, therefore, in her beginning vowed to God; yet now is she given over to the Devil of her love for you, and you of your love for her. Fair, sweet my friend,' saith the hermit, 'Let go this folly, which is so cruel, that you have taken in hand, and be repentant of these sins! So every day will I pray to the Saviour for you, that so truly as He pardoned His death to him that smote Him with a lance in His side, so may He pardon you of this sin that you have maintained, and that so you be repentant and truly confessed thereof, I may take the penance due thereunto upon myself!' 'Sir,' saith Lancelot, 'I thank you much, but I am not minded to renounce it, nor have I no wish to speak aught wherewith my heart accordeth not. I am willing enough to do penance as great as is enjoined of this sin, but my Lady the Queen will I serve so long as it may be her pleasure, and I may have her good will. So dearly do I love her that I

Lancelot loveth too well wish not even that any will should come to me to renounce her love, and God is so sweet and so full of right merciful mildness, as good men bear witness, that He will have pity upon us, for never no treason have I done toward her, nor she toward me.' 'Ha, fair sweet friend,' saith the hermit, 'Nought may you avail you of whatsoever I may say, wherefore God grant her such will and you also, that you may be able to do the will of Our Saviour. But so much am I fain to tell you, that and if you shall lie in the hostel of King Fisherman, yet never may you behold the Graal for the mortal sin that lieth at your heart.' 'May our Lord God,' saith Lancelot, 'counsel me therein at His pleasure and at His will!' 'So may He do!' saith the hermit, 'For of a truth you may know thereof am I right fain.'

XI

Lancelot taketh leave of the hermit, and is mounted forthwith and departeth from the hermitage. And evening draweth on, and he seeth that it is time to lodge him. And he espieth before him the castle of the rich King Fisherman. He seeth the bridges, broad and long, but they seem not to him the same as they had seemed to Messire Gawain. He beholdeth the rich entrance of the gateway there where Our Lord God was figured as He was set upon the rood, and seeth two lions that guard the entrance of the gate. Lancelot thinketh that sith Messire Gawain had passed through amidst the lions, he would do likewise. He goeth toward the gateway, and the lions that were **King** unchained prick up their ears and look at him. **Fisher-** Howbeit Lancelot goeth his way between them **man** without heeding them, and neither of them was fain to do him any hurt. He alighteth before the master-palace, and mounteth upward all armed. Two other knights come to meet him and receive him with right great joy, then they make him be seated on a couch in the midst of the hall and be disarmed of two servants. Two damsels bring him a right rich robe and make him be apparelled therewithal. Lancelot beholdeth the richness of the hall and seeth nought figured there save images of saints, men or women, and he seeth the hall hung about with cloths of silk in many places. The knights lead him before King Fisherman in a chamber where he lay right richly. He findeth the King, that lieth on a bed so rich and so fair apparelled as never was seen a better, and one damsel was at his head and another at his feet. Lancelot saluteth him right nobly, and the King answereth him full fairly as one that is a right worshipful man. And such a brightness of light was there in the chamber as that it seemed the sun were beaming on all sides, and albeit the night was dark, no candles, so far as Lancelot might espy, were lighted therewithin. 'Sir,' saith King Fisherman, 'Can you tell me tidings of my sister's son, that was son of Alain li Gros of the Valleys of Camelot, whom they call Perceval?' 'Sir,' saith Lancelot, 'I saw him not long time sithence in the house of King Hermit, his uncle.' 'Sir,' saith the King,

Lancelot seeth not the Graal

'They tell me he is a right good knight?' 'Sir,' saith Lancelot, 'He is the best knight of the world. I myself have felt the goodness of his knighthood and his valour, for right sorely did he wound me or ever I knew him or he me.' 'And what is your name?' saith the King. 'Sir, I am called Lancelot of the Lake, King Ban's son of Benoic.' 'Ha,' saith the King, 'You are nigh of our lineage, you ought to be good knight of right, and so are you as I have heard witness, Lancelot,' saith the King. 'Behold there the chapel where the most Holy Graal taketh his rest, that appeared to two knights that have been herewithin. I know not what was the name of the first, but never saw I any so gentle and quiet, nor had better likelihood to be good knight. It was through him that I have fallen into languishment. The second was Messire Gawain.' 'Sir,' saith Lancelot, 'The first was Perceval your nephew.' 'Ha!' saith King Fisherman, 'Take heed that you speak true!' 'Sir,' saith Lancelot, 'I ought to know him well!' 'Ha, God!' saith the King, 'Wherefore then did I know him not? Through him have I fallen into this languishment, and had I only known then that it was he, should I now be all whole of my limbs and of my body, and right instantly do I pray you, when you shall see him, that he come to see me or ever I die, and that he be fain to succour and help his mother, whose men have been slain, and whose land hath been reaved in such sort that never may she have it again save by him alone. And his sister hath gone in quest of him throughout all kingdoms.'

'Sir,' saith Lancelot, 'This will I tell him gladly, if ever I may find him in any place, but it is great adventure of finding him, for oft-times will he change his cognizance in divers fashion and conceal his name in many places.'

Lancelot departeth

XII

King Fisherman is right joyous of the tidings he hath heard of his nephew, wherefore he maketh Lancelot be honoured greatly. The knights seat them in the hall at a table of ivory at meat, and the King remaineth in his chamber. When they had washen, the table was dight of rich sets of vessels of gold and silver, and they were served of rich meats of venison of hart and wild boar. But the story witnesseth that the Graal appeared not at this feast. It held not aloof for that Lancelot was not one of the three knights of the world of the most renown and mightiest valour, but for his great sin as touching the Queen, whom he loved without repenting him thereof, for of nought did he think so much as of her, nor never might he remove his heart therefrom. When they had eaten they rose from the tables. Two damsels waited on Lancelot at his going to bed, and he lay on a right rich couch, nor were they willing to depart until such time as he was asleep. He rose on the morrow as soon as he saw the day, and went to hear mass. Then he took leave of King Fisherman and the knights and damsels, and issued forth of the castle between the two lions, and prayeth God that He allow him to see the Queen again betimes, for this is his most

A knight will not marry desire. He rideth until he hath left the castle far behind and entereth the forest, and is in right great desire to see Perceval, but the tidings of him were right far away. He looketh before him in the forest and seeth come right amidst the launde a knight, and a damsel clad in the richest robe of gold and silk that ever he had seen tofore.

XIII

The damsel came weeping by the side of the knight and prayed him oftentimes that he would have mercy upon her. The knight is still and holdeth his peace, and saith never a word. 'Ha, Sir,' saith the damsel to Lancelot, 'Be pleased to beseech this knight on my behalf.' 'In what manner?' saith Lancelot. 'Sir,' saith she, 'I will tell you. He hath shown me semblance of love for more than a year, and had me in covenant that he would take me to wife, and I apparelled myself in the richest garments that I had to come to him. But my father is of greater power and riches than is he, and therefore was not willing to allow the marriage. Wherefore come I with him in this manner, for I love him better than ever another knight beside. Now will he do nought of that he had me in covenant to do, for he loveth another, better, methinketh, than me. And this hath he done, as I surmise, to do shame to my friends and to me.' Lancelot seeth the damsel of right great beauty and weeping tenderly, whereof hath he passing great pity. 'Hold, Sir!' saith Lancelot to the knight,

'This shall you not do! You shall not do such shame to so fair a damsel as that you shall fail to keep covenant with her. For not a knight is there in the kingdom of Logres nor in that of Wales but ought to be right well pleased to have so fair a damsel to wife, and I pray and require that you do to the damsel that whereof you held her in covenant. This will be a right worshipful deed, and I pray and beseech that you do it, and thereof shall I be much beholden to you.' 'Sir,' saith the knight, 'I have no will thereunto, nor for no man will I do it, for ill would it beseem me.' 'By my head, then,' saith Lancelot, 'the basest knight are you that ever have I seen, nor ought dame nor damsel ever hereafter put trust in you, sith that you are minded to put such disgrace upon this lady.' 'Sir,' saith the knight, 'A worthier lover have I than this, and one that I more value; wherefore as touching this damsel will I do nought more than I have said.' 'And whither, then, mean you to take her?' saith Lancelot. 'I mean to take her to a hold of mine own that is in this forest, and to give her in charge to a dwarf of mine that looketh after my house, and I will marry her to some knight or some other man.' 'Now never God help me,' saith Lancelot, 'but this is foul churlishness you tell me, and, so you do not her will, it shall betide you ill of me myself, and, had you been armed as I am, you should have felt my first onset already.' 'Ha,' saith the damsel to Lancelot, 'Be not so ready to do him any hurt, for nought love I so well as I love his body,

a damsel he hath promised

Lancelot compelleth the knight whatsoever he do to me. But for God's sake pray him that he do me the honour he hath promised me.' 'Willingly,' saith Lancelot. 'Sir Knight, will you do this whereof you had the damsel in covenant?' 'Sir,' saith the knight, 'I have told you plainly that I will not.' 'By my head,' saith Lancelot, 'you shall do it, or otherwise sentence of death hath passed upon you, and this not so much for the sake of the damsel only, but for the churlishness that hath taken possession of you, that it be not a reproach to other knights. For promise that knight maketh to dame or damsel behoveth him to keep. And you, as you tell me, are knight, and no knight ought to do churlishly to his knowledge, and this churlishness is so far greater than another, that for no prayer that the damsel may make will I suffer that it shall be done, but that if you do not that whereof you held her in covenant, I shall slay you, for that I will not have this churlishness made a reproach to other knights.' He draweth his sword and would have come toward him, when the knight cometh over against him and saith to him: 'Slay me not. Tell me rather what you would have me do?' 'I would,' saith he, 'that you take the damsel to wife without denial.' 'Sir,' saith he, 'It pleaseth me better to take her than to die. Sir, I will do your will.' 'I thank you much therefor,' saith Lancelot. 'Damsel, is this your pleasure also?' 'Yea, Sir, but, so please you, take not your departure from us until such time as he shall have done that which you tell him.' 'I will well that so it be,' saith Lancelot, 'for love of you.' They ride together right through the forest, until they came to a chapel at a hermitage, and the hermit wedded them and made much joy thereof. When it cometh to after-mass, Lancelot would fain depart, but the damsel prayeth him right sweetly that he should come right to her father's house to witness that the knight had wedded her.

to marry the damsel

XIV

'Sir,' saith she, 'My father's hold is not far away.' 'Lady,' saith Lancelot, 'Willingly will I go sith that you beseech me thereof.' They ride so long right amidst the forest, that presently they come to the castle of the Vavasour, that was sitting on the bridge of his castle, right sorrowful and troubled because of his daughter. Lancelot is gone on before and alighteth. The Vavasour riseth up to meet him, and Lancelot recounteth to him how his daughter hath been wedded, and that he hath been at the wedding. Thereof the Vavasour maketh right great joy. Therewithal, behold you, the knight and the Vavasour's daughter that are straightway alighted, and the Vavasour thanketh Lancelot much of the honour he hath done his daughter. Therewith he departeth from the castle and rideth amidst the forest the day long, and meeteth a damsel and a dwarf that came a great gallop. 'Sir,' saith the damsel to Lancelot, 'From whence come you?' 'Damsel,' saith he, 'I come from the Vavasour's castle that is in this forest.' 'Did you meet,' saith she, 'a knight and a damsel on your way?' 'Yea,' saith Lancelot, 'He hath wedded her.' 'Say you true?' saith she. 'I tell you true,' saith Lancelot, 'But had I not been there, he would not have wedded her.' 'Shame and ill adventure may you have thereof, for you have reft me of the thing in the world that most I loved. And know you well of a truth that joy of him shall she never have, and if the knight had been armed as are you, never would he have done your will, but his own. And this is not the first harm you have done me; you and Messire Gawain between you have slain my uncle and my two cousins-german in the forest, whom behoved me bury in the chapel where you were, there where my dwarf that you see here was making the graves in the burial-ground.' 'Damsel,' saith Lancelot, 'True it is that I was there, but I departed from the grave-yard, honour safe.' 'True,' saith the dwarf, 'For the knights that were there were craven, and failed.' 'Fair friend,' saith Lancelot, 'Rather would I they should be coward toward me than hardy.' 'Lancelot,' saith the damsel, 'Much outrage have you done, for you slew the Knight of the Waste House, there whither the brachet led Messire Gawain, but had he there been known, he would not have departed so soon, for he was scarce better loved than you, and God grant you may find a knight that may abate the outrages that are in your heart and in his; for great rejoicing would there be thereof, for many a good knight have you slain, and I myself will bring about trouble for you, so quickly as I may.'

The other damsel

XV

Thereupon the dwarf smiteth the mule with his whip, and she departeth. Lancelot would answer none of her reviling, wherefore he departed forthwith, and rideth so long on his journeys that he is come back to the house of the good King Hermit, that maketh right great joy of him. And he telleth him that he hath been to the house of King Fisherman, his brother that lieth in languishment, and telleth him also how he hath been honoured in his hostel, and of the salutations that he sent him. King Hermit is right joyous thereof, and asketh him of his nephew, and he telleth him he hath seen him not since he departed thence. King Hermit asketh him whether he hath seen the Graal, and he telleth him he hath seen it not at all. 'I know well,' saith the King, 'wherefore this was so. And you had had the like desire to see the Graal that you have to see the Queen, the Graal would you have seen.' 'Sir,' saith Lancelot, 'The Queen do I desire to see for the sake of her good intent, her wisdom, courtesy and worth, and so ought every knight to do. For in herself hath she all honourable conditions that a lady may have.' 'God grant you good issue therein,' saith King Hermit, 'and that you do nought whereof He may visit you with His wrath at the Day of Judgment.' Lancelot lay the night in the hermitage, and on the morrow departed thence and took leave when he had heard mass, and cometh back as straight as he may to Pannenoisance on the sea of Wales, where were the King and Queen with great plenty of knights and barons.

Lancelot cometh back

BRANCH XI

TITLE I

Again of Perceval

THIS High History witnesseth whereof this account cometh, and saith that Perceval is in the kingdom of Logres, and came great pace toward the land of the Queen of the Tents to release the Damsel of the Car, that he had left in hostage on account of Clamados, that had put upon him the treason whereof behoved him to defend himself. But, or ever he entered into the land of the Queen of the Tents, he met the Damsel of the Car that was coming thence. She made right great joy of him, and told him that Clamados was dead of the wound that Meliot of Logres had dealt him, and that Meliot of Logres was heal. 'Sir,' saith she, 'The tents and the awnings are taken down, and the Queen hath withdrawn herself to the castle with her maidens, and by my coming back from thence may you well know that you are altogether quit. Wherefore I tell you that your sister goeth in quest of you, and that never had your mother so sore need of help as now she hath, nor never again shall your sister have joy at heart until such time as she shall have found you. She goeth seeking for you by all the kingdoms and strange countries in sore mis-ease, nor may she find any to tell her tidings of you.' Therewith Perceval departeth from the Damsel, without saying more, and rideth until he cometh into the kingdom of Wales to a castle that is seated above the sea upon a high rock, and it was called the Castle of Tallages. He seeth a knight issue from the castle and asketh whose hold it is, and he telleth him that it belonged to the Queen of the Maidens. He entereth into the first baily of the castle, and alighteth at the mounting-stage and setteth down his shield and his spear, and looketh toward the steps whereby one goeth up to the higher hall, and seeth upon them row upon row of knights and damsels. He cometh thitherward, but never a knight nor dame was there that gave him greeting of any kind. So he saluted them at large. He went his way right amidst them toward the door of the great hall, which he findeth shut, and rattled the ring so loud that it made the whole hall resound thereof. A knight cometh to open it and he entereth in. 'Sir Knight, welcome may you be!' 'Good adventure may you have!' saith Perceval. He lowereth his ventail and taketh off his helm. The knight leadeth him to the Queen's chamber, and she riseth to meet him, and maketh great joy of him, and maketh him sit beside her all armed.

The Castle of Tallages

II

With that, cometh a damsel and kneeleth before the Queen and saith: 'Lady, behold here the knight that was first at the Graal. I saw him in the court of the Queen of the Tents, there where he was appeached of treason and murder.' 'Now haste,' saith the Queen to the knight, 'Let sound the ivory horn upon the castle.' The knights and damsels that were sitting on the steps leapt up, and make right great joy, and the other knights likewise. They say that now they know well that they have done their penance. Thereupon they enter into the hall, and the Lady issueth from her chamber and taketh Perceval by the hand and goeth to meet them. 'Behold here,' saith she, 'the knight through whom you have had the pain and travail, and by whom you are now released therefrom!' 'Ha,' say the knights and dames, 'Welcome may he be!' 'By my head,' saith the Queen, 'so is he, for he is the knight of the world that I had most desire to see.' She maketh disarm him, and bring the rich robe of cloth of silk to apparel him. 'Sir,' saith the Queen, 'Four knights and three damsels have been under the steps at the entrance of the hall ever since such time as you were at the hostel of King Fisherman, there where you forgot to ask whereof the Graal might serve, nor never since have they had none other house nor hold wherein to eat nor to drink nor to lie, nor never since have they had no heart to make joy, nor would not now and you had not come hither. Wherefore ought you not to marvel that they make joy of your coming. Howbeit, on the other hand, sore need have we in this castle of your coming, for a knight warreth

A penance ended

upon me that is brother of King Fisherman, and his name is the King of Castle Mortal.' 'Lady,' saith he, 'He is my uncle, albeit I knew it not of a long time, nor of the good King Fisherman either, and the good King Hermit is my uncle also. But I tell you of a very truth, the King of Castle Mortal is the most fell and cruel that liveth, wherefore ought none to love him for the felony that is in him, for he hath begun to war upon King Fisherman my uncle, and challengeth him his castle, and would fain have the Lance and the Graal.' 'Sir,' saith the Queen, 'In like sort challengeth he my castle of me for that I am in aid of King Fisherman, and every week cometh he to an island that is in this sea, and oft-times cometh plundering before this castle and hath slain many of my knights and damsels, whereof God grant us vengeance upon him.' She taketh Perceval by the hand and leadeth him to the windows of the hall that were nighest the sea. 'Sir,' saith she, 'Now may you see the island, there, whereunto your uncle cometh in a galley, and in this island sojourneth he until he hath seen where to aim his blow and laid his plans. And here below, see, are my galleys that defend us thereof.'

The Queen of the Maidens

III

Perceval, as the history telleth, was much honoured at the castle of the Queen of the Maidens, that was right passing fair. The Queen loved him of a passing great love, but well she knew that she should never have her desire, nor any dame nor damsel that might set her intent thereon, for chaste was he and in chastity was fain to die. So long was he at the castle as that he heard tell his uncle was arrived at the island whither he wont to come. Perceval maketh arm him forthwith and entereth into a galley below the hall, and maketh him be rowed toward his uncle, that much marvelleth when he seeth him coming, for never aforetime durst no knight issue out alone from this castle to meet him, nor to come there where he was, body to body. But had he known that it was Perceval, he would not have marvelled. Thereupon the galley taketh the ground and Percival is issued forth. The Queen and the knights and her maidens are come to the windows of the castle to behold the bearing of the nephew and the uncle. The Queen would have sent over some of her knights with him, but Perceval would not. The King of Castle Mortal was tall and strong and hardy. He seeth his nephew come all armed, but knoweth him not. But Perceval knew him well, and kept his sword drawn and his shield on his arm, and sought out his uncle with right passing wrathfulness, and dealeth him a heavy buffet above upon his helm that he maketh him stoop withal. Howbeit, the King spareth him not, but smiteth him so passing stoutly that he had his helm all dinted in thereby. But Perceval attacketh him again, thinking to strike him above on the head, but the King swerveth aside and the blow falleth on the shield and cleaveth it right down as far as the boss. The

King of Castle Mortal draweth him backward and hath great shame within himself for that Perceval should thus fettle him, for he searcheth him with his sword in every part, and dealeth him great buffets in such sort that, and his habergeon had not been so strong and tough, he would have wounded him in many places.

<small>the King of Castle Mortal</small>

IV

The King himself giveth him blows so heavy that the Queen and all they that were at the windows marvelled how Perceval might abide such buffets. The King took witting of the shield that Perceval bare, and looketh on it of a long space. 'Knight,' saith he, 'Who gave you this shield, and on behalf of whom do you bear such an one?' 'I bear it on behalf of my father,' saith he. 'Did your father, then, bear a red shield with a white hart?' 'Yea!' saith Percival, 'Many a day.' 'Was your father, then, King Alain of the Valleys of Camelot?' 'My father was he without fail. No blame ought I to have of him, for a good knight was he and a loyal.' 'Are you the son of Yglais my sister, that was his wife?' 'Yea!' saith Perceval. 'Then are you my nephew,' saith the King of Castle Mortal, 'For she was my sister.' 'That misliketh me,' saith Perceval, 'For thereof have I neither worship nor honour, for the most disloyal are you of all my kindred, and I knew well when I came hither that it was you, and, for the great disloyalty that is in you, you war upon the best King that liveth and the most worshipful

The King fleeth man, and upon the Lady of this castle for that she aideth him in all that she may. But, please God, henceforward she shall have no need to guard her to the best of her power against so evil a man as are you, nor shall her castle never be obedient to you, nor the sacred hallows that the Good King hath in his keeping. For God loveth not you so much as He doth him, and so long as you war upon him, you do I defy and hold you as mine enemy.' The king wotteth well that his nephew holdeth him not over dear, and that he is eager to do him a hurt, and that he holdeth his sword in his fist and that he is well roofed-in of his helmet, and that he is raging like a lion. He misdoubteth him sore of his strength and his great hardiment. He hath well proven and essayed that he is the Best Knight of the world. He durst no longer abide his blows, but rather he turneth him full speed toward his galley, and leapeth thereinto forthwith. He pusheth out from the shore incontinent, and Perceval followeth him right to the beach, full heavy that he hath gotten him away. Then he crieth after him: 'Evil King, tell me not that I am of your kindred! Never yet did knight of my mother's lineage flee from another knight, save you alone! Now have I conquered this island, and never on no day hereafter be you so over-hardy as be seen therein again!' The King goeth his way as he that hath no mind to return, and Perceval cometh back again in his galley to the Queen's castle, and all they of the palace come forth to meet him with great joy. The Queen

asketh him how it is with him and whether he **Perceval**
is wounded? 'Lady,' saith he, 'Not at all, **returneth**
thank God.' She maketh disarm him, and
honoureth him at her pleasure, and commandeth
that all be obedient to him, and do his commandment so long as he shall please to be there.
Now feel they safer in the castle for that the
king hath so meanly departed thence, and it
well seemeth them that never will he dare
come back for dread of his nephew more than
of any other, whereof make they much joy
in common.

BRANCH XII

TITLE I

Lohot Arthur's son

NOW is the story silent about Perceval, and saith that King Arthur is at Pannenoisance in Wales, with great plenty of knights. Lancelot and Messire Gawain are repaired thither, whereof all the folk make great joy. The King asketh of Messire Gawain and Lancelot whether they have seen Lohot his son in none of these islands nor in none of these forests, and they answer him that they have seen him nowhere. 'I marvel much,' saith the King, 'what hath become of him, for no tidings have I heard of him beyond these, that Kay the Seneschal slew Logrin the giant, whose head he brought me, whereof I made great joy, and right willingly did I make Kay's lands the broader thereof, and well ought I to do him such favour, for he avenged me of him that did my land more hurt than any other, wherefore I love him greatly.' But, and the King had only known how Kay had wrought against him, he would not have so highly honoured his chivalry and his hardiment. The King sate one day at meat and Queen Guenievre at his side. Thereupon, behold you, a damsel that alighteth before the palace, then mounteth the steps of the hall and is come before the King and the Queen. 'Sir, I salute you as the sorest dismayed and most discounselled damsel that ever you have seen! Wherefore am I come to demand a boon of you for the nobleness and valour of your heart.' 'Damsel,' saith the King, 'God counsel you of His will and pleasure, and I myself am full fain to partake therein.' The damsel looketh at the shield that hangeth in the midst of the hall. 'Sir,' saith she, 'I beseech you that you deign grant me the aid of the knight that shall bear this shield from hence. For sorer need have I thereof than ever another of them that are discounselled.' 'Damsel,' saith the King, 'Full well shall I be pleased, so the knight be also fain to do as you say.' 'Sir,' saith she, 'And he be so good knight as he is reported, never will he refuse your prayer, nor would he mine, if only I were here at such time as he shall come. For, had I been able to find my brother that I have been seeking this long time, then well should I have been succoured long agone! But I have sought him in many lands, nor never could I learn where he is. Therefore, to my sorrow, behoveth me to ride all lonely by the strange islands and put my body in jeopardy of death, whereof ought these knights to have great pity.'

Of Perceval's sister

II

'Damsel,' saith the King, 'For this reason do I refuse you nought of that you wish, and right willingly will I put myself to trouble herein.' 'Sir,' saith she, 'Much thanks to

The brachet knoweth her

God thereof!' He maketh her be set at meat, and much honour be done her. When the cloths were drawn, the Queen leadeth her into her chamber with the maidens, and maketh much joy of her. The brachet that was brought thither with the shield was lying on a couch of straw. He would not know the Queen nor her damsels nor the knights that were in the court, but so soon as ever he heard the damsel he cometh to her and maketh greater joy of her than ever was brachet seen to make before. The Queen and her damsels marvelled much thereof, as did the damsel herself to whom the brachet made such joy, for never since that he was brought into the hall had they seen him rejoice of any. The Queen asked her whether she knew him. 'Certes, Lady, no, for never, so far as I know, have I seen him before.' The brachet will not leave her, but will be always on her lap, nor can she move anywhither but he followeth her. The damsel is long time in the court in this manner, albeit as she that had sore need of succour she remained in the chapel every day after that the Queen was come forth, and wept right tenderly before the image of the Saviour, and prayed right sweetly that His Mother would counsel her, for that she had been left in sore peril of losing her castle. The Queen asked her one day who her brother was. 'Lady,' saith she, 'one of the best knights of the world, whereof have I heard witness. But he departed from my father's and mother's hostel a right young squire. My father is since dead, and my Lady mother is left without help and **Dindrane** without counsel, wherefore hath a certain man **her story** reaved her of her land and her castles and slain her men. The very castle wherein she hath her hold would he have seized long agone had it not been for Messire Gawain that made it be safe-guarded against her enemies for a year. The term is now ended, and my Lady mother is in dread lest she shall lose her castle, for none other hold hath she. Wherefore is it that she hath sent me to seek for my brother, for she hath been told that he is a good knight, and for that I may not find him am I come to this court to beseech of King Arthur succour of the knight that shall bear away the shield, for I have heard tell that he is the Best Knight of the world; and, for the bounty that is in him will he therefore have pity on me.' 'Damsel,' saith the Queen, 'Would that you had found him, for great joy would it be to me that your mother were succoured, and God grant that he that ought to bear the shield come quickly, and grant him courage that he be fain to succour your mother.' 'So shall he be, please God, for never was good knight that was without pity.'

III

The Queen hath much pity of the damsel, for she was of right great beauty, and well might it be seen by her cheer and her semblant that no joy had she. She had told the Queen her name and the name of her father and mother, and the Queen told her that many

A wondrous ship a time had she heard tell of Alain li Gros, and that he was said to be a worshipful man and good knight. The King lay one night beside the Queen, and was awoke from his first sleep so that he might not go to sleep again. He rose and did on a great grey cape and issueth forth of the chamber and cometh to the windows of the hall that opened toward the sea, calm and untroubled, so that much pleasure had he of looking thereat and leaning at the windows. When he had been there of a long space, he looked out to sea and saw coming afar off as it were the shining of a candle in the midst of the sea. Much he marvelled what it might be. He looked at it until he espied what seemed him to be a ship wherein was the light, and he was minded not to move until such time as he should know whether a ship it were or something other. The longer he looketh at it, the better perceiveth he that it is a ship, and that it was coming with great rushing toward the castle as fast as it might. The King espieth it nigh at hand, but none seeth he within nor without save one old man, ancient and bald, of right passing seemliness that held the rudder of the ship. The ship was covered of a right rich cloth in the midst and the sail was lowered, for the sea was calm and quiet. The ship was arrived under the palace and was quite still. When the ship had taken ground, the King looketh thereat with much marvelling, and knoweth not who is there within, for not a soul heareth he speak. Him thinketh that he will go see what is within the ship, and he issueth

forth of the hall, and cometh thither where the **Arthur**
ship was arrived, but he might not come anigh **seeth it**
for the flowing of the sea. 'Sir,' saith he that
held the rudder, 'Allow me a little!' He
launcheth forth of the ship a little boat, and
the King entereth thereinto, and so cometh into
the great ship, and findeth a knight that lay all
armed upon a table of ivory, and had set his
shield at his head. At the head of his bed had
he two tall twisted links of wax in two candlesticks of gold, and the like at his feet, and his
hands were crossed upon his breast. The King
draweth nigh toward him and so looketh at
him, and seemed him that never had he seen
so comely a knight.

IV

'Sir,' saith the master of the ship, 'For God's
sake draw you back and let the knight rest, for
thereof hath he sore need.' 'Sir,' saith the
King, 'Who is the knight?' 'Sir, this would
he well tell you were he willing, but of me may
you know it not.' 'Will he depart forthwith
from hence?' saith the King. 'Sir,' saith the
master, 'Not before he hath been in this hall,
but he hath had sore travail and therefore he
taketh rest.' When the King heard say that
he would come into his palace, thereof had
he great joy. He cometh to the Queen's
chamber and telleth her how the ship is arrived.
The Queen riseth and two of her damsels with
her, and apparelleth her of a kirtle of cloth of
silk, furred of ermine, and cometh into the
midst of the hall. Thereupon behold you, the

Perceval landeth knight that cometh all armed and the master of the ship before him bearing the twisted link of wax in the candlestick of gold in front of him, and the knight held his sword all naked. 'Sir,' saith the Queen, 'Well may you be welcome!' 'Lady,' saith he, 'God grant you joy and good adventure.' 'Sir,' saith she, 'Please God we have nought to fear of you?' 'Lady,' saith he, 'No fear ought you to have!' The King seeth that he beareth the red shield with the white hart whereof he had heard tell. The brachet that was in the hall heareth the knight. He cometh racing toward him and leapeth about his legs and maketh great joy of him. And the knight playeth with him, then taketh the shield that hung at the column, and hangeth the other there, and cometh back thereafter toward the door of the hall. 'Lady,' saith the King, 'Pray the knight that he go not so hastily.' 'Sir,' saith the knight, 'No leisure have I to abide, but at some time shall you see me again.' The knights also say as much, and the King and Queen are right heavy of his departure, but they durst not press him beyond his will. He is entered into the ship, and the brachet with him. The master draweth the boat within, and so they depart and leave the castle behind. King Arthur abideth at Pannenoisance, and is right sorrowful of the knight, that he hath gone his way so soon. The knights arose throughout the castle when the day waxed light, and learnt the tidings of the knight that had borne the shield thence, and were right grieved for that they had not seen him. The damsel that had asked the boon and cometh to the King. 'Sir,' saith she, 'Did you taketh speak of my business to the knight?' 'Damsel,' his shield saith the King, 'Never a whit! to my sorrow, for he hath departed sooner than I would!' 'Sir,' saith she, 'You have done a wrong and a sin, but, please God, so good a King as are you shall not fail of his covenants to damsel so forlorn as am I.' The King was right sorrowful for that he had remembered not the damsel. She departeth from the court, and taketh leave of the King and Queen, and saith that she herself will go seek the knight, and that, so she may find him, she will hold the King quit of his covenant. Messire Gawain and Lancelot are returned to the court, and have heard the tidings of the knight that hath carried away the shield, and are right grieved that they have not seen him, and Messire Gawain more than enough, for that he had lien in his mother's house. Lancelot seeth the shield that he had left on the column, and knoweth it well, and saith, 'Now know I well that Perceval hath been here, for this shield was he wont to bear, and the like also his father bore.' 'Ha,' saith Messire Gawain, 'What ill-chance have I that I may not see the Good Knight!' 'Messire Gawain,' saith Lancelot, 'So nigh did I see him that methought he would have killed me, for never before did I essay onset so stout nor so cruel of force of arms, and I myself wounded him, and when he knew me he made right great joy of me. And I was with him at the house of King Hermit a long space until that I

Arthur forgetteth Dindrane

was healed.' 'Lancelot,' saith Messire Gawain, 'I would that he had wounded me, so I were not too sore harmed thereof, so that I might have been with him so long time as were you.' 'Lords,' saith the King, 'Behoveth you go on quest of him or I will go, for I am bound to beseech his aid on behalf of a damsel that asked me thereof, but she told me that, so she might find him first, I should be quit of her request.' 'Sir,' saith the Queen, 'You will do a right great service and you may counsel her herein, for sore discounselled is she. She hath told me that she was daughter of Alain li Gros of the Valleys of Camelot, and that her mother's name is Yglais, and her own Dindrane. 'Ha, Lady,' saith Messire Gawain, 'She is sister to the knight that hath borne away the shield, for I lay at her mother's house where I was right well lodged.' 'By my head,' saith the Queen, 'it may well be, for so soon as she came in hither, the brachet that would have acquaintance with none, made her great joy, and when the knight came to seek the shield, the brachet, that had remained in the hall, played gladly with him and went away with him.' 'By my faith,' saith Messire Gawain, 'I will go in quest of the knight, for right great desire have I to see him.' 'And I,' saith Lancelot, 'Never so glad have I been to see him aforetime as I should be now.' 'Howsoever it be,' saith the King, 'I pray you so speed my business that the damsel shall not be able to plain her of me.'

V

'Sir,' saith Lancelot, 'We will tell him and we may find him, that his sister is gone in quest of him, and that she hath been at your court.' The two knights depart from the court to enter on the quest of the Good Knight, and leave the castle far behind them and ride in the midst of a high forest until they find a cross in the midst of a launde, there where all the roads of the forest join together. 'Lancelot,' saith Messire Gawain, 'Choose which road soever you will, and so let each go by himself, so that we may the sooner hear tidings of the Good Knight, and let us meet together again at this cross at the end of a year and let either tell other how he hath sped, for please God in one place or another we shall hear tidings of him.' Lancelot taketh the way to the right, and Messire Gawain to the left. Therewithal they depart and commend them one another to God.

Lancelot and Gawain

BRANCH XIII

TITLE I

Of Messire Gawain

HERE the story is silent of Lancelot, and saith that Messire Gawain goeth a great pace riding, and prayeth God that He will so counsel him that he may find the knight. He rideth until the day cometh to decline, and he lay in the house of a hermit in the forest, that lodged him well. 'Sir,' saith the hermit to Messire Gawain, 'Whom do you go seek?' 'Sir,' saith he, 'I am in quest of a knight that I would see right gladly.' 'Sir,' saith the hermit, 'In this neighbourhood will you find no knight.' 'Wherefore not?' saith Messire Gawain, 'Be there no knights in this country?' 'There was wont to be plenty,' saith the hermit, 'But now no longer are there any, save one all alone in a castle and one all alone on the sea that have chased away and slain all the others.' 'And who is the one of the sea?' saith Messire Gawain. 'Sir,' saith the hermit, 'I know not who he is, save only that the sea is hard by here, where the ship runneth oftentimes wherein the knight is, and he repaireth to an island that is under the castle of the Queen of the Maidens, from whence he chased an uncle of his that warred upon the castle, and the other knights that he hath chased thence and slain were helping his uncle, so that now the castle is made sure. And the knights that might flee from this forest and this kingdom durst not repair thither for the knight, for they dread his hardiment and his great might, sith that they know well they might not long endure against him.' 'Sir,' saith Messire Gawain, 'Is it so long a space sithence that he hath haunted the sea?' 'Sir,' saith the hermit, 'It is scarce more than a twelvemonth.' 'And how nigh is this to the sea?' saith Messire Gawain. 'Sir,' saith the hermit, 'It is not more than two leagues Welsh. When I have gone forth to my toil, many a time have I seen the ship run close by me, and the knight, all armed, within, and meseemed he was of right great comeliness, and had as passing proud a look as any lion. But I can well tell you never was knight so dreaded in this kingdom as is he. The Queen of the Maidens would have lost her castle ere now but for him. Nor never sithence that he had chased his uncle from the island, hath he entered the Queen's castle even once, but from that time forth hath rather rowed about the sea and searched all the islands and stricken down all the proud in such sort that he is dreaded and warily avoided throughout all the kingdoms. The Queen of the Maidens is right sorrowful for that he cometh not to her castle, for so dear she holdeth him of very love, that and he should come and she might keep him so that he should never issue forth again, she would sooner lock him up with her there safe within.' 'Know you,' saith Messire Gawain, 'what shield the knight beareth?' 'Sir,' saith the hermit, 'I know not how to blazon it, for

Perceval haunteth the sea

The Queen of the Maidens

nought know I of arms. Three score years and more have I been in this hermitage, yet never saw I this kingdom before so dismayed as is it now.' Messire Gawain lay the night therewithin, and departed when he had heard mass. He draweth him as nigh the sea as he may, and rideth all along beside the shore and many a time draweth rein to look forth if he might see the knight's ship. But nowhere might he espy it. He hath ridden until he cometh to the castle of the Queen of the Maidens. When she knew that it was Messire Gawain, she made thereof great joy, and pointed him out the island whither Perceval had repaired, and from whence he had driven his uncle. 'Sir,' saith she to Messire Gawain, 'I plain me much of him, for never hath he been fain to enter herewithin, save the one time that he did battle with his uncle, but ever sithence hath he made repair to this island and rowed about this sea.' 'Lady,' saith Messire Gawain, 'and whereabout may he be now?' 'Sir, God help me,' saith she, 'I know not, for I have not seen him now of a long space, and no earthly man may know his intent nor his desire, nor whitherward he may turn.' Messire Gawain is right sorrowful for that he knoweth not where to seek him albeit he hath so late tidings of him. He lay at the castle and was greatly honoured, and on the morrow he heard mass and took leave of the Queen, and rideth all armed beside the seashore, for that the hermit had told him, and the Queen herself, that he goeth oftener by sea than by land. He entereth into a forest that was nigh the sea, and seeth a knight coming a great gallop as if one were chasing him to slay him. 'Sir knight,' saith Messire Gawain, 'Whither away so fast?' 'Sir, I am fleeing from the knight that hath slain all the others.' 'And who is the knight?' saith Messire Gawain. 'I know not who he is,' saith the knight, 'But and you go forward you are sure to find him.' 'Meseemeth,' saith Messire Gawain, 'that I have seen you aforetime.' 'Sir,' saith he, 'So have you! I am the Knight Coward that you met in the forest there where you conquered the knight of the shield party black and white, and I am man of the Damsel of the Car. Wherefore I pray you for God's sake that you do me no hurt, for the knight that I found down yonder hath a look so fierce that I thought I was dead when I saw it.' 'Need you fear nought of me,' saith Messire Gawain, 'For I love your Damsel well.' 'Sir,' saith the knight, 'I would that all the other knights would say as much in respect of me, for no fear have I save for myself alone.'

The Knight Coward

II

Messire Gawain departeth from the knight, and goeth his way amidst the forest that overshadowed the land as far as the seashore, and looketh forth from the top of a sand-hill, and seeth a knight armed on a tall destrier, and he had a shield of gold with a green cross. 'Ha, God,' saith Messire Gawain, 'Grant that this knight may be able to tell me tidings of him

I seek!' Thitherward goeth he a great gallop, and saluteth him worshipfully and he him again. 'Sir,' saith Messire Gawain, 'Can you tell me tidings of a knight that beareth a shield banded of argent and azure with a red cross?' 'Yea, Sir,' saith the knight, 'That can I well. At the assembly of the knights may you find him within forty days.' 'Sir,' saith Messire Gawain, 'Where will the assembly be?' 'In the Red Launde, where will be many a good knight. There shall you find him without fail.' Thereof hath Messire Gawain right great joy, and so departeth from the knight and the knight from him, and goeth back toward the sea a great gallop. But Messire Gawain saw not the ship whereinto he entered, for that it was anchored underneath the rock. The knight entered thereinto and put out to sea as he had wont to do. Howbeit Messire Gawain goeth his way toward the Red Launde where the assembly was to be, and desireth much the day that it shall be. He rideth until he cometh one eventide nigh to a castle that was of right fair seeming. He met a damsel that was following after a dead knight that two other knights bare upon a horse-bier, and she rode a great pace right amidst the forest. And Messire Gawain cometh to meet her and saluteth her, and she returned the salute as fairly as she might. 'Damsel,' saith Messire Gawain, 'Who lieth in this bier?' 'Sir, a knight that a certain man hath slain by great outrage.' 'And whither shall you ride this day?' 'Sir, I would fain be in the Red Launde, and thither

Gawain meeteth Perceval

will I take this knight, that was a right worshipful man for his age.' 'And wherefore will you take him there?' saith Messire Gawain. 'For that he that shall do best at the assembly of knights shall avenge this knight's death.'

The treacherous Vavasour

III

The damsel goeth her way thereupon. And Messire Gawain goeth to the castle that he had seen, and found none within save only one solitary knight, old and feeble, and a squire that waited upon him. Howbeit, Messire Gawain alighteth at the castle. The Vavasour lodged him well and willingly, and made his door be well shut fast and Messire Gawain be disarmed, and that night he showed him honour as well as he might. And when it came to the morrow and Messire Gawain was minded to depart thence, the Vavasour saith to him, 'Sir, you may not depart thus, for this door hath not been opened this long while save only yesterday, when I made it be opened before you, to the intent that you should meet on my behalf a certain knight that is fain to slay me, for that the King of Castle Mortal hath had his hold herewithin, he that warreth on the Queen of the Maidens. Wherefore I pray you that you help me to defend it against the knight.' 'What shield beareth he?' saith Messire Gawain. 'He beareth a golden shield with a green cross.' 'And what sort of knight is he?' saith Messire Gawain. 'Sir,' saith the Vavasour, 'A good knight and a hardy and a sure.' 'By my faith,' saith Messire Gawain,

Gawain again meeteth Perceval

'And you can tell me tidings of another knight whereof I am in quest, I will protect you against this one to the best I may, and if he will do nought for my prayer, I will safeguard you of my force.' 'What knight, then, do you go seek?' saith the Vavasour. 'Sir, a knight that is called Perceval, and he hath carried away from the court of King Arthur a shield banded argent and azure with a red cross on a band of gold. He will be at the assembly in the Red Launde. These tidings had I of the knight you dread so much.'

IV

Thereupon, whilst Messire Gawain was thus speaking to the Vavasour, behold you the Knight of the Golden Shield, that draweth rein in the midst of a launde that was between the castle and the forest. The Vavasour seeth him from the windows of the hall, and pointeth him out to Messire Gawain. Messire Gawain goeth and mounteth on his destrier, his shield at his neck and his spear in his fist, all armed, and issueth forth of the door when it had been unfastened, and cometh toward the knight, that awaited him on his horse. He seeth Messire Gawain coming, but moveth not, and Messire Gawain marvelleth much that the knight cometh not toward him, for him thinketh well that the Vavasour had told him true. But he had not, for never had the knight come thither to do the Vavasour any hurt, but on account of the knights that passed by that way that went to seek adventure, for right glad was he to see them albeit he was not minded to make himself known to any. Messire Gawain looketh before him and behind him and seeth that the door was made fast and the bridge drawn up so soon as he was departed thence, whereof he marvelled much and saith to the knight, 'Sir, is your intent nought but good only?' 'By my head,' saith he, 'Nought at all, and readily will I tell it you.' Thereupon, behold you a damsel that cometh a great pace, and held a whip wherewith she hurrieth her mule onward, and she draweth rein there where the two knights were. 'Ha, God!' saith she, 'Shall I ever find one to wreak me vengeance of the traitor Vavasour that dwelleth in this castle?' 'Is he then traitor?' saith Messire Gawain. 'Yea, Sir, the most traitor you saw ever! He lodged my brother the day before yesterday, and bore him on hand at night that a certain knight was warring upon him for that the way whereby the knights pass is here in front of this place, and lied to him so much as that my brother held him in covenant that he would assault a certain knight that he should point out to him, for love of him. This knight came passing hereby, that had no thought to do hurt neither to the Vavasour nor to my brother. The knight was right strong and hardy, and was born at the castle of Escavalon. My brother issued forth of the castle filled with fool-hardiness for the leasing of the Vavasour, and ran upon the knight without a word. The knight could do no less than avenge himself. They hurtled together so sore that their horses fell under them and their

The spears passed either through other's heart. Thus were both twain killed on this very piece of ground.

The damsel of the horse-bier

V

'The Vavasour took the arms and the horses and put them in safe keeping in his castle, and the bodies of the knights he left to the wild beasts, that would have devoured them had I not chanced to come thither with two knights that helped me bury them by yonder cross at the entrance of the forest.' 'By my head,' saith Messire Gawain, 'In like manner would he have wrought me mischief had I been minded to trust him; for he bore me in hand that this knight was warring upon him, and besought me that I should safeguard him against him. But our Lord God so helped me that I intermeddled not therein, for lightly might I have wrought folly.' 'By the name of God,' saith the other, 'Meseemeth it clear that the Vavasour would fain that knights should kill each other.' 'Sir,' saith the damsel, 'You say true; it is of his covetise of harness and horses that he entreateth the knights on this-wise.' 'Damsel,' saith Messire Gawain, 'Whither go you?' 'Sir,' saith she, 'After a knight that I have made be carried in a litter for the dead.' 'I saw him,' saith he, 'pass by here last night, full late last night.' The knight taketh leave of Messire Gawain, and Messire Gawain saith that he holdeth himself a churl in that he hath not asked him of his name. But the knight said, 'Fair Sir, I pray you of love that you ask not

my name until such time as I shall ask you of
yours.'

Josuias the hermit

VI

Messire Gawain would ask nought further of the knight, and the knight entered into the Lonely Forest and Messire Gawain goeth on his way. He meeteth neither knight nor damsel to whom he telleth not whom he goeth to seek, and they all say that he will be in the Red Launde. He lodged the night with a hermit. At night, the hermit asked Messire Gawain whence he came? 'Sir, from the land of the Queen of the Maidens.' 'Have you seen Perceval, the Good Knight that took the shield in King Arthur's court and left another there?' 'No, certes,' saith Messire Gawain, 'whereof am I right sorrowful. But a knight with a shield of gold and a green cross thereon told me that he would be at the Red Launde.' 'Sir,' saith the hermit, 'You say true, for it was he himself to whom you spake. To-night is the third night since he lay within yonder, and see here the brachet he brought from King Arthur's court, which he hath commanded me to convey to his uncle, King Hermit.' 'Alas!' saith Messire Gawain, 'What ill chance is mine if this be true!' 'Sir,' saith the hermit, 'I ought not to lie, neither to you nor other. By the brachet may you well know that this is true.' 'Sir,' saith Messire Gawain, 'Of custom beareth he no such shield.' 'I know well,' saith the hermit, 'what shield he ought to bear, and what shield he will bear hereafter.

Perceval's close counsel

But this doth he that he may not be known, and this shield took he in the hermitage of Joseus, the son of King Hermit, there where Lancelot was lodged, where he hanged the four thieves that would have broken into the hermitage by night. And within there hath remained the shield he brought from King Arthur's court, with Joseus the son of my sister, and they are as brother and sister between the twain, and you may know of very truth that albeit Joseus be hermit, no knight is there in Great Britain of his heart and hardiment.'

VII

'Certes,' saith Messire Gawain, 'It was sore mischance for me that I should see him yesterday before the castle where the knights pass by, and speak to him and ask him his name, but he besought me that I should not ask him his name until such time as he should ask me mine; and with that he departed from me and entered into the forest, and I came hitherward. Now am I so sorrowful that I know not what I may do for the best, for King Arthur sendeth me in quest of him, and Lancelot hath also gone to seek him in another part of the kingdom of Logres. But now hath too great mischance befallen me of this quest, for twice have I seen him and found him and spoken to him, and now have I lost him again.' 'Sir,' saith the hermit, 'He is so close and wary a knight, that he is fain never to waste a word, neither will he make false semblant to any nor speak word that he would not should be heard, nor do shame of his body to his knowledge, nor carnal sin, for **The Red** virgin and chaste is he and doth never outrage **Launde** to any.' 'I know well,' saith Messire Gawain, 'that all the valours and all the cleannesses that ought to be in a knight are in him, and therefore am I the more sorrowful that I am not of them that he knoweth, for a man is worth the more that hath acquaintance with a good knight.'

VIII

Messire Gawain lay the night in the hermit's house, right sorrowful, and in the morning departed when he had heard mass. Josephus the good clerk witnesseth us in this high history that this hermit had to name Josuias, and was a knight of great worship and valour, but he renounced all for the love of God, and was fain to set his body in banishment for Him. And all these adventures that you hear in this high record came to pass, Josephus telleth us, for the setting forward the law of the Saviour. All of them could he not record, but only these whereof he best remembered him, and whereof he knew for certain all the adventures by virtue of the Holy Spirit. This high record saith that Messire Gawain hath wandered so far that he is come into the Red Launde whereas the assembly of knights should be held. He looketh and seeth the tents pitched and the knights coming from all quarters. The most part were already armed within and before their tents. Messire Gawain looketh everywhere, thinking to see the knight he seeketh, but seemeth him

Gawain seeketh Perceval

he seeth him not, for no such shield seeth he as he beareth. All abashed is he thereof, for he hath seen all the tents and looked at all the arms. But the knight is not easy to recognise, for he hath changed his arms, and nigh enough is he to Messire Gawain, albeit you may well understand that he knoweth it not. And the tournament assembleth from all parts, and the divers fellowships come the one against other, and the melly of either upon other as they come together waxeth sore and marvellous. And Messire Gawain searcheth the ranks to find the knight, albeit when he meeteth knight in his way he cannot choose but do whatsoever a knight may do of arms, and yet more would he have done but for his fairness to seek out the knight. The damsel is at the head of the tournament, for that she would fain know the one that shall have the mastery and the prize therein. The knight that Messire Gawain seeketh is not at the head of the fellowships, but in the thickest of the press, and such feats of arms doth he that more may no knight do, and smiteth down the knights about him, that flee from him even as the deer-hound fleeth from the lion. 'By my faith,' saith Messire Gawain, 'sith that they have lied to me about the knight, I will seek him no more this day, but forget my discontent as best I may until evening.' He seeth the knight, but knoweth him not, for he had a white shield and cognisances of the same. And Messire Gawain cometh to him as fast as his horse may carry him, and the knight toward Messire Gawain. So passing stoutly they come together that they pierce their shields and below the boss. Their spears were so tough that they break not, and they draw them forth and come together again so strongly that the spears wherewith they smote each other amidst the breast were bended so that they unriveted the holdfasts of their shields, and they lost their stirrups, and the reins fly from their fists, and they stagger against the back saddlebows, and the horses stumbled so as that they all but fell. They straighten them in saddle and stirrup, and catch hold upon their reins, and then come together again, burning with wrath and fury like lions, and either smiteth on other with their spears that may endure no longer, for the shafts are all to-frushed as far as the fists in such sort that they that look on marvel them much how it came to pass that the points had not pierced their bodies. But God would not that the good knights should slay each other, rather would He that the one should know the true worth of the other. The habergeons safeguarded not their bodies, but the might of God in whom they believed, for in them had they all the valour that knight should have; and never did Messire Gawain depart from hostel wherein he had lien, but he first heard mass before he went if so he might, nor never found he dame nor damsel discounselled whereof he had not pity, nor did he ever churlishness to other knight, nor said nor thought it, and he came, as you have heard, of the most holy lineage of Josephus and the good King Fisherman.

and fighteth him unknown

Perceval departeth secretly

IX

The good knights were in the midst of the assembly, and right wrathful was the one against the other, and they held their swords naked and their shields on their arms and dealt each other huge buffets right in the midst of the helms. The most part of the knights come to them and tell them that the assembly waiteth for them to come thereunto. They have much pains to part them asunder, and then the melly beginneth again on all sides, and the evening cometh on that parteth them at last. And on this wise the assembly lasted for two days. The damsel that brought the knight on a bier in a coffin, dead, prayed the assembly of all the knights to declare which one of all the knights had done the best, for the knight that she made be carried might not be buried until such time as he were avenged. And they say that the knight of the white shield and the other with the shield sinople and the golden eagle had done better than all the other, but, for that the knight of the white shield had joined in the melly before the other, they therefore would give him the prize; but they judged that for the time that Messire Gawain had joined therein he had not done worse than the other knight. The damsel seeketh the knight of the white shield among the knights and throughout all the tents, but cannot find him, for already hath he departed. She cometh to Messire Gawain and saith: 'Sir, sith that I find not the knight of the white shield, you are he that

behoveth avenge the knight that lieth dead in The
the litter.' 'Damsel,' saith Messire Gawain, damsel
'Do me not this shame, for it hath been declared of the
that the other knight hath better done herein bier
than I.'

X

'Damsel, well you know that no honour should I have thereof, were I to emprise to do that whereof you beseech me, for you have said that behoveth none to avenge him, save only he that hath borne him best at this assembly, and that is he of the white shield, and, so God help me, this have I well felt and proven.'

XI

The damsel well understandeth that Messire Gawain speaketh reason. 'Ha, Sir,' saith she, 'He hath already departed hence and gone into the forest, and the most divers-seeming knight is he and the best that liveth, and great pains shall I have or ever I find him again.' 'The best?' saith Messire Gawain; 'How know you that?' 'I know it well,' saith she, 'For that in the house of King Fisherman did the Graal appear unto him for the goodness of his knighthood and the goodness of his heart and for the chastity of his body. But he forgat to ask that one should serve thereof, whence hath sore harm befallen the land. He came to the court of King Arthur, where he took a shield that none ought to bear save he alone. Up to this time have I well known his coming and going, but nought shall I know thereof hereafter for

Gawain sore grieved that he hath changed the cognisance of his shield and arms. And now am I entered into sore pain and travail to seek him, for I shall not have found him of a long space, and I came not to this assembly save for him alone.' 'Damsel,' saith Messire Gawain, 'You have told me tidings such as no gladness have I thereof, for I also am seeking him, but I know not how I may ever recognise him, for he willeth not to tell me his name, and too often changeth he his shield, and well I know that so I shall ever come in place where he hath changed his cognisance, and he shall come against me and I against him, I shall only know him by the buffets that he knoweth how to deal, for never in arms have I made acquaintance with so cruel a knight. But again would I suffer sorer blows than I have suffered yet, so only I might be where he is.' 'Sir,' saith the damsel, 'What is your name?' 'Damsel,' saith he, 'I am called Gawain.' With that he commendeth the damsel to God, and goeth his way in one direction and the damsel in another, and saith to herself that Perceval is the most marvellous knight of the world, that so often he discogniseth himself. For when one seeth him one may recognise him not. Messire Gawain rideth amidst the forest, and prayeth the Saviour lead him into such place as that he may find Perceval openly, in such sort that he may have his acquaintance and his love that so greatly he desireth.

BRANCH XIV

TITLE I

HEREWITHAL the story is silent of Messire Gawain, and saith that Lancelot seeketh Perceval in like manner as did Messire Gawain, and rideth until that he cometh to the hermitage where he hanged the thieves. Joseus made right great joy of him. He asked him whether he knew any tidings of the son of the Widow Lady. 'I have seen him sithence that he came from King Arthur's court but once only, and whither he is gone I know not.' 'Sir,' saith Lancelot, 'I would see him right fain. King Arthur sendeth for him by me.' 'Sir,' saith the hermit, 'I know not when I may see him again, for when once he departeth hence he is not easy to find.' Lancelot entereth the chapel with the hermit, and seeth the shield that Perceval brought from King Arthur's court beside the altar. 'Sir,' saith Lancelot, 'I see his shield yonder. Hide him not from me.' 'I will not do so,' saith the hermit. 'This shield, truly, is his, but he took with him another from hence, of gold with a green cross.' 'And know you no tidings of Messire Gawain?' 'I have not seen Messire Gawain sithence tofore I entered into this hermitage. But you have fallen into sore

The hatred on account of the four robbers that
Golden were knights whom you hanged. For their
Circlet kinsmen are searching for you in this forest and in other, and are thieves like as were the others, and they have their hold in this forest, wherein they bestow their robberies and plunder. Wherefore I pray you greatly be on your guard against them.' 'So will I,' saith Lancelot, 'please God.' He lay the night in the hermitage, and departeth on the morrow after that he hath heard mass, and prayeth God grant he may find Perceval or Messire Gawain. He goeth his way amidst the strange forests until that he cometh to a strong castle that was builded right seemly. He looketh before him and seeth a knight that was issued thereout, and was riding a great pace on a strong destrier, and carried a bird on his fist toward the forest.

II

When he saw Lancelot coming he drew up. 'Sir,' saith he, 'Be welcome.' 'Good adventure to you,' saith Lancelot. 'What castle is this?' 'Sir, it is the Castle of the Golden Circlet. And I go to meet the knights and dames that come to the castle, for this day is the day ordained for the adoration of the Golden Circlet.' 'What is the Golden Circlet?' saith Lancelot. 'Sir, it is the Crown of Thorns,' saith the knight, 'that the Saviour of the world had on His head when He was set upon the Rood. Wherefore the Queen of this castle hath set it in gold and precious stones in such sort that the knights and dames of this kingdom come to behold it once in the year. But it is said that the knight that was first at the Graal shall conquer it, and therefore is no strange knight allowed to enter. But, so please you, I will lead you to my own hold that is in this forest.' 'Right great thanks,' saith Lancelot, 'But as yet is it not time to take lodging.' He taketh leave of the knight, and so departeth and looketh at the castle, and saith that in right great worship should the knight be held that by the valour of his chivalry shall conquer so noble a hallow as is the Golden Circlet when it is kept safe in a place so strong. He goeth his way right amidst the forest, and looketh forth before him and seeth coming the damsel that hath the knight carried in the litter for the dead. 'Damsel,' saith Lancelot, 'Be welcome.' 'Sir, God give you good adventure! Sir,' saith the damsel, 'Greatly ought I to hate the knight that slew this knight, for that he hath forced me thus to lead him in this wise by fell and forest. So also ought I to mislike me much of the knight that it standeth upon to avenge him, whom I may not find.' 'Damsel,' saith Lancelot, 'Who slew this knight?' 'Sir,' saith she, 'The Lord of the Burning Dragon.' 'And who ought of right to avenge him?' 'Sir,' saith she, 'The knight that was in the Red Launde at the assembly, that jousted with Messire Gawain, and had the prize of the tournament.' 'Did he better than Messire Gawain?' saith Lancelot. 'Sir, so did they adjudge him; for that he was a longer time in the assembly.' 'A good knight was he, then,' saith Lancelot.

A robber hold

'Sith that he did better than Messire Gawain!' 'By my head,' saith the damsel, 'You say true, for he is the Best Knight of the World.' 'And what shield beareth he?' saith Lancelot. 'Sir,' saith the damsel, 'At the assembly he bore white arms, but before that, he had arms of another semblance, and one shield that he had was green, and one gold with a green cross.' 'Damsel,' saith he, 'Did Messire Gawain know him?' 'Sir, not at all, whereof is he right sorrowful.' 'Is he then,' saith he, 'Perceval, the son of the Widow Lady?' 'By my head, you say true!' 'Ha, God!' saith Lancelot, 'The more am I mazed how Messire Gawain knew him not. Damsel,' saith he, 'And know you whitherward they are gone?' 'Sir,' saith she, 'I know not whither, nor have I any tidings, neither of the one nor the other.' He departeth from the damsel and rideth until the sun was set. He found the rocks darkling and the forest right deep and perilous of seeming. He rode on, troubled in thought, and weary and full of vexation. Many a time looketh he to right and to left, and he may see any place where he may lodge. A dwarf espied him, but Lancelot saw him not. The dwarf goeth right along a by-way that is in the forest, and goeth to a little hold of robber-knights that lay out of the way, where was a damsel that kept watch over the hold. The robbers had another hold where was the damsel where the passing knights are deceived and entrapped. The dwarf cometh forthright to the damsel, and saith: 'Now shall we see what you will do, for see, here cometh the knight **A** that hanged your uncle and your three cousins **treacher-** german.' 'Now shall I have the best of him,' **ous** saith she, 'as for mine own share in this matter, **damsel** but take heed that you be garnished ready to boot.' 'By my head,' saith the dwarf, 'That will I, for, please God, he shall not escape us again, save he be dead.' The damsel was of passing great beauty and was clad right seemingly, but right treacherous was she of heart, nor no marvel was it thereof, for she came of the lineage of robbers and was nurtured on theft and robbery, and she herself had helped to murder many a knight. She is come upon the way, so that Lancelot hath to pass her, without her kerchief. She meeteth Lancelot and saluteth him and maketh him right great joy, of semblant. 'Sir,' saith she, 'Follow this path that goeth into the forest, and you will find a hold that my forefathers stablished for harbouring of such knights as might be passing through the forest. The night is dark already, and if you pass on further no hold will you find nearer than a score leagues Welsh.' 'Damsel,' saith Lancelot, 'Gramercy heartily of this that it pleaseth you to say, for right gladly will I harbour me here, for it is more than time to take lodging, and with you more willingly than another.'

III

On this wise they go their way talking, as far as the hold. There was none therewithin save only the dwarf, for the five robber knights were

Lancelot is wary in their hold at the lower end of the forest. The dwarf took Lancelot's horse, and stabled him, then went up into the hall above, and gave himself up wholly to serving him. 'Sir,' saith the damsel, 'Allow yourself to be disarmed, and have full assurance of safety.' 'Damsel,' saith he, 'Small trouble is it for me to wear mine arms, and lightly may I abide it.' 'Sir,' saith she, 'Please God, you shall not lie armed within yonder. Never yet did knight so that harboured therein.' But the more the damsel presseth him to disarm, the more it misliketh him, for the place seemeth him right dark and foul-seeming, wherefore will he not disarm nor disgarnish himself. 'Sir,' saith she, 'Meseemeth you are suspicious of something, but no call have you to misdoubt of aught here within, for the place is quite safe. I know not whether you have enemies?' 'Damsel,' saith Lancelot, 'Never yet knew I knight that was loved of everybody, yet sometimes might none tell the reason thereof.'

IV

Lancelot, so saith the story, would not disarm him, wherefore he made the table be set, and sate thereat beside the damsel at meat. He made his shield and his helmet and spear be brought into the hall. He leant back upon a rich couch that was therewithin, with his sword by his side, all armed. He was weary and the bed was soft, so he went to sleep. Howbeit, the dwarf mounteth on his horse that he had left still saddled, and goeth his way to the other hold where the robbers were, all five, that **Lancelot** were Lancelot's mortal enemies. The damsel **dreameth** remained all alone with him that she hated of a right deadly hate. She thought to herself that gladly would she slay him, and that, so she might compass it, she would be thereof held in greater worship of all the world, for well she knew that he was a good knight, and that one so good she had never slain. She filched away the sword that was at his side, then drew it from the scabbard, then looketh to see where she may lightliest smite him to slay him. She seeth that his head is so covered of armour that nought appeareth thereof save only the face, and she bethinketh her that one stroke nor two on the helmet would scarce hurt him greatly, but that and she might lift the skirt of his habergeon without awakening him she might well slay him, for so might she thrust the sword right through his heart. Meanwhile, as she was searching thus, Lancelot, that was sleeping and took no heed thereof, saw, so it seemed him, a little cur-dog come therewithin, and brought with him sundry great mongrel ban-dogs that ran upon him on all sides, and the little cur bit at him likewise among the others. The ban-dogs held him so fast that he might not get away from them. He seeth that a greyhound bitch had hold of his sword, and she had hands like a woman, and was fain to slay him. And it seemed him that he snatched the sword from her and slew the greyhound bitch and the biggest and most masterful of the ban-dogs and the little cur. He was scared of the dream

Lancelot's sword stolen

and started up and awoke, and felt the scabbard of his sword by his side, that the damsel had left there all empty, the which he perceived not, and soon thereafter he fell on sleep again. The dwarf that had stolen his horse cometh to the robber knights, and crieth to them, 'Up, Sirs, and haste you to come and avenge you of your mortal enemy that sent the best of your kindred out of the world with such shame! See, here is his horse that I bring you for a token!' He alighteth of the horse, and giveth him up to them. Right joyous are the robbers of the tidings he telleth them. The dwarf bringeth them all armed to the hold.

V

Lancelot was awake, all scared of the dream he had dreamed. He seeth them enter within all armed, and the damsel crieth to them: 'Now will it appear,' saith she, 'what you will do!' Lancelot hath leapt up, thinking to take his sword, but findeth the scabbard all empty. The damsel that held the sword was the first of all to run upon him, and the five knights and the dwarf set upon him from every side. He perceived that it was his own sword the damsel held, the one he prized above all other. He taketh his lance that was at his bed's-head and cometh toward the master of the knights at a great sweep, and smiteth him so fiercely that he thrusteth him right through the body so that the lance passeth a fathom beyond, and beareth him to the ground dead. His spear broke as he drew it back. He runneth to the damsel that held the sword, and **Lancelot and the robbers** wresteth it forth of her hands and holdeth it fast with his arm right against his flank and grippeth it to him right strait; albeit she would fain snatch it again from him by force, whereat Lancelot much marvelled. He swingeth it above him, and the four knights come back upon him. He thinketh to smite one with the sword, when the damsel leapeth in between them, thinking to hold Lancelot fast, and thereby the blow that should have fallen on one of the knights caught the damsel right through the head and slew her, whereof he was right sorrowful, howsoever she might have wrought against him.

VI

When the four knights saw the damsel dead, right grieved were they thereof. And the dwarf crieth out to them: 'Lords, now shall it be seen how you will avenge the sore mischief done you. So help me God, great shame may you have and you cannot conquer a single knight.' They run upon him again on all sides, but maugre all their heads he goeth thither where he thinketh to find his horse; but him findeth he not. Thereby well knoweth he that the dwarf hath made away with him, wherefore he redoubled his hardiment and his wrath waxed more and more. And the knights were not to be lightly apaid when they saw their lord dead and the damsel that was their cousin. Sore buffets they dealt him of their swords the while he defended himself as best he might. He caught the dwarf that was edging them on to do him hurt, and clave him as far as the shoulders, and wounded two of the knights right badly, and he himself was hurt in two places; but he might not depart from the house, nor was his horse there within, nor was there but a single entrance into the hall. The knights set themselves without the door and guard the issue, and Lancelot was within with them that were dead. He sate himself down at the top of the hall to rest himself, for he was sore spent with the blows he had given and received. When he had rested himself awhile, he riseth to his feet and seeth that they have sate them down in the entrance to the hall. He mounteth up to the windows and flingeth them down them that were dead within through the windows. Just then the day appeared, fair and clear, and the birds began to sing amidst the forest, whereof the hall was overshadowed. He maketh fast the door of the hall and barreth it and shutteth the knights without; and they say one to the other and swear it, that they will not depart thence until they have taken him or famished him to death. Little had Lancelot recked of their threats and he might have had his horse at will, but he was not so sure of his stroke afoot as a-horseback, as no knight never is. Him thinketh he may well abide the siege as long as God shall please, for the hall was well garnished of meat in right great joints. He is there within all alone, and the four knights without that keep watch that he goeth not, but neither

He slayeth sundry

wish nor will hath he to go forth afoot; but, and and he had had his horse, the great hardiment abideth that he hath in him would have made that he should go forth honourably, howsoever they without might have taken it and what grievance soever they might have had thereof.

BRANCH XV

TITLE I

Gawain and Joseus

HERE the story is silent of Lancelot, and talketh of Messire Gawain that goeth to seek Perceval, and is right heavy for that twice hath he found him when he knew him not. He cometh back again to the cross whereas he told Lancelot he would await him so he should come thither before him. He went and came to and fro by the forest more than eight days to wait for him, but could hear no tidings. He would not return to King Arthur's court, for had he gone thither in such case, he would have had blame thereof. He goeth back upon the quest and saith that he will never stint therein until he shall have found both Lancelot and Perceval. He cometh to the hermitage of Joseus, and alighted of his horse and found the young hermit Joseus, that received him well and made full great joy of him. He harboured the night therewithin. Messire Gawain asked him tidings of Perceval, and the hermit telleth him he hath not seen him since before the assembly of the Red Launde. 'And can you tell me where I may find him?' saith Messire Gawain. 'Not I,' saith the hermit, 'I cannot tell you whereabout he is.' While they were talking on this wise, straightway behold you a knight **Tidings** coming that hath arms of azure, and alighteth **of** at the hermitage to lodge there. The hermit **Perceval** receiveth him right gladly. Messire Gawain asketh him if he saw a knight with white arms ride amidst the forest. 'By my faith,' saith the knight, 'I have seen him this day and spoken with him, and he asked me and I could tell him tidings of a knight that beareth a shield of sinople with a golden eagle, and I told him, no. Afterward, I enquired wherefore he asked it, and he made answer that he had jousted at him in the Red Launde, nor never before had he found so sturdy assault of any knight, wherefore he was right sorrowful for that he was not acquainted with him, for the sake of his good knighthood.' 'By my faith,' saith Gawain, 'The knight is more sorrowful than he, for nought is there in the world he would gladlier see than him.' The knight espieth Messire Gawain's shield and saith, 'Ha, Sir, methinketh you are he.' 'Certes,' saith Messire Gawain, 'you say true. I am he against whom he jousted, and right glad am I that so good a knight smote upon my shield, and right sorrowful for that I knew him not; but tell me where I may find him?'

II

'Sir,' saith Joseus the Hermit, 'He will not have gone forth from this forest, for this is the place wherein he wonneth most willingly, and the shield that he brought from King Arthur's court is in this chapel.' So he

Perceval arriveth showeth the shield to Messire Gawain that maketh great joy thereof. 'Ha, Sir,' saith the knight of the white arms, 'Is your name Messire Gawain?' 'Fair Sir,' saith he, 'Gawain am I called.' 'Sir,' saith the knight, 'I have not ceased to seek you for a long while past. Meliot of Logres, that is your man, the son of the lady that was slain on your account, sendeth you word that Nabigant of the Rock hath slain his father on your account; wherefore he challengeth the land that hath fallen to him; and hereof he prayeth you that you will come to succour him as behoveth lord to do to his liege man.' 'By my faith,' saith Messire Gawain, 'Behoveth me not fail him therein, wherefore tell him I will succour him so soon as I may; but tell him I have emprised a business that I cannot leave but with loss of honour until such time as it be achieved.' They lay the night at the hermitage until after mass was sung on the morrow.

III

The knight departed and Messire Gawain remained. So when he was apparelled to mount, he looketh before him at the issue of the forest toward the hermitage, and seeth coming a knight on a tall horse, full speed and all armed, and he bore a shield like the one he saw Perceval bearing the first time. 'Sir,' saith he, 'Know you this knight that cometh there?' 'Truly, Sir, well do I know him. This is Perceval whom you seek, whom you so much desire to see!' 'God be praised thereof!' saith Messire Gawain, 'Inasmuch as he cometh hither.' He goeth afoot to meet him, and Perceval alighteth so soon as he seeth him. 'Sir,' saith Messire Gawain, 'Right welcome may you be!' 'Good joy may you have,' saith Perceval. 'Sir,' saith the hermit, 'Make great joy of him! this is Messire Gawain, King Arthur's nephew.' 'Thereof do I love him the better!' saith he. 'Honour and joy ought all they to do him that know him!' He throweth his arms on his neck, and so maketh him great joy. 'Sir,' saith he, 'Can you tell me tidings of a knight that was in the Red Launde at the assembly of knights?' 'What shield beareth he?' saith Messire Gawain. 'A red shield with a golden eagle,' saith Perceval. 'And more by token, never made I acquaintance with any so sturdy in battle as are he and Lancelot.' 'Fair sir, it pleaseth you to say so,' saith Messire Gawain. 'In the Red Launde was I at the assembly, and such arms bore I as these you blazon, and I jousted against a knight in white arms, of whom I know this, that all of knighthood that may be lodged in the body of a man is in him.' 'Sir,' saith Perceval to Messire Gawain, 'You know not how to blame any man.' So they hold one another by the hands, and go into the hermitage. 'Sir,' saith Messire Gawain, 'When you were in the court of King Arthur for the shield that is within yonder, your sister was also there, and prayed and besought the help of the knight that should bear away the shield, as being the most discounselled damsel in the world. The King

Gawain knoweth Perceval

Good knights' converse granted it her, and you bore away the shield. She asked your aid of the King as she that deemed not you were her brother, and said that if the King failed of his covenant, he would do great sin, whereof would he have much blame. The King was fain to do all he might to seek you, to make good that he had said, and sent us forth in quest of you, so that the quest lieth between me and Lancelot. He himself would have come had we been unwilling to go. Sir, I have found you three times without knowing you, albeit great desire had I to see you. This is the fourth time and I know you now, whereof I make myself right joyous; and much am I beholden to you of the fair lodging your mother gave me at Camelot; but right sore pity have I of her, for a right worshipful woman is she, and a widow lady and ancient, and fallen into much war without aid nor comfort, through the evil folk that harass her and reave her of her castles. She prayed me, weeping the while right sweetly, that and if I should find you that are her son, I should tell you of her plight, that your father is dead, and that she hath no succour nor aid to look for save from you alone, and if you succour her not shortly, she will lose her own one castle that she holdeth, and must needs become a beggar, for of the fifteen castles she wont to have in your father's time, she hath now only that of Camelot, nor of all her knights hath she but five to guard the castle. Wherefore I pray you on her behalf and for your own honour, that you will grant her herein of your counsel and your valour and your might, for of no chivalry that you may do may you rise to greater worship. And so sore need hath she herein as you hear me tell, nor would I that she should lose aught by default of message, for thereof should I have sin and she harm, and you yourself also, that have the power to amend it and ought of right so to do!' 'Well have you delivered yourself herein,' saith Perceval, 'And betimes will I succour her and our Lord God will.' 'You will do honour to yourself,' saith Messire Gawain. 'Thereof will you have praise with God and worship with the world.' 'Well know I,' saith Perceval, 'that in me ought she to have aid and counsel as of right, and that so I do not accordingly, I ought to have reproach and be blamed as recreant before the world.'

Perceval will aid his sister

IV

'In God's name,' saith the hermit, 'You speak according to the scripture, for he that honoureth not his father and mother neither believeth in God nor loveth Him.' 'All this know I well,' saith Perceval, 'And well pleased am I to be reminded thereof, and well know I also mine intent herein, albeit I tell it to none. But if any can tell me tidings of Lancelot, right willingly shall I hear them, and take it kindly of the teller thereof.' 'Sir,' saith Joseus, 'It is but just now since he lay here within, and asked me tidings of Messire Gawain, and I told him such as I knew. Another time before that, he lay here when the robbers assailed us that he hanged in the forest, and so hated is he thereof

Tidings of Lancelot

of their kinsfolk that and they may meet him, so they have the might, he is like to pay for it right dear, and in this forest won they rather than in any other. I told him as much, but he made light thereof in semblant, even as he will in deed also if their force be not too great.' 'By my head,' saith Perceval, 'I will not depart forth of this forest until I know tidings of him, if Messire Gawain will pledge himself thereto.' And Messire saith he desireth nothing better, sith that he hath found Perceval, for he may not be at ease until such time as he shall know tidings of Lancelot, for he hath great misgiving sith that he hath enemies in the forest.

v

Perceval and Messire Gawain sojourned that day in the forest in the hermitage, and the morrow Perceval took his shield that he brought from King Arthur's court, and left that which he brought with him, and Messire Gawain along with him that made himself right joyous of his company. They ride amidst the forest both twain, all armed, and at the right hour of noon they meet a knight that was coming a great gallop as though he were all scared. Perceval asketh him whence he cometh, that he seemeth so a-dread. 'Sir, I come from the forest of the robbers that won in this forest wherethrough you have to pass. They have chased me a full league Welsh to slay me, but they would not follow me further for a knight that they have beset in one of their

holds, that hath done them right sore mischief, **Lancelot**
for he hath hanged four of their knights and **needeth**
slain one, as well as the fairest damsel that was **succour**
in a kingdom. But right well had she deserved
the death for that she harboured knights with
fair semblant and showed them much honour,
and afterward brought about their death and
destruction, between herself and a dwarf that
she hath, that slew the knights.' 'And know
you who is the knight?' saith Perceval. 'Sir,'
saith the knight, 'Not I, for no leisure had I to
ask him, for sorer need had I to flee than to
stay. But I tell you that on account of the
meat that failed him in the hold wherein they
beset him, he issued forth raging like a lion,
nor would he have suffered himself be shut up
so long but for two wounds that he had upon
his body; for he cared not to issue forth of
the house until such time as they were healed,
and also for that he had no horse. And so
soon as he felt himself whole, he ventured
himself against the four knights, that were so
a-dread of him that they durst not come a-nigh.
And moreover he deigneth not to go a-foot,
wherefore if they now come a-nigh, it may not
be but he shall have one at least out of their
four horses, but they hold them heedfully
aloof.' 'Sir,' saith Perceval, 'Gramercy of
these tidings.' They were fain to depart from
the knight, but said he: 'Ha, Lords, allow
me so much as to see the destruction of this
evil folk that have wrought such mischief in
this forest! Sir,' saith he to Messire Gawain,
'I am cousin to the Poor Knight of the Waste

Forest that hath the two poor damsels to sister, there where you and Lancelot jousted between you, and when the knight that brought you tidings thereof died in the night.' 'By my faith,' saith Messire Gawain, 'These tidings know I well, for you say true, and your company hold I right dear for the love of the Poor Knight, for never yet saw I more courteous knight, nor more courteous damsels, nor better nurtured, and our Lord God grant them as much good as I would they should have.' Messire Gawain made the knight go before, for well knew he the robbers' hold, but loath enough had he been to go thither, had the knights not followed him behind. Lancelot was issued forth of the hold sword in hand, all armed, angry as a lion. The four knights were upon their horses all armed, but no mind had they come a-nigh him, for sore dreaded they the huge buffets he dealt, and his hardiment. One of them came forward before the others, and it seemed him shame that they might not vanquish one single knight. He goeth to smite Lancelot a great stroke of his sword above in the midst of his head, nor did Lancelot's sword fail of its stroke, for before he could draw back, Lancelot dealt him such a blow as smote off all of his leg at the thigh, so that he made him leave the saddlebows empty. Lancelot leapt up on the destrier, and now seemed him he was safer than before. The three robber-knights that yet remained whole ran upon him on all sides and began to press him of their swords in right sore wrath. Thereupon behold you, the knight cometh to the way that goeth to the hold and saith to Messire Gawain and Perceval, 'Now may you hear the clashing of swords and the melly.' Therewithal the two good knights smite horse with spur and come thither where the three robber-knights were assailing Lancelot. Each of the twain smiteth his own so wrathfully that they thrust their spears right through their bodies and bear them to the ground dead. Howbeit the third knight was fain to flee, but the knight that had come to show Messire Gawain the way took heart and hardiment from the confidence of the good knights, and smote him as he fled so sore that he pierced him with his spear to the heart and toppled him to the ground dead. And the one whose leg Lancelot had lopped off was so trampled underfoot of the knights that he had no life in him.

VI

When Lancelot knew Perceval and Messire Gawain he made great joy of them and they of him. 'Lancelot,' saith Messire Gawain, 'This knight that led us hither to save your life is cousin to the Poor Knight of the Waste Castle, the brother of the two poor damsels that lodged us so well. We will send him these horses, one for the knight that shall be the messenger, and the two to the lord of the Waste Castle, and this hold that we have taken shall be for the two damsels, and so shall we make them safe all the days of their life. This, methinketh, will be well.' 'Certes,' saith Perceval, 'You

The robbers' treasure speak of great courtesy.' 'Sir,' saith Lancelot, 'Messire Gawain hath said, and right willingly will I grant him all his wish.' 'Lords,' saith the knight, 'They have in this forest a hold where the knights stowed their plunder, for the sake whereof they murdered the passers by. If the goods remain there, they will be lost, for therein is so great store as might be of much worth to many folk that are poverty-stricken for want thereof.' They go to the hold and find right great treasure in a cave underground, and rich sets of vessels and rich ornaments of cloths and armours for horses, that they had thrown the one over another into a pit that was right broad. 'Certes,' saith he, 'Right well hath it been done to this evil folk that is destroyed!' 'Sir,' saith Lancelot, 'In like manner would they have dealt with me and killed me if they might; wherefore no sorrow have I save of the damsel that I slew, that was one of the fairest dames of the world. But I slew her not knowingly, for I meant rather to strike the knight, but she leapt between us, like the hardiest dame that saw I ever.' 'Sirs,' saith the knight, 'Perceval and Lancelot, by the counsel of Messire Gawain, granted the treasure to the two damsels, sisters to the Poor Knight of the Waste Castle, whereupon let them send for Joseus the Hermit and bid him guard the treasure until they shall come hither.' And Joseus said that he would do so, and is right glad that the robbers of the forest are made away withal, that had so often made assault upon him. He guarded the treasure and the **Perceval** hold right safely in the forest; but the dread **departeth** and the renown of the good knights that had freed the forest went far and wide. The knight that led the three destriers was right joyfully received at the Waste Castle; and when he told the message wherewith he was charged by Messire Gawain, the Poor Knight and two damsels made great joy thereof. Perceval taketh leave of Messire Gawain and Lancelot, and saith that never will he rest again until he shall have found his sister and his widow mother. They durst not gainsay him, for they know well that he is right, and he prayeth them right sweetly that they salute the King and Queen and all the good knights of the court, for, please God, he will go see them at an early day. But first he was fain to fulfil the promise King Arthur made to his sister, for he would not that the King should be blamed in any place as concerning him, nor by his default; and he himself would have the greater blame therein and he succoured her not, for the matter touched him nearer than it did King Arthur.

VII

With that the Good Knight departeth, and they commend him to God, and he them in like sort. Messire Gawain and Lancelot go their way back toward the court of King Arthur, and Perceval goeth amidst strange forests until he cometh to a forest far away, wherein, so it seemed him, he had never been before. And he passed through a land that seemed him to have been laid waste, for it was all void of folk. Wild beast only seeth he there, that ran through the open country. He entered into a forest in this waste country, and found a hermitage in the combe of a mountain. He alighted without and heard that the hermit was singing the service of the dead, and had begun the mass with a requiem between him and his clerk. He looketh and seeth a pall spread upon the ground before the altar as though it were over a corpse. He would not enter the chapel armed, wherefore he hearkened to the mass from without right reverently, and showed great devotion as he that loved God much and was a-dread. When the mass was sung, and the hermit was disarmed of the armour of Our Lord, he cometh to Perceval and saluteth him and Perceval him again. 'Sir,' saith Perceval, 'For whom have you done such service? meseemed that the corpse lay therewithin for whom the service was ordained.' 'You say truth,' saith the hermit. 'I have done it for Lohot, King Arthur's son, that lieth buried under this pall.' 'Who, then, hath slain him?' saith Perceval. 'That will I tell you plainly,' saith the hermit.

Of Lohot's death

VIII

'This wasted land about this forest wherethrough you have come is the beginning of the kingdom of Logres. There wont to be therein a Giant so big and horrible and cruel that none durst won within half a league round about, and he destroyed the land and wasted it in such sort as you see. Lohot was departed from the land and the court of King Arthur his father in quest of adventure, and by the will of God arrived at this forest, and fought against Logrin, right cruel as he was, and Logrin against him. As it pleased God, Lohot vanquished him; but Lohot had a marvellous custom: when he had slain a man, he slept upon him. A knight of King Arthur's court, that is called Kay the Seneschal, was come peradventure into this forest of Logres. He heard the Giant roar when Lohot dealt him the mortal blow. Thither came he as fast as he might, and found the King's son sleeping upon Logrin. He drew his sword and therewith cut off Lohot's head, and took the head and the body and set them in a coffin of stone. After that, he hacked his shield to pieces with his sword, that he should not be recognised; then came he to the Giant that lay dead, and so cut off his head, that was right huge and hideous, and hung it at his fore saddle-bow. Then went he to the court of King Arthur and presented it to him. The King made great joy thereof and all they of the court, and the King made broad his lands right freely for that he believed Kay had spoken true. I went,' saith the hermit, 'on the morrow to the piece of land where the Giant lay dead, as a damsel came within here to tell me with right great joy. I found the corpse of the Giant so big that I durst not come a-nigh it. The damsel led me to the coffin where the King's son was

Kay's treachery

lying. She asked the head of me as her guerdon, and I granted it to her willingly. She set it forthwith in a coffer laden with precious stones that was all garnished within of balsams. After that, she helped me carry the body into this chapel and enshroud and bury it.

IX

'Afterwards the damsel departed, nor have I never heard talk of her since, nor do I make remembrance hereof for that I would King Arthur should know it, nor for aught that I say thereof that he should do evil to the knight; for right sore sin should I have thereof, but deadly treason and disloyalty he wrought.' 'Sir,' saith Perceval, 'This is sore pity of the King's son, that he is dead in such manner, for I have heard witness that he ever waxed more and more in great chivalry, and, so the King knew thereof, Kay the Seneschal, that is not well-loved of all folk, would lose the court for ever more, or his life, so he might be taken, and this would be only right and just.' Perceval lay the night in the hermitage, and departed on the morrow when he had heard mass. He rideth through the forest as he that right gladly would hear tidings of his mother, nor never before hath he been so desirous thereof as is he now. He heard, at right hour of noon, a damsel under a tree that made greater dole than ever heard he damsel make before. She held her mule by the reins and was alighted a-foot and set herself on her knees toward the East. She stretched her hands up toward heaven and prayed right sweetly the Saviour of the World and His sweet Mother that they would send her succour betimes, for that the most discounselled damsel of the world was she, and never was alms given to damsel to counsel her so well bestowed as it would be upon her, for that needs must she go to the most perilous place that is in the world, and that, save she might bring some one with her, never would that she had to do be done.

Dindrane prayeth

X

Perceval drew himself up when he heard the damsel bemoaning thus. He was in the shadow of the forest so that she saw him not. The damsel cried out all weeping, 'Ha, King Arthur, great sin did you in forgetting to speak of my business to the knight that bare away the shield from your court, by whom would my mother have been succoured, that now must lose her castle presently save God grant counsel herein; and so unhappy am I, that I have gone through all the lands of Great Britain, yet may I hear no tidings of my brother, albeit they say that he is the Best Knight of the world. But what availeth us his knighthood, when we have neither aid nor succour thereof? So much the greater shame ought he to have of himself, if he love his mother, as she, that is the most gentle lady that liveth and the most loyal, hath hope that, and he knew, he would come thither. Either he is dead or he is in lands so far away that none may hear tidings of him. Ha, sweet Lady, Mother of Our Saviour, aid us when we

Perceval is not known may have no aid of any other! for if my lady mother loseth her castle, needs must we be forlorn wanderers in strange lands, for so have her brothers been long time; he that had the most power and valour lieth in languishment, the good King Fisherman that the King of Castle Mortal warreth on, albeit he also is my uncle, my mother's brother, and would fain reave my uncle, that is his brother, of his castle by his felony. Of a man so evil my lady mother looketh for neither aid nor succour. And the good King Pelles hath renounced his kingdom for the love of his Saviour, and hath entered into a hermitage. He likewise is brother of my mother, and behoveth him make war upon none, for the most worshipful hermit is he of the world. And all they on my father's side have died in arms. Eleven were there of them, and my father was the twelfth. Had they remained on live, well able would they have been to succour us, but the knight that was first at the Graal hath undone us, for through him our uncle fell in languishment, in whom should have been our surest succour.'

XI

At this word Perceval rode forward, and the damsel heareth him. She riseth up, and looketh backward and seeth the knight come, the shield at his neck banded argent and azure, with a red cross. She clasped her two hands toward heaven, and saith, 'Ha, sweet Lady that didst bear the Saviour of the World, you have not forgotten me, nor never may be discounselled he nor she that calleth upon you with the heart. Here see I the knight come of whom we shall have aid and succour, and our Lord God grant him will to do His pleasure, and lend him courage and strength to protect us!' She goeth to meet him, and holdeth his stirrup and would have kissed his foot, but he avoideth it and crieth to her: 'Ill do you herein, damsel!' And therewith she melteth in tears of weeping and prayeth him right sweetly. 'Sir,' saith she, 'Of such pity as God had of His most sweet Mother on that day He took His death, when He beheld Her at the foot of the cross, have pity and mercy of my lady mother and of me. For, and your aid fail us, we know not to whom to fly for rescue, for I have been told that you are the Best Knight of the world. And for obtaining of your help went I to King Arthur's court. Wherefore succour us for pity's sake and God's and for nought beside, for, so please you, it is your duty so to do, albeit, had you been my brother that is also such a knight as you, whom I cannot find, I might have called upon you of a greater right. Sir,' saith she, 'Do you remember you of the brachet you had at the court waiting for you until such time as you should come for the shield, and that went away with you, how he would never make joy nor know any save me alone? By this know I well that if you knew the soreness of our need you would succour us. But King Arthur, that should have prayed you thereof, forgat it.' 'Damsel,' saith he, 'So much hath he done

Dindrane prayeth succour

that he hath not failed of his covenant with you, for he sent for me by the two best knights of his court, and, so I may speed, so much will I do herein as that God and he shall be well pleased thereof.'

The holy altar-cloth

XII

The damsel had right great joy of the knight that he should grant her his aid, but she knew not he was her brother, or otherwise she would have doubled her joy. Perceval knoweth well that she is his sister, but he would not yet discover himself and manifest his pity outwardly. He helpeth the damsel to mount again and they rode on together. 'Sir,' saith the damsel, 'Needs must I go to-night by myself to the Grave-yard Perilous.' 'Wherefore go you thither?' saith Perceval. 'Sir,' saith she, 'I have made vow thereof, and moreover a holy hermit hath told me that the knight that warreth upon us may not be overcome of no knight, save I bring him not some of the cloth wherewith the altar in the chapel of the Grave-yard Perilous is covered. The cloth is of the most holiest, for our Lord God was covered therewith in the Holy Sepulchre, on the third day when He came back from death to life. Nor none may enter the holy grave-yard that bringeth another with him, wherefore behoveth me go by myself, and may God save my life this night, for the place is sore perilous, and so ought I greatly to hate him that hath procured me this dolour and travail. Sir,' saith she, 'You will go your way toward the castle of Camelot: there is the Widow Lady my mother, that awaiteth the return and the succour of the Good Knight, and may you remember to succour and aid us when you shall see how sore is our need of succour.'

The Graveyard Perilous

XIII

'Damsel,' saith Perceval, 'So God allow me I will aid you to the utmost of my power.' 'Sir,' saith she, 'See, this is my way, that is but little frequented, for I tell you that no knight durst tread therein without great peril and great dread. And our Lord God have your body in keeping, for mine own this night shall be in sore jeopardy and hazard.' Perceval departeth from the damsel, his sister, and hath right great pity for that she goeth in so perilous place all alone. Natheless would he not forbid her, for he knew well that she might not go thither with him nor with other, sith that such was the custom of the grave-yard that twain might not pass the entrance, wherefore needs must one remain without. Perceval was not willing that his sister should break her vow, for never none of his lineage did at any time disloyalty nor base deed knowingly, nor failed of nought that they had in covenant, save only the King of Castle Mortal, from whom he had as much evil as he had good of the others.

XIV

The damsel goeth her way all alone and all forlorn toward the grave-yard and the deep of the forest, all dark and shadowy. She hath ridden until the sun was set and the night draweth nigh. She looketh before her and seeth a cross, high and wide and thick. And on this cross was the figure of Our Lord graven, whereof is she greatly comforted. She draweth nigh the cross, and so kisseth and adoreth it, and prayeth the Saviour of the world that was nailed on Holy Rood that He would bring her forth of the burial-ground with honour. The cross was at the entrance of the grave-yard, that was right spacious, for, from such time as the land was first peopled of folk, and that knights began to seek adventure by the forest, not a knight had died in the forest, that was full great of breadth and length, but his body was borne thither, nor might never knight there be buried that had not received baptism and had repented him not of his sins at his death.

The knights' ghosts

XV

Thereinto entered the damsel all alone, and found great multitude of tombs and coffins. Nor none need wonder whether she had shuddering and fear, for such place must needs be dreadful to a lonely damsel, there where lay so many knights that had been slain in arms. Josephus the good clerk witnesseth us that within the grave-yard might no evil spirit meddle, for that Saint Andrew the apostle had blessed it with his hand. But never might no hermit remain within for the evil things that appeared each night all round about, that took the shapes of the knights that were dead in the forest, whereof the bodies lay not in the blessed burial-ground.

XVI

The altar-cloth lifteth

The damsel beholdeth their sepulchres all round about the grave-yard whereinto she was come. She seeth them surrounded of knights, all black, and spears had they withal, and came one against another, and made such uproar and alarm as it seemed all the forest resounded thereof. The most part held swords all red as of fire, and ran either upon other, and gashed one another's hands and feet and nose and face. And great was the clashing they made, but they could not come a-nigh the grave-yard. The damsel seeth them, and hath such affright thereof that she nigh fell to the ground in a swoon. The mule whereon she sate draweth wide his nostrils and goeth in much fear. The damsel signeth her of the cross and commendeth her to the Saviour and to His sweet Mother. She looketh before her to the head of the grave-yard, and seeth the chapel, small and ancient. She smiteth her mule with her whip, and cometh thitherward and alighteth. She entered therewithin and found a great brightness of light. Within was an image of Our Lady, to whom she prayeth right sweetly that She will preserve her senses and her life and enable her to depart in safety from this perilous place. She seeth above the altar the most holy cloth for the which she was come thither, that was right ancient, and a smell came thereof so sweet and glorious that no sweetness of the world might equal it. The damsel cometh toward the altar thinking to take the cloth, but it goeth up into

Dindrane her prayer the air as if the wind had lifted it, and was so high that she might not reach it above an ancient crucifix that was there within. 'Ha, God!' saith the damsel, 'It is for my sin and my disloyalty that this most holy cloth thus draweth itself away from me!'

XVII

'Fair Father God, never did I evil to none, nor never did I shame nor sinned deadly in myself, nor never wrought against your will, so far as in me lay, but rather do I serve you and love and fear you and your sweet Mother; and all the tribulation I receive, accept I in patience for your love, for well I know that such is your pleasure, nor have I no will to set myself against nought that pleaseth you.

XVIII

'When it shall please you, you will release me and my mother of the grief and tribulation wherein we are. For well you know that they have reaved her of her castles by wrong, and of her land, for that she is a Widow Lady without help. Lord, you who have all the world at your mercy and do your commandment in all things, grant me betimes to hear tidings of my brother and he be on live, for sore need have we of him. And so lend force to the knight and power against all our enemies, that for your love and for pity is fain to succour and aid my mother that is sore discounselled. Lord, well might it beseem you to remember of your pity and the sweetness that is in you,

and of compassion that she hath been un- *She is*
righteously disherited, and that no succour nor *answered*
aid nor counsel hath she, save of you alone.
You are her affiance and her succour, and
therefore ought you to remember that the good
knight Joseph of Abarimacie, that took down
your Body when it hung upon the rood, was
her own uncle. Better loved he to take down
your Body than all the gold and all the fee that
Pilate might give him. Lord, good right of
very truth had he so to do, for he took you in
his arms beside the rood, and laid your Body in
the holy sepulchre, wherein were you covered
of the sovran cloth for the which have I come
in hither. Lord, grant it be your pleasure
that I may have it, for love of the knight by
whom it was set in this chapel; sith that I
am of his lineage it ought well to manifest
itself in this sore need, so it come according
to your pleasure.' Forthwith the cloth came
down above the altar, and she straightway found
taken away therefrom as much as it pleased Our
Lord she should have. Josephus telleth us of
a truth, that never did none enter into the
chapel that might touch the cloth save only
this one damsel. She set her face to it and
her mouth or ever the cloth removed.

XIX

Thereafter, she took the piece that God
would and set it near herself full worshipfully,
but still the stour went on of the evil spirits
round about the church-yard, and they dealt
one another blows so sore that all the forest

A Voice resounded thereof, and it seemed that it was all set on fire of the flame that issued from them. Great fear would the damsel have had of them, had she not comforted herself in God and in His dear, sweet Mother, and the most holy cloth that was within there. A Voice appeared upon the stroke of midnight from above the chapel, and speaketh to the souls whereof the bodies lie within the grave-yard: 'How sore loss hath befallen you of late, and all other whose bodies lie in other hallowed church-yards by the forests of this kingdom! For the good King Fisherman is dead that made every day our service be done in the most holy chapel there where the most Holy Graal every day appeared, and where the Mother of God abode from the Saturday until the Monday that the service was finished. And now hath the King of Castle Mortal seized the castle in such sort that never sithence hath the Holy Graal appeared, and all the other hallows are hidden, so that none knoweth what hath become of the priests that served in the chapel, nor the twelve ancient knights, nor the damsels that were therein. And you, damsel, that are within, have no affiance in the aid of strange knight in this need, for succoured may you never be save of your brother only!'

XX

With that the Voice is still, and a wailing and a lamentation goeth up from the bodies that lay in the church-yard, so dolorous that no man is there in the world but should have

pity thereof, and all the evil spirits that were
without departed groaning and making so mighty
uproar at their going away that it seemed all
the earth trembled. The damsel heard the
tidings of her uncle that was dead, and fell on
the ground in a swoon, and when she raised
herself, took on to lament and cried: 'Ha,
God! Now have we lost the most comfort
and the best friend that we had, and hereof am
I again discomforted that I may not be succoured
in this my next need by the Good Knight of
whom I thought to have succour and aid, and
that was so fain to render it. Now shall I
know not what to ask of him, for he would
grant it right willingly, and may God be as
pleased with him thereof as if he had done
it.' The damsel was in sore misdoubting and
dismay, for she knew not who the knight was,
and great misgiving had she of her uncle's death
and right sore sorrow. She was in the chapel
until it was day, and then commended herself
to God and departed and mounted on her mule
and issued forth of the church-yard full speed,
all alone.

_{above the chapel}

XXI

The story saith that the damsel went her way toward her mother's castle as straight as she might, but sore dismayed was she of the Voice that had told her she might not be succoured save of her brother alone. She hath ridden so far of her journeys that she is come to the Valley of Camelot, and seeth her mother's castle that was surrounded of great

Dindrane joineth Perceval rivers, and seeth Perceval, that was alighted under the shadow of a tree at the top of the forest in order that he might behold his mother's castle, whence he went forth squire what time he slew the Knight of the Red Shield. When he had looked well at the castle and the country round about, much pleasure had he thereof, and mounted again forthwith. Thereupon, behold you, the damsel cometh. 'Sir,' saith she, 'In sore travail and jeopardy have I been sithence that last I saw you, and tidings have I heard as bad as may be, and right grievous for my mother and myself. For King Fisherman my uncle is dead, and another of my uncles, the King of Castle Mortal, hath seized his castle, albeit my lady mother ought rather to have it, or I, or my brother.' 'Is it true,' saith Perceval, 'that he is dead?' 'Yea, certes, Sir, I know it of a truth.' 'So help me God!' saith he, 'This misliketh me right sore. I thought not that he would die so soon, for I have not been to see him of a long time.'

XXII

'Sir,' saith she, 'I am much discomforted as concerning you, for I have likewise been told that no force nor aid of any knight may avail to succour nor aid me from this day forward save my brother's help alone. Wherefore, and it be so, we have lost all, for my lady mother hath respite to be in her castle only until the fifteenth day from to-day, and I know not where to seek my brother, and the day is so nigh as you hear. Now behoveth us do the best we may and

abandon this castle betimes, nor know I any **The**
refuge that we now may have save only King **Widow**
Pelles in the hermitage. I would fain that my **Lady**
lady mother were there, for he would not fail
us.' Perceval is silent, and hath great pity in
his heart of this that the damsel saith. She
followeth him weeping, and pointeth out to him
the Valleys of Camelot and the castles that were
shut in by combes and mountains, and the broad
meadow-lands and the forest that girded them
about. 'Sir,' saith she, 'All this hath the Lord
of the Moors reaved of my lady mother, and
nought coveteth he so much as to have this
castle, and have it he will, betimes.'

XXIII

When they had ridden until that they drew
nigh the castle, the Lady was at the windows
of the hall and knew her daughter. 'Ha,
God!' saith the Lady, 'I see there my daughter
coming, and a knight with her. Fair Father
God, grant of your pleasure that it be my son,
for and it be not he, I have lost my castle and
my heirs are disherited.' Perceval cometh
nigh the castle in company with his sister, and
knoweth again the chapel that stood upon four
columns of marble between the forest and the
castle, there where his father told him how
much ought he to love good knights, and that
none earthly thing might be of greater worth,
and how none might know yet who lay in the
coffin until such time as the Best Knight of the
world should come thither, but that then should
it be known. Perceval would fain have passed

Perceval is known by the chapel, but the damsel saith to him: 'Sir, no knight passeth hereby save he go first to see the coffin within the chapel.' He alighteth and setteth the damsel to the ground, and layeth down his spear and shield and cometh toward the tomb, that was right fair and rich. He set his hand above it. So soon as he came nigh, the sepulchre openeth on one side, so that one saw him that was within the coffin. The damsel falleth at his feet for joy. The Lady had a custom such that every time a knight stopped at the coffin she made the five ancient knights that she had with her in the castle accompany her, wherein they would never fail her, and bring her as far as the chapel. So soon as she saw the coffin open and the joy her daughter made, she knew that it was her son, and ran to him and embraced him and kissed him and began to make the greatest joy that ever lady made.

XXIV

'Now know I well,' saith she, 'that our Lord God hath not forgotten me. Sith that I have my son again, the tribulations and the wrongs that have been done me grieve me nought any more. Sir,' saith she to her son, 'Now is it well known and proven that you are the Best Knight of the world! For otherwise never would the coffin have opened, nor would any have known who he is that you now see openly.' She maketh her chaplain take certain letters that were sealed with gold in the coffin. He looketh thereat and readeth, and then saith

that these letters witness of him that lieth in the **The**
coffin that he was one of them that helped to **tomb**
un-nail Our Lord from the cross. They **openeth**
looked beside him and found the pincers all
bloody wherewith the nails were drawn, but
they might not take them away, nor the body,
nor the coffin, according as Josephus telleth us,
for as soon as Perceval was forth of the chapel,
the coffin closed again and joined together even
as it was before. The Widow Lady led her
son with right great joy into her castle, and
recounted to him all the shame that had been
done her, and also how Messire Gawain had
made safe the castle for a year by his good
knighthood.

XXV

'Fair son,' saith she, 'now is the term drawn
nigh when I should have lost my castle and you
had not come. But now know I well that it
shall be safe-guarded of you. He that coveteth this castle is one of the most outrageous
knights on live. And he hath reaved me of
my land and the Valleys of Camelot without
reasonable occasion. But, please God, you
will well repair the harm he hath done you,
for nought claim I any longer of the land since
you are come. But so avenge your shame as
to increase your honour, for none ought to allow
his right to be minished of an evil man, and
the mischiefs that have been done me for that
I had no aid, let them not wax cold in you, for
a shame done to one valiant and strong ought
not to wax cold in him, but rankle and prick

**Perce-
val's
mother**
in him, so ought he to have his enemies in remembrance without making semblant, but so much as he shall show in his cheer and making semblant and his menaces, so much ought he to make good in deed when he shall come in place. For one cannot do too much hurt to an enemy, save only one is willing to let him be for God's sake. But truth it is that the scripture saith, that one ought not to do evil to one's enemies, but pray God that He amend them. I would fain that our enemies were such that they might amend toward us, and that they would do as much good to us without harming themselves as they have done evil, on condition that my anger and yours were forgone against them. Mine own anger I freely forbear against them so far forth as concerneth myself, for no need have I to wish evil to none, and Solomon telleth how the sinner that curseth other sinner curseth himself likewise.

XXVI

'Fair son, this castle is yours, and this land round about whereof I have been reft ought to be yours of right, for it falleth to you on behalf of your father and me. Wherefore send to the Lord of the Moors that hath reft it from me, that he render it to you. I make no further claim, for I pass it on to you; for nought have I now to do with any land save only so much as will be enough wherein to bury my body when I die, nor shall I now live much longer since King Fisherman my brother is dead, whereof right sorrowful am I at heart, and still more sorrowful should I be were it not for your coming. And, son, I tell you plainly that you have great blame of his death, for you are the knight through whom he fell first into languishment, for now at last I know well that and if you had afterwards gone back and so made the demand that you made not at the first, he would have come back to health. But our Lord God willed it so to be, wherefore well beseemeth us to yield to His will and pleasure.' **The Lord of the Moors**

XXVII

Perceval hath heard his mother, but right little hath he answered her, albeit greatly is he pleased with whatsoever she hath said. His face is to-flushed of hardiment, and courage hath taken hold on him. His mother looketh at him right fainly, and hath him disarmed and apparelled in a right rich robe. So comely a knight was he that in all the world might not be found one of better seeming nor better shapen of body. The Lord of the Moors, that made full certain of having his mother's castle, knew of Perceval's coming. He was not at all dismayed in semblant, nor would he stint to ride by fell nor forest, and every day he weened in his pride that the castle should be his own at the hour and the term he had set thereof. One of the five knights of the Widow Lady was one day gone into the Lonely Forest after hart and hind, and had taken thereof at his will. He was returning back to the castle and the huntsmen with him, when the Lord of the Moors

A knight slain met him and told him he had done great hardiment in shooting with the bow in the forest, and the knight made answer that the forest was not his of right, but the Lady's of Camelot and her son's that had repaired thither.

XXVIII

The Lord of the Moors waxed wroth. He held a sword in his hand and thrust him therewith through the body and slew him. The knight was borne dead to the castle of Camelot before the Widow Lady and her son. 'Fair son,' saith the Widow Lady, 'More presents of such-like kind the Lord of the Moors sendeth me than I would. Never may he be satisfied of harming my land and shedding the blood of the bodies of my knights. Now may you well know how many a hurt he hath done me sithence that your father hath been dead and you were no longer at the castle, sith that this hath he done me even now that you are here. You have the name of Perceval on this account, that tofore you were born, he had begun to reave your father of the Valleys of Camelot, for your father was an old knight and all his brethren were dead, and therefore he gave you this name in baptism, for that he would remind you of the mischief done to him and to you, and that you might help to retrieve it and you should have the power.' The Dame maketh shroud the knight, for whom she is full sorrowful, and on the morrow hath mass sung and burieth him. Perceval made arm two of the old knights with him, then issued forth of the

castle and entered the great dark forest. He **Perceval**
rode until he came before a castle, and met five **taketh**
knights that issued forth all armed. He asked **prisoners**
whose men they were. They answer, the
Lord's of the Moors, and that he goeth seek
the son of the Widow Lady that is in the
forest. 'If we may deliver him up to our
lord, good guerdon shall we have thereof.'
'By my faith,' saith Perceval, 'You have not
far to seek. I am here!'

XXIX

Perceval smiteth his horse of his spurs and
cometh to the first in such sort that he passeth
his spear right through his body and beareth
him to the ground dead. The other two
knights each smote his man so that they
wounded them in the body right sore. The
other two would fain have fled, but Perceval
preventeth them, and they gave themselves up
prisoners for fear of death. He bringeth all
four to the castle of Camelot and presenteth
them to his lady mother. 'Lady,' saith he,
'see here the quittance for your knight that
was slain, and the fifth also remaineth lying on
the piece of ground shent in like manner as
was your own.' 'Fair son,' saith she, 'I
should have better loved peace after another
sort, and so it might be.' 'Lady,' saith he,
'Thus is it now. One ought to make war
against the warrior, and be at peace with the
peaceable.' The knights are put in prison.
The tidings are come to the Lord of the
Moors that the son of the Widow Lady hath

More prisoners slain one of his knights and carried off four to prison. Thereof hath he right great wrath at heart, and sweareth and standeth to it that never will he be at rest until he shall have either taken or slain him, and that, so there were any knight in his land that would deliver him up, he would give him one of the best castles in his country. The more part are keen to take Perceval. Eight came for that intent before him all armed in the forest of Camelot, and hunted and drove wild deer in the purlieus of the forest so that they of the castle saw them.

XXX

Perceval was in his mother's chapel, where he heard mass; and when the mass was sung, his sister said: 'Fair brother, see here the most holy cloth that I brought from the chapel of the Grave-yard Perilous. Kiss it and touch it with your face, for a holy hermit told me that never should our land be conquered back until such time as you should have hereof.' Perceval kisseth it, then toucheth his eyes and face therewith. Afterward he goeth to arm him, and the four knights with him; then he issueth forth of the chamber and mounteth on his horse, then goeth out of the gateway like a lion unchained. He sitteth on a tall horse all covered. He cometh nigh the eight knights that were all armed, man and horse, and asketh them what folk they be and what they seek, and they say that they are enemies of the Widow Lady and her son. 'Then you do I

defy!' saith Perceval. He cometh to them a **Perceval**
great run, and the four knights with him, and **taketh**
each one overthroweth his own man so roughly **their**
that either he is wounded in his body or maimed **lord**
of arm or leg. The rest held the melly to the
utmost they might endure. Perceval made take
them and bring to the castle, and the other five
that they had overthrown. The Lord of the
Moors was come to shoot with a bow, and
he heard the noise of the knights, and cometh
thitherward a great gallop all armed. 'Sir,'
saith one of the old knights to Perceval, 'Look!
here is the Lord of the Moors coming, that
hath reft your mother of her land and slain her
men. Of him will it be good to take vengeance.
See, how boldly he cometh.' Perceval looketh
on him as he that loveth him not, and cometh
toward him as hard as his horse may carry
him, and smiteth him right through the breast
so strongly that he beareth to the ground him
and his horse together all in a heap. He
alighteth to the ground and draweth his sword.
'How?' saith the Lord of the Moors, 'Would
you then slay me and put me in worse plight
than I am?' 'By my head,' saith Perceval,
'No, not so swiftly, but I will slay you enough,
betimes!' 'So it seemeth you,' saith the
Lord of the Moors, 'But it shall not be yet!'
He leapeth up on his feet and runneth on
Perceval, sword drawn, as one that fain would
harm him if he might. But Perceval defendeth
himself as good knight should, and giveth such
a buffet at the outset as smiteth off his arm
together with his sword. The knights that

Perceval wreaketh came after fled back all discomfited when they saw their lord wounded. And Perceval made lift him on a horse and carry him to the castle and presenteth him to his mother. 'Lady,' saith he, 'See here the Lord of the Moors! Well might you expect him eftsoons, sith that you were to have yielded him up your castle the day after to-morrow!'

XXXI

'Lady,' saith the Lord of the Moors, 'Your son hath wounded me and taken my knights and myself likewise. I will yield you up your castle albeit I hold it mine as of right, on condition you cry me quit.' 'And who shall repay her,' saith Perceval, 'for the shame that you have done her, for her knights that you have slain, whereof never had you pity? Now, so help me God, if she have mercy or pity upon you, never hereafter will I trouble to come to her aid how sore soever may be her need. Such pity and none other as you have had for her and my sister will I have for you. Our Lord God commanded in both the Old Law and the New, that justice should be done upon man-slayers and traitors, and justice will I do upon you that His commandment be not transgressed.' He hath a great vat made ready in the midst of the court, and maketh the eleven knights be brought. He maketh their heads be stricken off into the vat and bleed therein as much blood as might come from them, and then made the heads and the bodies be drawn forth so that nought was there but blood in the vat. After that, he made disarm the Lord of the Moors and be brought before the vat wherein was great abundance of blood. He made bind his feet and his hands right strait, and after that saith: 'Never might you be satisfied of the blood of the knights of my lady mother, now will I satisfy you of the blood of your own knights!' He maketh hang him by the feet in the vat, so that his head were in the blood as far as the shoulders, and so maketh him be held there until that he was drowned and quenched. After that, he made carry his body and the bodies of the other knights and their heads, and made them be cast into an ancient charnel that was beside an old chapel in the forest, and the vat together with the blood made he be cast into the river, so that the water thereof was all bloody. The tidings came to the castles that the son of the Widow Lady had slain the Lord of the Moors and the best of his knights. Thereof were they in sore misgiving, and the most part said that the like also would he do to them save they held themselves at his commandment. They brought him the keys of all the castles that had been reft of his mother, and all the knights that had before renounced their allegiance returned thereunto and pledged themselves to be at his will for dread of death. All the land was assured in safety, nor was there nought to trouble the Lady's joy save only that King Fisherman her brother was dead, whereof she was right sorrowful and sore afflicted.

a bloody vengeance

XXXII

The Damsel of the Car — One day the Widow Lady sate at meat, and there was great plenty of knights in the hall. Percival sate him beside his sister. Thereupon, behold you the Damsel of the Car that came with the other two damsels before the Widow Lady and her son, and saluted them right nobly. 'Damsel,' saith Perceval, 'Good adventure may you have!' 'Sir,' saith she, 'You have speeded right well of your business here, now go speed it elsewhere, for thereof is the need right sore. King Hermit, that is your mother's brother, sendeth you word that, and you come not with haste into the land that was King Fisherman's your uncle, the New Law that God hath stablished will be sore brought low. For the King of Castle Mortal, that hath seized the land and castle, hath made be cried throughout all the country how all they that would fain maintain the Old Law and abandon the New shall have protection of him and counsel and aid, and they that will not shall be destroyed and outlawed.' 'Ha, fair son,' saith the Widow Lady, 'Now have you heard the great disloyalty of the evil man that is my brother, whereof am I right sorrowful, for that he is of my kindred.' 'Lady,' saith Perceval, 'Your brother nor my uncle is he no longer, sith that he denieth God! Rather is he our mortal enemy that we ought of right to hate more than any stranger!'

XXXIII

'Fair son,' saith the Widow Lady, 'I pray and beseech you that the Law of the Saviour be not set aside in forgetfulness and neglect there where you may exalt it, for better Lord in no wise may you serve, nor one that better knoweth how to bestow fair guerdon. Fair son, none may be good knight that serveth Him not and loveth Him. Take heed that you be swift in His service nor delay not for no intent, but be ever at His commandment alike at eventide as in the morning, so shall you not bely your lineage. And the Lord God grant you good intent therein and good will to go on even as you have begun.' The Widow Lady, that much loved her son, riseth up from the tables, and all the other knights, and seemeth it that she is Lady of her land in such sort as that never was she better. But full often doth she give thanks to the Saviour of the World with her whole heart, and prayeth Him of His pleasure grant her son length of life for the amendment both of soul and body. Perceval was with his mother of a long space, and with his sister, and was much feared and honoured of all the knights of the land, alike for his great wisdom and great pains-taking, as well as for the valour of his knighthood.

Perceval's mother's counsel

END OF VOL. I

Printed by T. and A. CONSTABLE, Printers to Her Majesty
at the Edinburgh University Press

www.ingramcontent.com/pod-product-compliance
Lightning Source LLC
Chambersburg PA
CBHW022055230426
43672CB00008B/1182